New Literacies around the Globe

D1532004

The increasing popularity of digitally mediated communication is prompting us to radically rethink literacy and its role in education; at the same time, national policies have promulgated a view of literacy focused on the skills and classroom routines associated with print, bolstered by regimes of accountability and assessments. As a result, teachers are caught between two competing discourses: one upholding a traditional conception of literacy reiterated by politicians and policymakers, and the other encouraging a more radical take on 21st-century literacies driven by leading-edge thinkers and researchers. There is a pressing need for a book which engages researchers in international dialogue around new literacies, their implications for policy and practice, and how they might articulate across national boundaries.

Drawing on cutting edge research from the USA, Canada, UK, Australia and South Africa, this book is a pedagogical and policy-driven call for change. It explores studies of literacy practices in varied contexts through a refreshingly dialogic style, interspersed with commentaries on the significance of the work described for education. The book concludes on the 'conversation' developed to identify key recommendations for policymakers through a Charter for Literacy Pedagogies.

Cathy Burnett is Reader in the Department of Teacher Education at Sheffield Hallam University, UK, where she leads the Language and Literacy Research Group.

Julia Davies is a Senior Lecturer in The School of Education at The University of Sheffield, UK, where she codirects The Centre for the Study of Literacies.

Guy Merchant is Professor of Literacy in Education at Sheffield Hallam University, UK, where he specialises in research into digital literacy in formal and informal educational settings.

Jennifer Rowsell is Professor and Canada Research Chair in Multiliteracies at Brock University's Faculty of Education, Canada.

Routledge Research in Literacy

EDITED BY DAVID BARTON, *Lancaster University, UK.*

New Literacies around the Globe

Policy and Pedagogy

**Edited by Cathy Burnett, Julia Davies,
Guy Merchant, and Jennifer Rowsell**

Routledge
Taylor & Francis Group

NEW YORK AND LONDON

First published 2014
by Routledge
711 Third Avenue, New York, NY 10017, USA

and by Routledge
2 Park Square, Milton Park, Abingdon, Oxfordshire OX14 4RN

First issued in paperback 2016

*Routledge is an imprint of the Taylor & Francis Group,
an informa business*

Library of Congress Cataloging-in-Publication Data
New literacies around the globe : policy and pedagogy / edited by
    Cathy Burnett, Julia Davies, Guy Merchant, and Jennifer Roswell.
        pages cm — (Routledge research in literacy)
    Includes bibliographical references and index.
    1. Literacy.   2. Technological literacy.   3. Globalization.   I. Burnett,
Cathy.
    LC149.N48 2014
    379.2'4—dc23
    2014003965

Typeset in Sabon
by IBT Global.

ISBN 13: 978-1-138-28666-5 (pbk)
ISBN 13: 978-0-415-71956-8 (hbk)

Contents

Figures

Tables

Foreword
Literacy and a New Global Citizenry?

Peter Freebody

The title of this volume invites us to see literacy both in a new outfit of its own and as part of extensive new ensemble of social, cultural and economic connections. But as we recover from our drawn-out millennial dose of global 'innovativ-itis', our resistances may be up, and we may find ourselves looking more sceptically at the terms 'new' and 'global'. We may wonder, as the old challenges facing literacy educators reconfigure around us, what new understandings and opportunities actually do appear in these new global times.

WHAT'S NEW ABOUT LITERACY?

Socrates worried about literacy. Plato records that the philosopher who arguably invented dialogic inquiry into human morality, at least in the Western tradition, spat out these tetchy comments in an exchange with Phaedrus:

> This discovery of yours, this writing, will produce forgetfulness in the minds of those who learn to use it . . . they will trust to the external written letters and not use their own memories; you give your students not truth, but only the appearance of truth; they will read many things and will have learned nothing; they will therefore seem to know many things, when they are, for the most part, ignorant and hard to get along with, having the show of wisdom without the reality . . . if you ask [written words] a question, they just give you the same answer over and over again. (Plato, 360 BCE, Socrates in dialogue with Phaedrus, Sections 275e–277a)

So Socrates worried that having read would be a self-deceiving substitute for having thought, a concern that neatly summarises much of the debate over the teaching of reading over the last forty years. But Socrates's observations here were part of a larger view he had of the significance of dialogue (Saunders, 1987): that genuine dialogue involves skilful management, truthfulness and the treatment of matters that are important to the participants; that it is only through genuine dialogue that the seeds of true knowledge and wisdom can be planted; and that only the organic processes of genuine dialogue can help people gradually grow their own and help others grow knowledge and wisdom and, from these, be "as happy as any human being can be" (276e–277a).

Showing us the details of specific illustrations of 'new literacies across the globe', the contributors to this volume also bring us back to a version of Socrates's apprehensions about literacy. This volume is built on two related ideas about literacy: (1) that new technological conditions, and the social and economic processes they support, have produced new communicational and interpretive demands on learners, workers and citizens, demands that are seriously under-recognised—both their prevalence in out-of-school life and the distinctiveness of the experiences that they provide—in most contemporary educational settings; (2) that a key element of these new conditions is the interplay between local and global settings, pervasive and profound in its operation and in its implications for education. The notion is that these combine to create genuinely new imperatives for literacy education as a domain of both practice and research.

One new aspect of literacy study emerging from these observations is a broad acceptance that 'being literate' is best considered an open-textured idea that covers a range of highly variable capabilities relevant to the sites of our everyday activities. The material, intellectual, social and institutional conditions of literacy's uses are integral to our understandings of what it is and how it can be developed in learners; they are conditions that are not just incidental features of the 'bucket' in which a particular instance of an idealised 'literacy' might take place. 'Being literate' refers to the linguistic, psychological and cultural work that can be done in light of the materials to be used or made, in the here-and-now (Freebody, Barton, & Chan, 2014). This work both shapes and is shaped by the particularities of daily use. Developing adequate literacy resources with this view in mind seems to present us, and perhaps even Socrates, with a new and more complex array of educational resources and challenges.

Two other features of literacy education seem to amount to genuinely new developments. First, some have argued, for example Apple (1989), that in times of internal pressures arising from redistributions of cultural, economic or political dominance, or in times of pressures arising from external economic competition, one tendency of contemporary developed societies is to lay the blame at the feet of schoolteachers, particularly primary schoolteachers, and most particularly those teaching literacy in primary schools. Contemplating the reasons why inadequate literacy education might have enjoyed such durability as an explanation for cultural and economic shortfalls is informative: perhaps 'uncompetitive' literacy test scores are an explanation that domesticates the problem, staging for us a scene that is personal, local and peopled by known characters. Perhaps 'the literacy problem' also allows us temporarily to defer or avoid debates about the nature, consequences, and sustainability of the economic, social, moral, environmental and intellectual features of contemporary societies. Literacy, we now almost take for granted, has become a political commodity, traded by schools, educational jurisdictions and systems and nation states.

Second, literacy has recently become a major economic commodity. Literacy products and programs for schools, teachers and parents sell well in many countries. But the commoditisation of literacy is also an issue for those who study it and formulate policies about it. Proprietary rights over the domain 'literacy' are contested among academic disciplinary groups and in bureaucracies. The success or otherwise of ownership claims has implications for promotion, research and development grants, personal and corporate status, publications and access to graduate students and assistants. The present volume puts on display a body of anthropological and sociological work in literacy that began to grow in earnest only about thirty years ago; the contributors refer to historical, psychological and linguistic traditions in the study of literacy to contrast their approaches with what they characterise as the more restrictive and potentially counterproductive consequences of these traditions. The intensity and consequentiality of these ownership struggles, and the difficulties that well-intentioned practitioners and policymakers might face in drawing out from them some principles for their own actions, seem to be new.

WHAT'S GLOBAL ABOUT LITERACY?

Globalisation and literacy can be related in at least two senses. The first invites us to consider how we can now access the words of people, communities and organisations from outside our own demographic, culture, ethnic group, and nation with ease. We can indeed, through visual communication technologies, come almost instantaneously face to face with others, effectively at will. In a widely referenced text on globalisation, Held, McGrew, Goldblatt, & Perraton, (1999) have suggested considering the effects of globalisation in terms of four variables: extensity (breadth of reach of products, ideas, money and people), intensity (density of interconnections and flows), velocity (speed of travel and communications), and impact (principally on decisions, institutional structures and practices and the distribution of wealth and power). As both an enabling process and a product, literacy has the capacity to score strongly on all four of these variables and is the key factor in the spread of many other aspects of modernity (e.g., institutionalised health care and research, transnational political decision making).

Although globalisation's potential for cultural and economic imperialism and the gradual fading away of local custom is clear in many respects, we might think that literacy would be exempt from such a charge. But this only works if we maintain an idealised notion of literacy. When we consider the global spread of particular literacy practices, we are alerted to the selective traditions that have, at least since ancient times (Thomas, 2008), arisen in certain sites. The potential of those selective practices being forcibly transplanted in new cultures makes the charge at least plausible (Freebody & Freiberg, 2008).

A second sense in which literacy and globalisation can be related concerns the effects on individual experience of these processes. The apparently resolutely here-and-now nature of our daily experiences can evolve into an awareness that these experiences are constantly, and often rapidly and deeply, shaped and reshaped by products, ideas, money and people, potentially from anywhere. We can then start to see around us, as do the contributors to this volume, the ongoing interplay of standardisation and hybridity and the particular threats and opportunities they may present to minority cultures.

As an instance, Levinson (2007) conducted a long, detailed study of the hostile attitudes among British Gypsies toward formal, school-based literacy education. Among his conclusions were that the well-intentioned pursuit of an idealised version of communication through literacy—as it is publicly known or assumed to be (see Lemphane and Prinsloo, this volume)—suits and advances the interests of some groups over others. These Gypsy communities knew this, and they foresaw its negative consequences for the maintenance of their culture. Levinson advised that even the brief glimpse his study provided of the usually invisible knowledge, understandings and communication practices of the Gypsy communities should lead us to 'speculate as to the alternative literacies that we have all forfeited' (p. 33).

A NEW LITERATE GLOBAL PUBLIC?

In his book *The Return of the Public* (2010), Dan Hind makes the case for a new global citizenry, with new literacy practices at its centre. He begins by describing the changing character of public action and agency across a variety of societies, ancient, medieval and modern. He argues for the more active participation of an increasingly autonomous public in the evolution of democratically based transformations of public life.

> Both the public service ethos and neoliberalism seek to do without a population operating as an autonomous public. In the first, well-meaning technocrats, who are properly responsive to the reasonable demands of the population, deliver the best of all possible worlds. In the second, market forces are left to do the work. (p. 202)

> In the absence of public institutions where collective responses to structural problems can be developed the individual is left alone in a horribly

uneven struggle with those who currently control the terms of debate and the systems of description. (p. 148)

Hind recalls Dewey's call for 'a great community' based on conversation and debate among equals as a means for both understanding and influencing the otherwise impersonal systems of modern power. Dewey pointed out that genuine, efficacious debate and discussion—and the praxis of experiencing agency in changing public understandings, judgments, and actions—become self-perpetuating as citizens come to appreciate the true force of an active public that insists on its democratic rights of participation.

Hind outlines a number of practical strategies such as ongoing plebiscites on topics urgently needing research funding, and much more broadly based and formally organised online forums for public exchange and debate. His strategies are based on revised conceptions of governance and governing elites and the better exploitation of new forms of access to information and mass communication. The goal is to work constantly toward what Hind calls a "commonwealth of descriptions" as the basis for actions affecting public life and its private consequences. Each strategy calls for expanded educational efforts around a reformed version of literacy—as skill, capacity and disposition.

These ideas evoke a big new agenda for literate public life that speaks to current public disputes, such as those about the value of scientific inquiry, the gathering, storage and use of 'intelligence' by government agencies on the everyday lives of citizens, decisions by members of the political class about what aspects of what they know can be 'safely' made available to those who elected them and who pay their salaries. These are complex challenges presented by a world that contains both 21st-century modes of global interaction side by side with 18th-century conceptions of how we relate to one another, communities, nations and the land. Hind's point is that these are not just challenges for the political/bureaucratic classes but challenges as well to us all as individuals and as 'a public'. Any productive, generalisable responses to that challenge will, in the end, be a literate accomplishment.

A COMMONWEALTH OF LITERATE DESCRIPTIONS: THE CASE OF WHERE WE LIVE

One example of the consequences of a lack of individual and collective agency in the literate production of a commonwealth of descriptions concerns where humans live. The example relates to a problem that can be resolved only through sophisticated literacy practices, not through more prolonged or extensive face-to-face discussions; it is a problem calling for a particular 'commonwealth of description'.

Recently attracting media attention in my homeland, Australia, was an extended occupation and protest at James Price Point on the far northwest coast of the continent (see Wilderness Society, 2013). A proposal was before government that would turn this largely uninhabited stretch of coastline into probably the largest natural gas hub in the world.

In making their case, the protestors pointed to the species that would be endangered, including migrating whales, and to valued features of the natural heritage, including a dinosaur track, internationally recognised as unique, along the nearby peninsula. Their case also included a simple statement about the distinctive beauty of this strip of coast. Along with government, conservationists and the developers, two Australian Aboriginal groups were in dispute over the proposed natural gas hub. One group had secured an arrangement with the developers whereby they would receive a portion of the profits for the development of their community, enabling them, they believed, to develop appropriate services and to access the kinds of resources that most non-Aboriginal Australians have taken for granted for decades. The other group pointed to the heritage significance of this stretch of land for the traditional Aboriginal inhabitants and owners, and to the need for it to remain as it is.

Regardless of our assessment of the final decision made in this instance, we can ask questions about the possibility of a 'commonwealth of description': How do a nation, a government, business interests, and a people conduct a good-faith debate over these claims, involving as they do incommensurate definitions of 'the land'? What sort of thing is 'land'? What is 'a rural environment'? 'Agricultural land'? 'Heritage land'? 'Natural land'? (The Supreme Court ruling that finally overturned the approval to mine at James Price Point was headlined by the Wilderness Society '*Victory for Australia's nature*'.) How does a nation come to a decision that, even if not consensual, is at least generally understood?

These are primordial questions about where we live and how we relate to one another because of where we live. They are new inflections of old questions. Both the agricultural revolution that began 11,000 years ago and the industrial revolution that began 350 years ago centred on and generated a new set of oppositions to do with people, as individuals and collectives, and the land as habitation, resource and retreat (Williams, 1958/1983). The unstable settlements that developed around those oppositions remain with us in modern industrialised societies today. As populations grow and spread and as agricultural and industrial technologies expand their reach, the contradictions and tensions that those settlements temporarily covered have reappeared with evermore urgency and consequentiality.

So what does literacy education have to do with land, country and nature? Donehower, Hogg, & Schell (2012) set out to show how literacy and English education are implicated in how questions about land, country and nature are, and could be, answered. Their aim was to show how deeply, and in how many surprisingly different ways, literacy and language practices are implicated in how 'how rural spaces and people relate—through representation or interaction—to urban and suburban areas and ultimately to the global community' (p. xiii). Donehower and colleagues developed a recognition that literacy policies and practices around curriculum, peda-gogical training and assessment regimes are, whatever else they may be, organic products of urban experience. The instincts arising from that par-ticular experience are for standardisation, actuarial forms of accountabil-ity, competitiveness and for a strong distinction between, on the one hand, intellectual work, and, on the other, social and manual work.

The absence of a 'commonwealth of descriptions' means that explana-tions for the widening socioeconomic discrepancies between rural and urban centres resort to the material resourcing of schools or maybe to the 'cultural deficiencies' of rural families. The work of Donehower and col-leagues shows many new, practical ways of using literacy teaching and learning to resist the 'deruralisation' of youngsters' educational experience, but the backdrop against which all of these make sense is that some current literacy and English education practices silently collude in the economic and cultural marginalisation of people and places.

THE AGENDA FOR LITERACY STUDIES

From the groundbreaking anthropological work of Street (1984), Heath (1983) and the New Literacy Studies group (e.g., Pahl & Rowsell, 2006), we have viewed the inadequacy of most descriptions of individual and col-lective literacy practices. These approaches have questioned not so much the reliability or the construct or predictive validity of the assessment of those practices but rather the relevance of most of the premises underlying and providing warrant to literacy education—most critically what is left out of conventional approaches to schooling literacy.

Much of the literature on relationships among globalisation, technol-ogy and literacy education points to the lack of articulation between educational policies to do with literacy and those to do with the uses of technology in classrooms (Burnett & Bailey, this volume, develop this point). From a research perspective, and in particular a research per-spective that draws on anthropological orientations, this is exactly the analytic point. How is it that some (and not other) textual affordances—the traces, forces, and flows of other times, places, cultures, ideologies, political, and economic conditions—have historically been ignored in everyday institutionalised educational practice? What are the conse-quences of ignoring these (and not the other) affordances with regard to preparing learners for domestic, social, civic and work life? Why is it that these omissions, so apparent from an anthropological perspective, have for generations been so comfortably accommodated in current policy and practice? And what disruptions would eventuate if the "communica-tional repertoires that are frequently left silent" (Rowsell & Burgess, this volume) were activated?

Clearly social justice and communication are interconnected in global settings. Sorrels (2012) has mapped the opportunities for and the challenges to the development of a less docile and more active, informed and equitable citizenry, showing the need for detailed ongoing study of these interconnections as they are acted out in everyday settings. The following chapters provide us with admirable levels of detail and a generally equally admirable resistance to providing grand-narrative explanations of how literacy works in these specific social and cultural settings. For a literacy educator, a key point to consider in light of these accounts is the development of theoretical and empirical programs that give us insight into the conditions, beliefs, and understandings that hold in place current practices to do with the teaching and assessment of literacy in schools. Without empirically grounded, theoretically informed understandings of those homeostatic forces, we are left with faux naïve accounts of literacy, social justice, and globalisation that are peopled by kindly but myopic, change-resistant and possibly benighted educational authorities, who just happen to miss, over and over again, the rich complexities and multiplicities so obvious to social scientists.

But, of course, these are unsatisfactory accounts, for researchers and practitioners alike, precisely because many of literacy's riches haven't been missed; they've been omitted. Documenting and theorising those persistent, transnational omissions maybe the next important literacy research program—one that might bring back some patina to 'new' and 'global'.

Acknowledgments

The editors would like to thank Peter Freebody for writing the foreword and all contributors for their excellent chapters, which provide such diverse insights into literacies in different localities. We would also like to thank the children and young people whose literacies practices are presented in this volume, as well as the teachers whose committed and innovative work enabled the practices described in educational settings. We very much appreciate the time taken by colleagues to read and comment on drafts of this work, in particular Kathy Mills, Sally Ng, Carol Taylor and Karen Wohlwend. We are also very grateful to Jennifer Colautti for her survey of international responses to '21st-century literacies', which informs Chapter 1. Finally, we would like to thank those at Routledge for their support in producing this volume and for devising the current title for this book, which prompted us to rethink our understandings of relationships between the local and 'global.'

1 Changing Contexts for 21st Century Literacies

INTRODUCTION

This volume brings together the work of innovative literacy researchers and asks how their work might inform educational practice, and how literacy educators might, as a result, best prepare children and young people for the future. We contend that everyday literacy practices are changing rapidly in the face of new sociotechnical arrangements, and that these changes impact on students and schools in surprising and often unpredictable ways imbricated, as they are, with wider social, cultural and economic change. Other changes are widespread as well—education systems too, are in flux. Curriculum and policy reforms in many parts of the world have themselves produced considerable uncertainty, often propelling issues of communication, language and literacy to centre stage. And along with all this, there have been changes in the ways in which we think about literacy, and changes in the ways in which it is theorised and researched.

Ways of looking at literacy have developed in significant ways since its re-conceptualisation as a social practice (Street, 1985). The evolution of a tradition that is often described as the New Literacy Studies (Gee, 1991; Street, 1995), and some of the more recent directions that this has taken, are reflected in the chapters that follow. These newer directions have involved shifts in the object of study, so for example, literacy—or literacies have mutated and diversified as different populations have explored and taken up the possibilities offered by new media and digital communication. In fact from a social practice perspective, how we describe and define literacy, and ultimately what counts as literate behaviour is inseparable from its context—and that context, as we have outlined, is rapidly changing. These changes in the communicative context suggest that literacies are increasingly multiple, multimodal and mediated through new technology.

The chapters in this book bring together literacy research from across the globe, yet even with our best intentions to take a global view, we are aware of the partiality of the perspective we offer. In generating theories which attempt to conceptualise literacy irrespective of cultural and social context, it is the specific detail of particular instances that often test them to breaking point. As we see in the following chapters, viewing specific instances of practice against broader cultural frameworks, and across cultural spaces, emphasises how crucial context is—but at the same time, as we shall see context itself is a problematic concept. Thus we cannot assume that all social settings treat technologies in the same way.

The social model of literacy proposed by The New London Group (Cope & Kalantzis, 1999) and enshrined in the New Literacy Studies (e.g. Barton & Hamilton, 1998; Gee, 1991; and Street, 1984) signalled a significant step change in literacy studies away from what was a predominantly psychological model. In the psychological model, where emphasis is placed on a regulative understanding of literacy, the teaching of discreet skills such as those of spelling and grammar, for example, are paramount. As Street (1984) identified, such teaching tends to be about those skills that can be easily assessed and assigned to age groups (reading ages are typical of this genre). This approach depends upon an assumption that what is taught is transferable to any context; the objective is to identify ways in which learners can be taught how to do things; how teachers can assess skills acquired, and on how positive interventions to accelerate or support learning may be effected. This point of view has been construed negatively by many of those who have adapted a sociocultural perspective of literacy. For example Gee comments that:

> . . . the traditional view of literacy as the ability to read and write rips literacy out of its sociocultural contexts and treats it as an asocial cognitive skill with little or nothing to do with human relationships.
>
> (Gee, 1996:46).

In the social model of literacy, the emphasis of research has been less prescriptive and more descriptive (see Cameron, 1995). The social paradigm has sought to describe ways in which literacy is used by individuals and groups; to this end much of the research (e.g. Barton & Hamilton, 1998; Barton et al 2007; Street, 2001; Tusting, 2013) has been ethnographic in texture. In many ways New Literacy Studies (NLS) research has a history of being democratic, seeking to value what literacy participants are doing, as opposed to assessing against a particular standard or set criteria; literacy researchers have watched how people do things; researchers learn from their research participants what literacy is—the users are the experts. NLS research is about understanding what people do, understanding literacy as an aspect of human behaviour. Within NLS the idea of context has been fundamental. Associated with this, as has been much documented, two key concepts which have been much used within the field—the literacy 'event' and the literacy 'practice'. Arrow & Finch (2013:131) explain that the term 'event' refers to specific interactions, modes of communication and text that in turn constitute literacy practices (Barton & Hamilton, 2005). Events are therefore observable instantiations of practice—and we can conceptualise practices as an extrapolated understanding of an array of associated events, so that we can talk about the practices of letter writing, game design or graphic novel writing, for example. Notwithstanding the above, and as some of the chapters in this volume suggest, it is sometimes difficult to isolate the boundaries of specific events, and that contexts whilst important, are also difficult to define. The move away from what Street referred to as 'the autonomous model of literacy', has not resolved our problems; indeed choosing to understand from the users what literacy is, as opposed to simply viewing it as a code, we have expanded our purview immeasurably in our attempt to capture the changing nature of literacy as a lived experience.

In preparing this volume we were keen to capture the essence of changes in how literacy is used and described. We were keen to show not only how these changes are reflected in the different ages and stages of the student population, varying as they do between and within communities, but also in different parts of the world, too. In many ways this is a challenging task, demanding a full study in its own right, so instead we have attempted to illustrate what we think are significant themes, by selectively including a variety of studies that point up key issues, but yet work together to help us in teasing out some more general tendencies and themes in literacies around the globe. In order to achieve this, an editorial commentary is woven through the chapters that follow, providing a coherent thread that draws on each chapter, indicating connections between the chapters, and binding them together in order that they can address current concerns in literacy policy and pedagogy.

In this introductory chapter we set out the context for that work, beginning with an exploration of discourses of globalism in order to identify the ways in which the concepts of 'global' and 'local' are taken up by the editors and contributors. We then identify what we see as the major influences that are shaping literacy policy and curriculum, illustrating these with some selective examples from different parts of the world. We conclude with a brief discussion of the different ways in which 'newness' is represented in this work. It is not then our intention to provide some sort of overview of (new) literacies, but rather to look at some important contemporary issues and how they are being addressed and interpreted in different ways, and in different contexts.

AROUND THE GLOBE?

It's perhaps inevitable that the phrase 'around the globe' when used in a contemporary context, conjures up the idea of globalisation with all its associations with universalism, interconnection, late capitalism and so on (Law, 2004). However, this book is not about globalisation, or the globalisation of education, or even about global education, although we will be addressing the spread of educational ideologies, the different ways in which technologies are taken up in education, and the effects of population mobility—all of which could be characterised as manifestations of what Appadurai (1996) refers to as 'global flow'. But by doing this we are not suggesting that there is movement towards an era of open and democratic sharing of ideas about literacy pedagogy, or that all educators and policy-makers have an equal voice in the current debate, yet we are interested in the ways in which influence works. So in this respect our critique of the global follows that of Massey, who argues that:

> The imagination of globalisation in terms of unbounded free space, that powerful rhetoric of neoliberalism around 'free trade', just as was modernity's view of space, is a pivotal element in an overweaning political discourse. It is a discourse which is dominantly produced in the countries of the world's North (though acquiesced in by many a government in the South). It has its institutions and its professionals. It is normative; and it has effects.
>
> (Massey, 2005:83)

Instead of 'global' we could, as an alternative, place our emphasis on an idea like 'translocal assemblages' (McFarlane, 2009). This is suggestive of the ways in which complex and multiple forces coalesce as place-based events—events that are partly constituted by the exchange of 'ideas, knowledge, practices, materials and resources across sites' (McFarlane, 2009:561). Not so easy to include in a book title, but a more fitting account of how discourses of language and power intersect with socioeconomic status and the ownership of mobile technologies in South Africa (Chapter 2), and a better description of the multiple social networking practices of newly arrived migrants in Canada than that afforded by globalisation (see Chapter 7).

However, ideas do travel between localities, and although there is nothing new in this, their influence is increasingly felt in education. Whether this is the spread of practical classroom ideas like the use of De Bono's 'Thinking Hats' (Nichols, 2006), pedagogic literacy theory such as the genre approach (Hyland, 2002), or larger scale ideological influence, such as that exerted by Hirsch and his US-based Core Knowledge Foundation on the English National Curriculum (Abrams, 2012), it is clear that a variety of influences come to bear upon practitioners and policymakers, and it is likely that the rapid diffusion of information on the internet has increased the volume and spread of ideas such as these. However, we strongly contend that this does not lead to homogeneity, since it is quite clear that local interpretation always determines how ideas are understood, interpreted and how they interact with other forces—to put it another way, we might replace the idea of 'the global' as an undifferentiated universal space with an understanding that 'the global is situated, specific and materially constructed in the practices which make each specificity' (Law, 2004: 563).

Technologies travel, too, particularly as multinational corporations seek out new markets for their products, but access to them, and the uses to which they are then put, are also patterned by a nexus of influences. A number of researchers in this collection focus their gaze on the use of mobile technologies, but in each instance the challenges, interpretations and practices are distinct. Take for example, the complex ways in which trainee hairdressers perform identity in their interconnecting web of on/offline practices, embedded as they are in the night-time economy of a city in the North of England (Chapter 5), and contrast it with the work of teachers and first-graders working with portable technologies in US Mid-West (Chapter 3). For all the widespread circulation of digital devices, their application could not be more heterogeneous. A singular narrative of the transformative effect of technology falls then at the first hurdle, with or without recourse to cautions against technological determinism. Yet still the materiality of these devices matters, and the ways in which they impact on literacy practices and literacy educators is important to consider, even if the result paints a complex and diverse picture.

Discourses of globalisation have also been particularly influential in political rhetoric. The inevitability of competition in the global economy was a key theme in the UK for New Labour governments (Watson & Hay, 2003), and the circulation of these and related ideas has no doubt fuelled the increased interest in international comparisons of educational performance. As a result, the idea of benchmark standards that allow for comparison across very different contexts—from Chicago to Paris to Singapore continues to seduce education policymakers whose reputation often rides on such measures. Dominant amongst these are the OECD's comparative measure of educational performance, the Programme for International Student Achievement (PISA) which covers 65 member countries from Albania to Vietnam, and the Progress in International Reading Literacy Study (PIRLS) with a similar international reach across 35 countries. But of course the extent to which these measures are genuinely international is questionable. China, with an estimated population of 1.3 billion is not included in either, and although the country's rapid economic growth led to membership of the World Trade Organisation (WT0) in 2001, and subsequent reform of basic education, it has yet to compete in this arena. Nevertheless, the rhetoric of global economic competitiveness cuts across a wide segment of policy reform and is repeatedly framed in terms of an educational emphasis on 21st Century skills.

21ST CENTURY LITERACIES AROUND THE GLOBE

With all the above caveats in mind, to take seriously the idea of new literacies around the globe we became interested in how this idea is framed within curriculum and policy. What do different policy initiatives identify as 'new' literacies, practices and epistemologies in the face of modern-day complexities? The phrase '21st century literacy' has become a fashionable, even a pervasive way of describing new literacies, and it carries with it the built-in assumption that we think and act differently when we use new technologies and new media.[1] This assumption often fuels the call for radical curriculum reform and the adoption of new pedagogies and in its extreme form is even used to challenge the relevance of educational institutions themselves (Merchant, 2012). Around the globe, different countries have offered their own distinctive interpretation of 21st century skills. In this section, we profile a selection of initiatives that relate to themes featured in the chapters that follow. These are certainly not comprehensive, have had varying levels of impact and some have now been superseded by other policies. They do, however, exemplify different ways in which '21st century skills' have been conceived by policy-makers.

In the UK, the New Labour vision of a 21st Century Schools System (DCSF, 2009) set out a surprisingly conservative view of the conditions and dispositions required for the 21st century. Good literacy, numeracy and ICT skills are repeatedly mentioned—sometimes abbreviated as 'basic skills', but there is little to suggest any change here, or for that matter, any recognition of new literacies. Subsequent reform in education provision in England has been even more retrogressive with the emphasis being placed on phonics in the initial stages of schooling, and then spelling and grammar later on. The discrete and often decontextualised presentation of literacy-as-a-basic-skill has characterised recent policy initiatives. And in further changes, even the ICT curriculum has been abandoned, soon to be replaced by computing and coding—the latter, in an influential report, being referred to as 'the new Latin' (Livingstone & Hope, 2011). Interestingly though, this area of the curriculum is the one that is most influenced by the rhetoric of global economic competitiveness: 'High-tech, knowledge-intensive sectors and, in the case of video games, major generators of intellectual property, these industries have all the attributes the UK needs to succeed in the 21st century' (Livingstone & Hope, 2011: 4), and this is used as a platform for arguing for a more specialised and technical kind of digital literacy. This is a rather different take on videogame technology than that offered by Beavis in Chapter 6.

If literacy education in England is characterised by a strict adherence to standards and accountability, Finland with its impressive track record as a front-runner in PISA scores, has a reputation for educational innovation and exemplary pedagogical frameworks. The Finnish government has invested heavily in teacher education and has been committed to a decentralised curriculum with high levels of teacher autonomy. Finland is one of four founding members of the 21st Century Skills Project, with a government strategy that underlines how 'Knowledge, creativity and innovation are the cornerstones of society and its development' (MoE, Finland, 2003). In a report on education in Finland (MoE, Finland, 2012), the measures required to equip students for the 21st century are outlined. These are listed as: better access to the arts and arts education; internationalisation; education and working life; and, lifelong learning. Being a part of the global initiative, Assessment and Teaching of 21st Century Skills Project (ATCS, 2013), Finland subscribes to the constellation of skills that the ATCS emphasises: 1. Collaborative problem solving—which represents the idea of working together to solve a common challenge, involving the contribution and exchange of ideas, knowledge or resources to achieve the goal, and 2. ICT literacy—which includes learning through digital media, such as social networking and simulations, as well as technological awareness. It is suggested that each of these elements enables individuals to function effectively in social networks and contribute to the development of social and intellectual capital. We will see how some of these skills are reflected and refined by the work of contributors to this volume.

Like Finland, Singapore is a partner in the ATCS initiative discussed above. And in addition, the Singapore Ministry of Education is implementing a new framework to enhance the development of 21st century competencies in students: 'This will underpin the holistic education that our schools provide to better prepare our students to thrive in a fast-changing and highly-connected world' (MoE, Singapore, 2012: 2). The Singapore Ministry of Education aims to prepare young people for the 'new digital age' by promoting civic literacy, global awareness and cross-cultural skills; critical and inventive thinking; and information and communication skills. The Singapore framework stresses self-awareness, self-management, social awareness, relationship management, and responsible decision-making (MoE, Singapore, 2010). Rather than specifying digital literacy skills, the Singaporean framework spotlights such skills as confidence; being a concerned citizen; self-directed learner; and, active contributor. In a recent initiative to promote new literacies a MoE working party is helping to generate more opportunities for students to create through critical and responsible use of ICT, to curate through developing socio-cultural sensitivity and awareness, and to connect through critical and inventive thinking within the national curriculum.

In response to rapid economic growth and modernisation China has recently instituted a substantial programme of educational reform. This incorporates a shift from a knowledge-based and teacher-led approach to one which incorporates learning through inquiry and discussion, alongside the application of knowledge and appropriate use of technology (Leung & Ruan, 2012). The Yuwen curriculum places a new emphasis on individuality and individual expression whilst upholding traditional standards in Chinese language and literacy such as character recognition, reading and writing. Moving towards a learner-centred education, it is hoped that students will develop flexibility and problem solving skills for the 21st Century. In a Ministry of Education document the Chinese government set out its goals for the information technology curriculum. These include:

a) to cultivate students' interest in and awareness of information technologies; b) to acquire basic ICT knowledge and skills; c) to develop an understanding of the impact of ICTs on human lives and conditions; d) to develop competence in locating, communicating, processing, and utilising information; e) to use technologies in responsible and ethical manners; f) to use technologies to support life-long learning and collaborative learning. Guidance also calls for the integration of ICTs into the teaching of other school subjects (Ge et al., 2012). There are many parallels here with work in this volume, but the challenges faced by the scale of change and the wide diversity of the Chinese population are, of course, distinctive.

In contrast, Australia has been involved in a number of initiatives that have explored innovative approaches to teaching and learning for the 21st century. Australia, along with Finland, the US and Singapore is involved in the ATCS outlined above. In addition to this, Australia's Digital Education Revolution (DER) was an initiative that provided funding for all aspects of digital education in schools including major school infrastructure, teacher training, curriculum design and assessment and community engagement. Focusing on the development and distribution of digital resources to support students' development of 21st century skills, building the capacity of teachers to deliver digital education (including inquiry-based learning), and supporting teachers in the development of ICT based pedagogical strategies, and formative assessment to support students' learning in and outside the classroom were key features of this initiative. Again, many of the same concepts associated with '21st century thinking' appeared in this work—these included an emphasis on inquiry-based approaches, focusing on digital teaching methods, and problem-solving.

In the US, publicly and privately-funded initiatives promote new ways of teaching and learning in the 21st century. As well as the ATCS model, the recently announced federal ConnectEd Initiative aims to equip schools with 21st century technology, providing highspeed broadband to 99% of students in the United States within 5 years. Another initiative—the 21st Century Community Learning Centers Program—is also impacting on practice. This program is an example of a federal effort to improve academic achievement by extending learning opportunities. The programme, funded by the US Department of Education and administered by the states, seeks to provide opportunities for academic enrichment, youth development and other activities for students before and after school, as well as during the summer. It also offers families opportunities for literacy and related educational development. Some examples of provision include: arts and music education activities, recreational activities, language skills, telecommunications and technology education programs, drug and violence prevention, entrepreneurial education programs, programs that promote parental involvement and family literacy. Key to this is the wish to expand the idea of the classroom involving mentors, employers, and artists working together in new ways to get students involved and interested in their own learning and making connections beyond the school. In addition, a patchwork of initiatives and grant programs offered by private foundations, corporations, and state and local government fund K-12 schools to provide digital technologies such as "1-to-1" tablets. In other places, schools are changing policies to institute BYOD programs that allow students to "bring your own device" such as mobile phones and tablets. All of these initiatives sit alongside what is presented as an integrated approach to literacy and technology in the Common Core State Standards, which are designed to frame education in the US (National Governors Association, 2012).

As an overall statement on 'digital learning', the Canadian government commissioned the Media Awareness Network (2010) to write a consultation paper on media and digital literacy. Echoing concerns raised by other national governments, it was felt that Canada had fallen behind a number of other countries in the development of what has come to be known as the digital economy. In this document, policy developers discuss what digital literacy includes and in doing so they go beyond simple technology skills to include a deeper understanding of, and ultimately the ability to create a wide range of content with various digital tools. *Use, understand,* and *create* are three verbs that underpin their view of the active competencies of a digitally literate individual.

Several provinces have proposed different versions of a 21st century curriculum. The 21st Century Education platform in British Columbia provides a vision for the school system that aims to prepare students to be successful in a rapidly changing world. It is rooted in a personalised, learner-centred approach and based on the idea that traditional skills like literacy and numeracy need to be applied in different ways. These would include: critical thinking and problem solving; creativity and innovation; technological literacy; communications and media literacy; collaboration and teamwork; personal organisation; motivation, self-regulation and adaptability; ethics, civic responsibility and cross-cultural awareness. Ontario emphasises many similar skills with a focus on changing classroom, school and board practices in order to respond to new challenges in education, to better meet student needs and expectations, and to anticipate what will be required in a knowledge-intensive and increasingly connected society.

Whilst this is by no stretch of the imagination a representative sample of policy imperatives, we think it does help to show how the idea of 21st Century skills has been interpreted and re-interpreted in different contexts. Some of the key themes that emerge are:

- a recognition of the changing practices associated with the increase of digital connectivity;
- an emphasis on learning both *with* and *about* technology;
- a restatement of the importance of basic skills;
- a recognition of the importance of soft skills such as collaboration and problem-solving;

- a view that flexibility, creativity and innovation are important;
- a recognition that learning continues outside of school contexts, and beyond the span of compulsory education;
- an idea that quite specific skills are needed to compete in the digital economy.

Playing across these themes is an overarching concern that the 21st Century poses new challenges for education systems, and that these will be best met by re-emphasising some familiar aspects of schooling (skills and ways of working) and adding on others. These are set against ideas about nurturing economic competitiveness in a hi-tech global future. Throughout these initiatives and aspirational statements there is also a set of assumptions about what is new—and it is this concept of newness that is central our book. In what follows we turn our attention to the 'new' of new literacies.

WHAT IS 'NEW'?

It would be hard to read contemporary sources on literacy education without noting the ubiquity of the adjective 'new', which is used to describe everything from theoretical orientation (as in New Literacy Studies or New Literacies), to practices and their associated habits of mind (Lankshear & Knobel, 2010), or the technologies that are used and the texts that are produced (Kress, 2003). New ways of making meaning and emerging modes of communication and interaction, have been variously described as 'new media', 'new' or 'digital' literacies, and they certainly do represent a significant change in everyday practices and one that invites fresh thinking about how we work with children and young people in formal educational settings. However, such is the rate of change that practices that once seemed new, quickly become established and taken for granted. Take, for example, a practice like blogging, once at the cutting edge of writing about new literacies and now, at least in some instances, an institutionalised activity. These uses of 'newness', have been useful in fuelling research and professional interest in the changes outlined above, but it is important to highlight how 'the new' surfaces in this volume and some of the particular issues that are raised. First let's look at some of the problems associated with these ideas about 'the new'.

One rather unfortunate consequence of our love affair with 'the new' is that it can create a rather unhealthy polarisation. Established or traditional practices can unwittingly be cast as redundant, dull or boring in the haste to valorise what is exciting, of the moment, and with all the allure of the 'shiny', stylish and fashionable (Davies, 2007). However, the idea that established print-based practices have been replaced by newer forms is patently untrue, and despite a whole raft of moral panics about declining literacy standards, the neglect of literary fiction, and the prevalence of uncritical reading, there is little evidence to support these assertions. In fact it is probably the case that we are now reading and writing more, and in more varied forms than ever before. Literacy practices associated with new media *add* to the existing range, rather than replacing it. This is picked up at a number of points in this book, for instance in Chapter 3, in which we see young children making use of a range of representational resources, and in Chapter 8 where familiar story-sharing routines are supplemented by the use of new technologies.

Another caution in the use of 'the new' in literacy studies and literacy education relates to the ways in which this has often been imagined as a universal phenomenon. But as we know, what is new in one context may not be new in another, and vice versa. This is particularly noticeable when we consider the impact of technology, which clearly has uneven take up across different populations. This raises the difficult question of whether or not we think, act, and communicate in distinctively different ways in the so-called 'digital age', and indeed whether the digital age is in itself a universal phenomenon. There is now a substantial body of work that addresses these questions from the early writings of McLuhan (1964), to the more recent contributions of Manovich (2001), Gee (2003), Kress (2003), Lankshear & Knobel (2010) and so on.

In assembling this book, our strategy has been to spotlight research into practices within specific contexts that focus on situated engagement with technologies. This strategy highlights the multiplicity of social practices that co-exist, and helps us to draw out what is *new* about new literacies in these particular contexts. With the dramatic shift from print to digital media (Snyder, 1998), there has been an acknowledgement across fields and disciplines that communication is in a state of flux. Unfortunately, as we have observed, within some educational discourses, there tends to be a set of rather nebulous ideas about new approaches to learning and teaching. Although the policy developments outlined in the previous section offer some alternatives, they are often vague and intangible with an emphasis on good intentions rather than practicalities.

Part of the problem lies in an assumption that digital technologies make us *better* thinkers and communicators. A utopian rhetoric informs some of what is said about technologies and '21ˢᵗ century' policy and pedagogy, and this utopianism sometimes derails moves to explore 'new' approaches. Part of the work of this volume is to provide a critique of this rhetoric and to ask more searching questions about students, meaning-making, and the media they use.

This volume raises some of these critical questions. For example, how do the wider discourses of gender, race, nationality and social class play out in new literacies? Differences in access and use, as well as differences in resources and levels of connectivity are all pressing issues and they are all too often rendered silent within discussions about new literacies. Given their importance, and the ways in which they pattern experience, they raise significant issues for all educators regardless of their specific orientation to 21st Century practices. And what of the representational and semiotic resources that are involved in the use of new technologies—for instance, is book-sharing a radically different experience when the print book is replaced by the iPad? As we see in Chapter 8, there are continuities and discontinuities. And what of the connections between online and offline worlds, and how do we conceptualise these? Contributors to this volume humanise movements across online and offline worlds so that they are rendered part of the everyday, and long upheld distinctions begin to blur. These are just a few of the many issues that are raised in what follows.

OUTLINE OF THE BOOK

The book looks selectively at telling cases of new literacies in different parts of the world. There are inevitably gaps in representation, but our intention is to provide a thread that ties local contexts to global ones. The first study is based in South Africa, and here Prinsloo and Lemphane throw social class into relief by contrasting how a middle class family interacts and accesses technologies as compared with the limited access a working class family has to digital tools and technologies. Unique in the book for its more polemical statement about 'new' literacies and technologies in relation to larger issues like race and social class, the chapter launches the collection with a situated, place-based approach to technology and digital tools. In the second chapter, Wohlwend and Buchholz, working in the US Mid-West encourage us to take a broad perspective on meaning making and to refine conceptions of communicational practices focusing on the multiple meaning-making practices of early years settings.

This is followed by a study located in a primary school in the North of England. Burnett and Bailey usher readers into the world of *Minecraft*, exploring the improvisational qualities of meaning-making in hybrid on/offline spaces, and consider the implications of this for how we see collaboration. This is followed by Davies who traces the textual exchanges of three young women as they communicate across contexts, weaving their face-to-face and online lives together. Based in the UK, the activities of these young women provide a nuanced perspective on the visual and semiotic complexities of identity as it is mediated through the everyday traffic of texts. In a return to classroom practices, Beavis gives the collection a view on video games as new narrative forms that carry the potential for innovative ways to explore and lift out literary and aesthetic dimensions of texts. Based on her work in Australian classrooms she demonstrates how reading is fused with action as children and young people engage with these new textual forms.

Set in Canada, Rowsell and Burgess present a research study on four Facebook users and the sophisticated linguistic and communicative practices they use to navigate different linguistic systems and transcultural domains. Moving into the world of apps, and more specifically story apps, in an early years context in England, Merchant displays the multi-sensory complexity of touch-based technologies. Delving into the intricacies of gesture and touch, Merchant sheds new light on evolving ways that we use, interact, and think through mobile technologies. Finally, Williams offers a contrastive picture of schooled and institutionalised conceptions of literacy juxtaposed against what actually happens when young adults make meaning in everyday practices through mobile devices.

The book concludes with a reflection on the themes explored in the chapters and commentaries. Rather than focusing on literacy as fixed and individualised, it is suggested that literacy in educational contexts needs to embrace the diverse, collaborative and provisional nature of contemporary meaning-making. The chapter ends with a Charter for Literacy Education which outlines a series of principles to underpin literacy policy and practice.

NOTES

1. See the NCTE (2010) Position Statement for a useful definition of 21st Century Literacies.

2 Global Forms and Assemblages

Children's Digital Literacy Practices in Unequal South African Settings[1]

Polo Lemphane and Mastin Prinsloo

INTRODUCTION

Over the last decade, many studies in literacy and in new media in education have merged two key sets of theoretical resources: firstly, the Literacy Studies (or 'New Literacy Studies') orientation to the study of literacies as social practices that vary across sites and have an ideological or political dimension (Street, 1984) and, secondly, Multimodal Studies which show how literacy activities are inextricably linked with other modes of communication, visual, kinaesthetic and so on (Jewitt, 2008; Kress 2010). Explicitly brought together in Kress and Street (2006) and in Pahl and Rowsell (2006), these two resources have since commonly been drawn on together in literacy and new media studies on the basis that they complement each other. As Street (2012: 1) put it: 'Multimodality and Literacy Studies, brought together, fill out a larger more nuanced picture of social positionings and communication by building an equal recognition of practices, texts, contexts, space, and time'.

This larger picture that Street mentions is certainly needed when the literacy practices studied are electronic, multimedia, screen-based and translocal, but what does it mean to give 'equal recognition' to all of those categories? The focus on multimodality, which Kress outlines, draws on theories of text where the unit of analysis is text in context, whereas Literacy Studies has a focus in which the unit of analysis is that of reading and writing embedded in social activity. These two perspectives direct researcher attention somewhat differently, we suggest, and offer different ways of interpreting what happens when material selves merge with digitally constructed images and activities. The multimodalities lens foregrounds aspects of design and production in considering how immaterial selves are constructed by the affordances of (socially shaped) resources of image, print, sound, gesture, separately and in combination to communicate particular kinds of representations and indentifications in specific ways. The Literacy Studies perspective, in contrast, foregrounds the *socially shaped* aspect. For example, we notice that the representations that individuals produce of themselves as they engage online and in digitalised space are constructed with resources that are globally available and familiar (e.g., the bits and pieces selected to construct a personal avatar). However, what they mean and why and how they are assembled are profoundly informed by concrete, material, located social realities, which are primarily available only to enthnographic analysis and less to social semiotic analyses of text design which assume that key features of design grammar are somehow pregiven.

These issues become more acute and most visible the further one is from the design centres or when the centre itself becomes a site of increasing diversity or 'superdiversity', as Vertovec (2007) and Blommaert and Rampton (2011) tell us is now the case with contemporary European cities. In Africa this is not a new point. The partial transformations of literacy, religion and Western culture that happened in Africa before, during and after colonialism are a case in point, where "(m)oney and commodities, literacy and Christendom . . . were variously and ingeniously redeployed to bear a host of new meanings as non-Western peoples . . . fashioned their own visions of modernity" (Comaroff & Comaroff, 1992: 51). In considering digital media usage in a globalised, diversified/homogenised world, the point can still be made that functions performed by particular modes and resources for communication in one place can be altered in another place, pointing to the complex and socially variable nature of form-function relationships in translocal communication (Hymes, 1996). The way in which 'signs of writing' (Harris, 1995) get inserted in sociocultural activity may differ significantly; consequently there may be important differences in what these (similar or identical) forms *do* in diverse settings. The same interactive multimedia screen might therefore not be functionally the same across these settings when users bring their differences to this screen. At the same time we do no doubt need to attend to both the socially variable and the multimodal aspects of youths' engagements with electronic media resources so as to make sense of them.

We can think of the messages and potentials of digital communications that become available through global electronic communications networks as *global forms* (Collier, 2006), or widely distributed meaning-making or semiotic/organisational resources, that are assembled and adapted in distinctive ways at local and regional levels and articulated in specific situations. Other examples of global forms that get unpredictably assembled include those of international workplace standards (ISOs), as they get invoked, positioned and bypassed in actual workplaces (Kleifgen, 2005), or *neoliberalism* as a logic of governing in Ong's (2007) analysis. Ong sees neoliberalism as a mobile technology and a migratory set of practices that get appropriated in new assemblages in African societies, and elsewhere. Such forms interact with other resources and elements in actual contexts in a mix of global constructs and more localised discourses and preoccupations. These interactions might be called the *actual* global, where the assemblage and its consequences are not predicted simply by the characteristics of the global forms, as they make up only part of what is combined. We can therefore focus on the specificity of the actual global and the sometimes unexpected nature of assemblages that grounded research throws up as a way of enquiring as to how immaterialised forms of self resonate with both material and imagined realities.

Such a perspective points us to what can be called 'the social life' of digital media, the ways that their uses are socially shaped and distinctive with regard to their embedded uses in particular settings. This is also an orientation that argues against a macro/micro conceptual frame in respect to the relationships between global and local. It fits well with an approach that sees a nonlinearity about contemporary processes of global integration (Law, 2004) and Kwa's (2002) preference for 'looking down' at the detail rather than 'looking up' for an overarching narrative (Burnett et al., 2014; Law, 2004). This is a view of the global and global integration that expects some imbalances between cause and effect, unpredictable outcomes, and self-organising, emergent structures, as suggested by Featherstone (2006: 370), who points out that 'the management of uncertainty, task predictability and orderly performances were much easier to facilitate in the "relatively complex" organisations of modern industrial societies'. A global society, on the other hand, he writes, 'entails a different form of complexity: one emanating more from microstructural arrangements that institute self-organising principles and patterns'. These arguments lead us to take a closer look at how digitalised multimedia resources are engaged with differently in contexts of social diversity while we continue to pay attention to the modal features of the (multimodal) resources used for constructing complex refigurations of the material and immaterial, of the concrete and the imaginary.

We turn to our comparative case study to examine the language and literacy practices of children in two households in Cape Town.[2] We examine children's early multimodal engagements with electronic media across contrasting socioeconomic settings and enquire how language and literacy resources are drawn on and merged with what kinds of interests, activities and identification processes and with what kinds of contrasts across these sites. We describe how differently situated children and already coded digitalised resources position each other, where children draw on widely circulating forms and resources as well as locally developed constructs of value, status and identity. We show that the unpredictable assemblage of intentions and resources results in immaterialities that appear both familiar and conventional but that are also situated and located as regards their specific imaginings or immaterialities.

RESEARCH SITES

We studied and contrasted two cases in the research we draw on in this chapter, both Cape Town families whose 'heritage language' in both cases is a Sotho language (Setswana, in one case, and Sesotho or South Sotho, in the other). One family lived in Khayelitsha, a crowded shack settlement (also sometimes referred to as an informal settlement area, or a squatter settlement, or a slum) outside Cape Town. Their home was a shack made from corrugated iron sheets and masonite, about 3½ by 4½ square metres, divided into several rooms by masonite dividers, in which the family of two parents and five children lived. The mother worked as a domestic worker but was working only on Saturdays at this time. The father was a contract labourer on construction sites who had intermittent work. For the duration of the fieldwork he was not working. The major source of monthly household income at such times was by way of state-funded child grants. The parents came to Cape Town from the Eastern Cape to look for work in Cape Town. The mother had completed six years of schooling, whereas the father had completed two. The family got water from a public tap, which was approximately 60 metres from their house. They had a connection to the city's electricity grid, and neighbours who did not have a connection charged their phones in the Mahlale home and sometimes paid R10 for a haircut. A prominent device in the house was the television set, used for watching videos, one church video in particular, rather than live broadcasts. The TV attracted regular visitors from the neighbourhood. Seats were reserved for adults, and children usually sat on the floor. The parents spoke both Sesotho and isiXhosa to their visitors and friends in the neighbourhood and to their children, who always responded in isiXhosa (the predominant language in their neighbourhood and at their school), although they incorporated Sotho terms and phrases occasionally. There were two mobile phones in the family, belonging to the parents and used interchangeably by them, exclusively for making and taking voice calls and not for texting or any other purpose. One of the phones had features that included FM radio and two preinstalled animated games, which were played by the children when they could get access to the phone. This phone had a relatively long-lasting battery compared with the other one and the parents valued it for communicating with family and friends. As a result, the children were allowed limited access to it. There was almost no evidence of printed matter in this household.

The second family in our contrasting case studies lived in a middle-class suburb. The parents were working professionals, one as a quantity surveyor and the other as a project manager. Their three children were at middle-class monolingual English, fee-paying schools and were raised by their parents as English language speakers, while the parents themselves were bilingual speakers of Setswana, which was their first language, and English, which is the lingua franca of commerce, government and the middle-classes in South Africa. As 'black middle-class' professionals, the parents are part of a relatively recent but rapidly growing demographic in South Africa.[3] The parents, who are 'skilled migrants' to Cape Town, frequently speak Setswana between themselves, but not with their children. Their children strongly identify as Anglo-American. Given the opportunity to self-select their pseudonyms for Lemphane's original study (Lemphane, 2012), the 8-year-old girl said she would like to be known as 'Ashley', which was a name she liked and had formerly given to a doll of hers. She picked Bolton as the family surname, borrowing it from the TV series 'The Boltons', which features the admired lead actor from the McGyver series. Her 14-year-old brother chose the name Lars, from an X-box game character whom he admired, and his 10-year-old brother chose the name Josh, on the basis that it was a name he had formerly used for his avatar on the 'virtual life' online simulation game that the children often played. They lived in a comfortable house with Internet connectivity, electricity and running water and had ample space in which to study and play. They were free to use the desktop computer at any time for schoolwork purposes but were allowed to play on it on weekends only. They watched television and played on a PlayStation connected to a TV in a bedroom.

RESEARCH FOCUS

Data were collected for a period of three months, from June to August 2011. The research model was that of contrastive ethnographic-style case studies (Heath & Street, 2008). Each family was visited on alternate weekends, when both children and their parents were at home. Lemphane, the coauthor of this chapter, observed and recorded activities while children played with particular digital media; she also carried out unstructured and semistructured interviews. Collected data included recordings of conversations and researcher discussions with children and parents, photographs of children at play in their environment, screenshots of electronic images and text, as well as field notes.

We focus in this chapter on examples of children communicating and playing with each other and with electronic media resources. We are interested in the contrasts across the two families and what these might signal as to how multimodal electronic resources get situated in their uses and purposes by the larger social dynamics that shape these children's diverging social trajectories. We are interested in differentials and contrasts or presences and absences in terms of digital media and technologies and what is and what is not materialised in the homes of our two contrasting case studies. In our analysis of the research findings here, we start with the Mahlale family, focusing on children's electronic media engagements and the shapes that these take.

THE MAHLALE CHILDREN AT PLAY

We start with a widely observed point that has been made with regard to Cape Town, to the rest of South Africa and also with regard to the rest of Africa, namely that most people do not have computer access but do have mobile phone access and that Internet activity is predominantly phone-based for most people, rather than computer-based. Whereas in 2000 only one in a hundred sub-Saharan Africans had access to a mobile phone, the figure is now greater than one in two (54% in 2012), with South Africa having (Deloitte, 2012) a considerably higher ratio, closer to a 100% access rate if one takes into account how phone use is widely shared within townships and informal settlements. Widespread mobile phone availability has led to calls for out-of-school educational interventions that are based on the mobile phone (Vosloo, 2012). However, such calls do not always examine the particularities or quality of working-class or underclass children's access and engagement with mobile phones or consider that their educational potentials might not be simply premised on the fact of the availability of the resources. Our study here offers a more complex view of the social factors that shape usage in ways that complicate the story about educational potential.

The first point to note is that the Mahlale children had no computer access at all and were allowed only limited access to their parents' mobile phones, in particular because prolonged play with the phone caused the battery to run down and also because their mother, at least, did not see any educational value in children's digital play. The conversation below starts to illustrate this point. The exchange is between their father and a visitor.

Mr Lebaka:	He!, ena ea hau ea sebetsa founu! Ha e na tsatsi la mahala. [This phone of yours really works! It does not have a free day]
Mr Mahlale:	E ea qeta betri (*Softly*) [It will exhaust the battery]
Mr Lebake:	Ha e ka siuoa chacheng mono feela, ba e bona feela . . . [If it is left there on the charger, and they see it . . .] (giggles from the children)

The children had taken the mobile phone off the charger when Mr. Mahlale was not looking. The children had two strategies to get hold of a phone: One was to wait for a phone to be put on the charger, so that they could take it and play with it; the other was to ask visitors to their home if they could 'see' their phones. When they 'saw' a phone, the children played with it to see what games it had, how its recording mode worked, as well as examining the different ringing tones it had. The children's mother was even more reluctant than their father to give them access to the phones. We note here a contrast with Marsh's (2004) findings that the working-class parents in her study in the north of England were supportive of their children's playing with new media.

The conversation below was between Thabang, her mother Mathabang and the researcher:

1.	*Lemphane:*	Ha le bapale ka fono tsatsing lee? [Are you not playing with the phone today?]
2.	*Thabang:*	Foune ea ntate haeo. [Father's phone is not there.]
3.	*Lemphane:*	Ha le sebelise ea 'M'e? [Don't you use your mother's?]
4.	*Thabang:*	Rea e sebelisa. (*Nervously*) [We use it.]
5.	*'Mathabang:*	Ba tseba hore 'na ha ke tšoane le ntat'oa bona, 'na ke bohale. [They know that I am not like their father. I am strict.]

The children were never seen to make phone calls or send SMSs. Their parents' restrictions regarding children's use of mobile phones, as they protected these costly resources, gave the children limited access to digital play. Not only was their access restricted but the conditions of play were also constrained by the limited space available in the home as well as the parents' attitudes to children's noise. When they played inside, the children often had to play silently so as not to annoy their parents or visitors in the crowded collective space which they all occupied.

The children's digital play consisted mostly of silently playing or silently watching each other play the one available game on the cheaper and older Vodafone 150, to which they had greater access (see Figure 2.1).

Figure 2.1   The only game on the mobile phone.

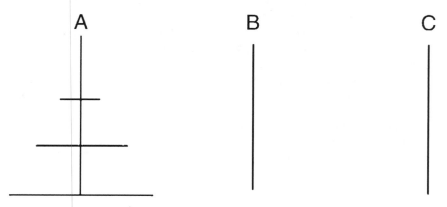

Figure 2.2   The ring game.

The task in the game was to move three rings from one pole and stack them on the next pole in the same order, as the diagram in Figure 2.2. illustrates. Success would lead to the next level with an additional ring, and so on.

Although the game apparently has some value for teaching logic and strategy, it provides limited opportunities for language development. Despite the narrow scope of the game, the children enjoyed it and had played it many times. But we note that it provides a different kind of play opportunity to the more familiar first-person 'virtual reality' games of cell phones and online gaming. In terms of the material/immateriality theme that runs through the collection, their play here does not take them into realms of fantasy or play identities where immaterial/material selves can emerge.

LANGUAGE, NEW MEDIA AND IDENTIFICATION PRACTICES

When the children did have space to talk while playing the relatively restricted game above, their talk tended not to be about the game but about other things. But their fantasies and longings had a rootedness that contrasts with the immaterial selves constructed and projected globally by the middle-class children in the second family that we talk about later in this study. In the conversation below, Thato dreams of having a 'PlayStation' while he is playing the rings game on the phone. The other children explore his fantasy with him.

1. *Thato:*   *Abanye abantwana esikolweni baphatha iplaystation badlale yona* [Some children take PlayStation to school and play with it]
2. *Thabang:*   *Uyaxoka* [You are lying]
3. *Nthabiseng: Hayibo Mputi* [No Mputi]
4. *Thabang:*   *Ifakwa etivini iplaystation* [It is connected to a TV]
5. *Thabang:*   *Yimalini iplaystation ?* [How much is PlayStation]
6. *Thato:*   *Ninety rand* [Ninety rand]
7. *Thabang:*   *Phi?* [Where?]
8. *Thato:*   *Apha Machaeneng* [There at the Chinese shop]
9. *Nthabiseng: Machaeneng* [At the Chinese shop]
10. *Thabang:*   *Ewe bendifuna ukudlala, iphum'nento ezinintsi, ifuneka iconnektwe etivini. Xa uzofuna umntu umdlalise wenze imali* [Yes, in order to play it, it needs many things, it needs to be connected to a TV. When someone needs to play, make him/her pay and make money]
11. *Nthabiseng: Utheng'amagwinya* [You buy fat cakes]
12. *Thabang:*   *For electricity le abadlala ngayo* [For electricity which they play with]
13. *Nthabiseng: Hayibo, Ndithenge is'kipa sePirates* [No, I buy pirates T-shirt

14. *Thabang:*   *Umntu xa efuna ukudlala, udlala nge-rand iplaystation.*
                 [Anyone who wants to play, plays the PlayStation for
                 one rand]
15. *Nthabiseng: Ewe ungena nge-randi* [Yes, they will enter with one rand]
16. *Thabang:*   *'Cause umbani* [Because electricity]
17. *Nthabiseng:* Ewe uyamoshakala umbani ungena nge-randi. [Yes,
                 electricity is expended; you have to enter with one rand]

There are some interesting elements in the children's discussion, the first of
which is the question as to why the children talk about the PlayStation as they
do. It is a surprise to hear that it only costs R90 (less than US$9). Secondly, it
is notable that they think first of its exchange value rather than its use value—
that they could use it, if they had one, to get *vetkoek* (fatcakes), football club
supporter T-shirts (Pirates FC, a glamour club based in Soweto) and electricity. The PlayStation, it turns out, against our expectations, is something local
and specific. What they have in mind is actually a cheap, more limited electronic toy that they have seen on sale locally, with only a few basic games on
it, not as unattainable as first seemed to be the case, though still aspirational
and out of reach at this time. The 'Chinese shop' raises echoes of global
trade, but the reality is one of thousands of similar low-cost outlets scattered
throughout poorer urban and residential sites across South Africa, staffed by
immigrant Chinese with limited English language resources, selling cheap
imitations of popular goods to poorer people. Lastly, the children's sense
that the PlayStation could be a potential money-making artefact probably
reflects the influence of both their parents and their wider environment in
a neighbourhood where few people have reliable income sources and everything that has value is considered tradeable. We see here examples of what
Blommaert and Rampton (2011) refer to as globalised 'superdiversity', where
there is a complex blend of 'local' and 'global' resources and such concepts as
'PlayStation' and 'Chinese shop' take on local meanings while maintaining,
for us, global echoes in a complex blend of the material and immaterial, the
imagined and the concrete.

THE BOLTON CHILDREN'S SEMIOTIC WORLD

The Bolton children absorbed the cultural capital that English language
resources, digital hardware and unlimited broadband connectivity in their
home afforded them by way of connections to global middle-class cultural
flows. One telling example was the nature of their play in the virtual world
of IMVU (IMVU, 2014), a '2nd life' teenage site that advertises itself as
'the world's largest 3D Chat and Dress Up Community', a favourite site of
8-year-old Ashley and 10-year-old Josh, where they selected avatars to represent themselves, made virtual friends and participated in online written
conversation. Ashley explained: 'It's just like your own mini-life!" The site

provided participants with credits, which the children referred to as money. With the credits they bought clothes for their avatars, cared for virtual pets, bought houses, saved 'money' and kept up friendships online.

Ashley used her avatar to communicate imagined things about herself and her eligibility to engage in the IMVU world. This eight-year-old African, dark-skinned girl projected herself through her selected avatar as a fair-skinned teenager (see Figure 2.3) whom she named Jessica Hawks. Jessica Hawks had long blonde hair (most of the time), wore a stylish jacket, leggings and high-heeled shoes. This name and image together form a motivated and interested sign, following Kress's (2010: 6) lead here, through which Ashley constructed an online presence for herself. The sign simultaneously indexes the dominance of Anglo-American stereotypes in this virtual world, along with Ashley's absorption of their hegemonic status in this domain. Ashley's materiality merges with Jessica Hawks' immateriality in ways that, as we can see here, are deeply situated and historically shaped.

Ashley's choice of avatar, of course, was limited to what was available for selection on the site, which were mostly white teenage avatars. In addition to using the avatar as a semiotic resource to communicate things about her online self and to identify with available signs of glamour and status, Ashley also on occasion experimented with different versions of her online self, changing her hair colour at one point and buying clothes and boots.

Figure 2.3   Jessica Hawks—Ashley's on-line avatar.

In the conversation below, Josh is surprised by Ashley's modifications:

1. *Josh:*   Is that you?
2. *Ashley:* Yeah.
3. *Josh:*   You buy a lot of stuff!
4. *Ashley:* No, I've had these boots for a long time. [Field notes]

It is apparent from this exchange that the children identified their online personae as 'themselves', but online. Merchant's (2009: 52) observation that avatars gave children in his study a sense of ambiguity of presence would seem to apply here as well. Children in Merchant's study spoke of their experience of 'being in the computer' and 'seeing yourself'.

Besides 'dressing up', the children also took part in chat-room interactions, characterised by rapid typed conversations with other avatars. IMVU chat-room settings included hospital, classroom, hotel and aeroplane settings, all of them comfortably middle class, as in the example below of a hotel chat room.

IMVU members' presence in a chat room is marked by their avatars as well as their names above their heads, as in Figure 2.4. ('Guest_' was used as a title followed by the name of the participant/avatar in IMVU chat rooms.) This mix of image and writing as identity markers indicates that children engaged with both visual and linguistic modalities in relation to themselves and others. Participants joined in on conversations by typing in their utterances. Turn taking was determined by the speed of electronic

Figure 2.4   Ashley's avatar and another avatar in the jacuzzi at the hotel.

transmission as well as the speed of participants' responses (as noted also in Merchant 2009:300). Online writing, in chat rooms as on mobile phones, requires familiarity and skill in a particular repertoire, register and genre, although it is easy for participants to engage as legitimate peripheral participants (Lave & Wenger, 1991) while they learn and assimilate the resources needed for skilful participation in this community of practice and social semiotic domain.

1. *Guest_cherx1 has joined the chat*
2. *Guest_grc1997:*   babe
3. *Guest_Magdalaniia:*   yes srry iM 15
4. *Guest_zacyblond:*   RUN
5. *Guest_Magdalaniia:*   yuu
6. *Guest_grc1997:*   15
7. *Guest_JessicaHawks:*   hi
8. *Guest_Magdalaniia:*   when yur birthday
9. *Guest_GirTheRobotisAwesome:* i'm soooooooo bored
10. *Guest_grc1997:*   ccan u send me some credits
11. *Guest_Vegasprincess97:*   hi
12. *Guest_zacyblond:*   RUN
13. *Guest_JessicaHawks:*   me too
14. *Guest_grc1997:*   12–22–95
15. *Guest_grc1997:*   u
16. *Guest_Vegasprincess97:*   hi
17. *Guest_cherx1:*   hey
18. *Guest_JessicaHawks:*   so do u like to swim?
19. *Guest_GirTheRobotisAwesome:* heyyyy pppl
20. *Guest_GirTheRobotisAwesome:* ppl
21. *Guest_cherx1:*   u all ok
[Chat-room conversation]

Although there is little coherence or apparent substance in the above exchange, there is evidence of domain-specific skill in the writing (or txtspk), including the use of contractions, punctuation, capital letters and letters repeated to communicate affect or get attention (line 9: soooooooo bored; line 19: heyyyy pppl), while there is no policing for consistency in orthography, punctuation or abbreviations. The effect of txtspk is to allow a written form that is close to speech and uncluttered by inflexible rules, allowing for rapid writing as well as displays of creativity as well as attitude. The rules of standard grammar and orthography can be variably bent for communicative effect. This flexibility offers children encouragement to develop phonemic and phonetic awareness (a sense of what the distinct sounds are in speech and how to represent them in the signs of writing), because it takes skill and know-how to successfully break rules for purposes of shared peer communication.

Figure 2.5   'Teenagers' flirting in a chat site.

Avatar-based play on IMVU also offered opportunities for interactive sociodramatic play and role experimentation. For 10-year-old Josh, flirting with (apparently) teenage girls was clearly an enjoyable activity, invoking for us, with some irony, Vygotsky's well-known comment about the importance of play as a channel for young children's learning (although Vygotsky was thinking of three-year-olds): 'In play a child always behaves beyond his average age, above his daily behaviour; in play it is as though he were a head taller than himself' (Vygotsky 1978: 102).

Josh named his avatar 'TonyAlvaBieber', probably to signal his 'coolness' and his access to global youth culture as a Tony Alva (skateboarding) and Justin Bieber (pop music) fan. Figure 2.5 shows Josh's avatar and two others in an aeroplane lounge setting.

Josh used a mouse to move his avatar (the one wearing a jacket in the above screen shot), read others' chat and typed in his replies, which appeared at the bottom of the screen.

1. *Guest_abbibold:*   so u want me to leave
2. *Guest_abbibold:*   hey i told u to stay over there
3. *Guest_LatinoTrini:*   no we would like u to stay if u like
4. *Guest_TonyAlvaBieber:*   lol
5. *Guest_abbibold:*   lol
6. *Guest_TonyAlvaBieber:*   u like her??
7. *Guest_TonyAlvaBieber:*   lol
8. *Guest_abbibold:*   guysdont follow me
9. *Guest_abbibold:*   sit over there

10. *Guest_TonyAlvaBieber:*	okay i won't
11. *Guest_abbibold:*	ok
12. *Guest_LatinoTrini:*	haha
13. *Guest_LatinoTrini:*	she seems shy tony haha
14. *Guest_TonyAlvaBieber:*	not shure about latino
15. *Guest_abbibold:*	i`m not shy
16. *Guest_TonyAlvaBieber:*	u are
17. *Guest_TonyAlvaBieber:*	lol
18. *Guest_LatinoTrini:*	haha
19. *Guest_abbibold:*	i`m not shy
20. *Guest_TonyAlvaBieber:*	admit it
21. *Guest_abbibold:*	i`m not
22. *Guest_TonyAlvaBieber:*	ur shy
23. *Guest_LatinoTrini:*	so why u sitting so far then
24. *Guest_abbibold:*	really noooooooooo
25. *Guest_LatinoTrini:*	anddont want us to come closer lol
26. *Guest_TonyAlvaBieber:*	U shy
27. *Guest_abbibold:*	because i`m the only girl on this plane
28. *Guest_abbibold:*	i`m not shy
29. *Guest_abbibold:*	lol
30. *Guest_TonyAlvaBieber:*	if aren't why u sittin so far away??
31. *Guest_LatinoTrini:*	huh lol
32. *Guest_TonyAlvaBieber:*	yeah why??
33. *Guest_LatinoTrini:*	what about a 3sum see i not shy lol
34. *Guest_LatinoTrini:*	LOL
35. *Guest_abbibold:*	if i was shy i wouldn`t be talking to u guys
36. *Guest_abbibold:*	lol
37. *Guest_abbibold:*	a 3sum nice one but noooooooo
38. *Guest_LatinoTrini:*	well then here is not fun lol
39. *Guest_LatinoTrini:*	what else can we do gosh lol
40. *Guest_abbibold:*	lol
41. *Guest_TonyAlvaBieber:*	nothin
42. *Guest_TonyAlvaBieber:*	where u going??
43. *Guest_abbibold:*	u guys can have a 2sum

[Chat-room conversation]

The two boys, TonyAlvaBieber and LatinoTrini, joined up to flirt with the girl, Abbibold. As Walton (2009) has pointed out with regard to South African teenagers' online chat, activity is prominently associated with flirting; in this example, Josh is getting some early practice in virtual flirting. The two boys teased Abbibold about her 'shyness' and constructed her as the object of their joint attention. They used insider terms *Haha* (line 13) and *Lol* (line 17) to communicate attitudes, humour and solidarity. They abbreviated each other's names ('tony', line 13, and 'latino', line 14), probably to signal familiarity and collaboration. LatinoTrini's suggestion of a

3-sum (line 33) suggests that he is probably older and more a teenager than Josh, and Abbibold's smart clincher (u guys can have a 2sum, line 43) suggest that she is a teenager too and enjoying the attention as well as the power she holds here. Josh manages to preserve face in this exchange despite his preteenage inexperience.

The literacy practice, which is a talklike written interaction, encouraged the Bolton children to read and write back to their online friends. The children's participation in chat rooms helped them to become familiar with new media practices and also allowed them to develop confidence in themselves as meaning-makers while taking on and experimenting with particular social personae. They are able to accumulate residues of experience with literacy as a resource for embedded communication of a particular kind that is linked to pleasurable social interactivity.

IMPLICATIONS OF CHILDREN'S DIFFERENT ENCOUNTERS WITH NEW MEDIA

Our research on children's language activity has focused on questions of language and the use of new media resources. The contrasting language movements of the groups of children, to monolingual English in the case of the Boltons and to a colloquial version of isiXhosa on the part of the Mahlale children, point to their contrasting class trajectories and consequently to their likely contrasting futures, in school and beyond. While the Bolton children are learning to think of themselves as legitimate participants in local, online, globally connected middle-class English language—based culture, the Mahlale children are acquiring linguistic resources that are localised, indexical of their sub-elite status and not associated with success in schooling (Bloch, 2009; Fleisch, 2008). English is the language of the political and economic elite in South Africa as much as in Tanzania, Kenya and elsewhere in Anglophone Africa (Blommaert, 2005), and we see here evidence of elite-reproduction processes and examples of English language gatekeeping functions.

As relatively privileged migrants, the Boltons are able to benefit from their mobility more than the less privileged Mahlale family precisely because of their affinity with dominant ideologies of language that define what counts as legitimate and authentic language. For the Boltons, online reading and writing practices using flexible English language registers give them tacit knowledge and practical skills that are likely to become second nature to them, part of their youthful identity practices, which they can draw on and adapt in school language, literacy and learning contexts. The schools where children do well in South Africa favour those children who bring monolingual, standard English language resources to school over those who bring code-switched multilingual versions of African languages as their primary resources. These dynamics help to explain why the Bolton parents show no interest in the maintenance of 'heritage language' for their children or in passing on their own bilingualism. They instead follow what is at present a common though not universal pattern amongst the emerging middle classes in South Africa of a 'straight for English' approach to their children's language acquisition, at home and at school. This approach is strongly shaped by the status that English language fluency holds in popular perception and in practice, in a context where levels of social inequalities are amongst the world's highest and where languages serve social gatekeeping or excluding functions.

Although it is widely understood that the development and diffusion of information and communication technologies are having a profound effect on modern life, our attention is thus drawn to how differently they are engaged with across these two contexts. Such varying access is, of course, of a social nature as well as a technological nature, and the Mahlale parents' attitudes to their children's use of cell phones for play purposes, particularly their mother's, lead to their access being further restricted. For the Bolton children there is also a perhaps lamentable element of their online play where they seem to feel obliged to pose as different to what they are, with a resulting vacuousness in their online chat. In contrast, the Mahlale children's PlayStation fantasies appear more real and rooted in their own worlds.

In conclusion, we would like to emphasise the particularities of children's engagements in each setting—that is, the way in which they engaged with new media devices as global forms or as placed resources (Prinsloo, 2005) that are assembled along with located preoccupations and resources and indicative of wider social dynamics. The examples of these placed and unpredictable combinations of elements that we have drawn attention to are the Bolton children's avatars, which were light-skinned and had Anglo names. We can see this as an instance where children in Africa participating in global middle-class culture are learning how to manage their historically inscribed *black* bodies in what are predominantly and hegemonically *white* spaces at this time. Because of the overtly racialised history of South African political struggles of the past, one might have expected a stronger resistance to accepting these dominant signs. Although it is uncertain that the Bolton children will always be as at ease with these identity practices as they now appear to be, we can nonetheless read this as part of a larger process where class differences amongst African children take on globalised cultural dimensions, by way of language practices and online media practices, that sharpen differences between middle-class children and poorer children.

In the case of the Mahlale children, we see a very different kind of engagement to that of the Boltons. Their limited access to mobile phones in crowded living conditions where children are cautioned not to make noise does not allow them to engage with the developmental potentials of these resources, nor do they have the sociocultural backgrounds or linguistic resources to engage with the new media. As we noticed, the Mahlale children's fantasies moved quickly to the potential of trading access to such resources for profit, thus pointing to the particularities and foci that characterise their social worlds. We can see how both groups of children display localised responses to global resources and that the differences between the two groups of children as regards their language practices and media engagements point to substantial social inequalities, which they bring to school and then experience in school as judgements about their individualised 'abilities', where school strategies in language and literacy are not alive to the social and linguistic diversity that characterises contemporary social settings.

EDITORS' COMMENTARY

In this chapter Lemphane and Prinsloo provide perspectives on children's engagements with electronic media in two diverse communities in Cape Town. We see how, in the more affluent family setting, children's activities are infused by wider transnational discourses about power and ethnicity. In contrast, in the less affluent setting, the children have limited access to digital tools. This raises questions about what happens as things (devices and the texts they mediate) cross sites. Like Auld et al.'s work, which has explored the localised ways in which mobile phones are used by Indigenous Australian communities (Auld et al., 2012), Lemphane and Prinsloo remind us that mobility is not unproblematic and that our understanding of texts and devices as mobile must be counterbalanced by the notion of literacies as 'placed resources' (Prinsloo, 2005). Lemphane and Prinsloo provide us with instances of what they call the 'actual global', in which digital devices and the texts they mediate 'interact with other resources and elements in actual contexts in a mix of global constructs and more localised discourses and preoccupations.' Whilst devices and the texts they mediate move between locations, what happens with these devices and texts is indexed in complex ways to social, cultural, economic and political flows.

Lemphane and Prinsloo draw our attention to how users routinely employ resources in ways not envisaged by their designers, demonstrating how sociocultural contexts are significant to the technological affordances that are taken up. Engagements with digital devices are suffused with both local and translocal discourses and the mediating influence of wealth. It may be useful here to distinguish between ideas of 'value' and 'worth', where value relates to monetary (and other) exchange rates and worth relates to use. Whilst there are high levels of mobile phone ownership in South Africa, the practices associated with these devices are patterned by differences in the value and worth. In one of the family settings the children's mother valued the phone as a precious communication device and so disapproved of the children playing with it, partly because making calls was so expensive and caused the battery to run down. When children did access the phone they played covertly, in silence and away from the gaze of their parents. In fantasising about owning a Playstation, however, they considered its value in economic terms, focusing on what they could exchange it for rather than its worth in providing play opportunities. Meanwhile the children in the affluent setting had easy access to electricity and digital connectivity. They used English proficiently and were thus able to access the cultural goods associated with that language; they played with avatars and projected themselves as white, using Anglo names and the English language. Their privileged access to material resources amplified their ability to access spaces of power.

Material goods, important resources such as electricity and access to use powerful forms of language are key to the ability of children and young people to participate in society. Lemphane and Prinsloo argue that inequalities are likely to be magnified as children enter school. Both sets of children in their study play agentively with resources available to them and will be participants in a range of language and literacy practices. However, a lack of familiarity with privileged literacy practices may be experienced in school 'as judgements about their individualised "abilities", where school strategies in language and literacy are not alive to the social and linguistic diversity that characterises contemporary social settings.' The illusion that new technologies are global resources working to flatten inequalities may itself sharpen and entrench divisions.

In the next chapter, Wolhwend and Buchholz consider children's meaning-making practices in a very different locality: a first-grade classroom in the US Midwest. They explore what happens if we shift the focus of the literacy curriculum and, by adopting what they call a 'strength orientation', provide resources and opportunities that enable children to draw on the diverse meaning-making experiences they bring with them to school. Describing the meaning-making of the children they observed, Wohlwend and Buchholz present proposals for reframing early literacy within a 'new media literacies nexus' and consider the implications this has for teaching, resourcing and assessing literacy. Importantly, their argument moves beyond advocating a shift from paper-based to digital practices (from one polarity to another), proposing instead a broadening and deepening of literacy provision in educational contexts—provision based on a view of literacies as the use of multiple media, with the production of digital and print texts productively entwined with a range of other forms of meaning-making.

NOTES

1. This chapter draws directly in part on Lemphane and Prinsloo, 'Children's digital literacy practices in unequal South African settings', which is to appear in the *Journal of Multilingual and Multicultural Development* in 2014, in a special issue on 'Promoting Multilingual Literacy in Diverse African Communities', edited by Bonny Norton.

2. The data reported on in this chapter were recorded by Polo Lemphane as part of her research for her Masters minor dissertation (Lemphane, 2012) and were also reported on in Lemphane and Prinsloo (in press), from which this chapter draws directly. Names of research participants used here are not their real ones. This work is part of a wider research project on children's home and school literacies that is partly funded by the National Research Foundation (NRF) South Africa. The arguments are ours, however, not those of the NRF.

3. 'The black middle class' in South Africa, as an identifiable demographic for marketing purposes, had grown from 1.7 million in 2003 to 4.5 million individuals early in 2013, according to the University of Cape Town's Unilever Institute of Strategic Marketing. This is available at http://www.unileverinstitute.co.za

3 Paper Pterodactyls and Popsicle Sticks
Expanding School Literacy through Filmmaking and Toymaking

Karen E. Wohlwend and Beth A. Buchholz

INTRODUCTION

In a time of high-stakes testing, pushed-down scripted instruction and intense teacher accountability in elementary school, play-based and child-friendly learning in early-childhood classrooms is increasingly set aside to make room for broad-based intervention aimed at preventing low test scores. To reclaim emergent, child-friendly, and learner-directed curricula, it is necessary to revisit the extensive early literacy research base on children's play (Dyson, 2003; Paley, 2004; Wohlwend, 2011; for comprehensive sources on early literacy research, see Larson & Marsh, 2013; Marsh, 2010; Pahl & Rowsell, 2012). At the same time, there is an equally compelling need to update early literacy curricula to better utilise the digital technologies so prevalent in modern childhoods (Alper, 2013; Burnett, 2010). We are living in a digital era when we finally have sophisticated and user-friendly technologies that are just right for little fingers to operate and to easily capture children's play texts. Specifically, touch screens on phones and tablets are mobile and responsive, with filmmaking apps that are simple and intuitive. These new tools seem designed for early-childhood teachers to use with their students. To be clear, we do not intend to invoke an old/new binary and either/or choice, often constructed around print and digital tools. Rather, we follow the children's lead to see how they are using and making texts with *all* the multiple resources they find around them, from paper and pencils to tape and popsicle sticks to cameras and digital video. Elsewhere, we have argued that play is a productive literacy with reconstructive potential to help children participate more fully in school cultures (Wohlwend, 2011). In our recent work on literacy playshops, we showed that video storying is a particularly powerful form of storytelling with toys, which invites invention and collaboration among players (Wohlwend, Buchholz, Wessel Powell, Coggin, & Husbye, 2013). In this chapter, we examine how young children in a combined kindergarten/first grade classroom, when encouraged to make their own digital films and paper toys, achieve academic goals consistent with prevailing standards for literacy but also, importantly, enact and tap into their individual literacy proficiencies and media interests.

We examine children's classroom play and storying from a *strength orientation*; that is, we recognise young children as richly resourced literacy learners who come to us already knowing much about their worlds. For example, children bring cinematic awareness and literary knowledge to video storying, resources gained through their interactions with favorite films, video games, and toys in popular media franchises (Medina & Wohlwend, 2014). This perspective aligns with ethnographic work that finds literacy in everyday ways of making meaning with ordinary artifacts in children's homes (Gregory, Long, & Volk, 2004; Pahl & Rowsell, 2010)—ways that contribute to children's cultural repertoires (Gutiérrez & Rogoff, 2003) and technical knowledges through experiences in family and community life (González, Moll, & Amanti, 2005; Scollon & Scollon, 1981). Further, this strength orientation recognises early-childhood teachers as knowledgeable professionals and responsive kid watchers who can build upon children's interests to develop responsive play-based literacy curricula.

NEXUS OF SCHOOL LITERACY

Literacy research has documented widespread trends in school policies, classroom routines and literacy programs that increasingly skew classroom practice to fit academic standards, anticipated test items, and teacher accountability criteria (Dyson, 2008; Ravitch, 2010; Stipek, 2006). We use the term *School Literacy* to refer to a particular nexus of widely circulating glocalised practices, justified by global discourses and enacted locally in classrooms. In this nexus, global discourses of accountability and standardisation are materialised at the classroom level in literacy routines—such as the turn taking and page turning among readers in a scripted reading group. However, the nexus of School Literacy in a given classroom is not a monolithic set of practices but encompasses additional, often contradictory educational discourses. In the classroom in this case, School Literacy included discourses of print productivity, cooperative learning, and individual achievement materialised through popular literacy curricular models such as writing workshop and balanced literacy.

We pause here to unpack another term—*nexus of practice*—an important concept that helps us look closely and critically at educational practices including those we advocate. A nexus of practice is a cluster of taken-for-granted practices that make up expected and usually unexamined ways of doing things (Scollon, 2001). Nexus analysis (Scollon & Scollon, 2004) is a methodology that blends discourse analysis and action research to promote social change. It involves engaging in, navigating and changing the nexus to address the inequities that are upheld by our shared acceptance of commonplace practices. As educators, nexus analysis helps us look critically at our own tried and true practices with the most ordinary literacy tools to understand who benefits and who does not in our educational traditions.

ENGAGING THE NEXUS

To engage the nexus of School Literacy, we partnered with teachers in small study groups to work through shared inquiry toward teachers' goals. In this study, we collaborated with six early-childhood teachers in teacher study groups to develop media literacy and filmmaking curricula—what we have termed *literacy playshops* (Wohlwend, et al., 2013), which combine collaborative play, storying, and media production. We focus here on one study group. During one school year, Karen met twice a month with two teachers who taught as a team in a first-grade classroom with about fifty 5- to 7-year-old children. Beth and three members of the research team visited this classroom four times per week during one semester, video-recording play and filmmaking activities, children's films and puppet shows and teacher study-group sessions. Key to the teachers' discussions and curricular planning were readings on current perspectives and recent research on global children's media and critical literacies. Informed by cutting-edge research, the teachers explored digital media technologies, challenged their own perceptions of parental beliefs about media and expanded literacy curricula in ways that aligned with school goals and missions (e.g., meeting state literacy benchmarks).

NAVIGATING THE NEXUS

To navigate the nexus in a particular place, we examine everyday routines with commonplace materials to uncover the implicit nexus of practice (Scollon & Scollon, 2004). Routines elicit automatic cooperation from students and acceptance as just the normal way of doing things at school. One indicator that value is placed on particular literacy practices and materials is the number of routines created to institutionalise and ensure their expected uses. School Literacy routines are often established at the beginning of each school year and made habitual through daily repetition. For example, in early-childhood classrooms with a writing workshop curriculum, we expect to see a buzz of activity: children talking, drawing and writing books with paper and pencils or word processing software as they plan and produce first drafts, confer with teachers and peers, craft revisions and share their work in the author's chair at the front of the class. Here are a few examples of tacit routines and expectations for working with paper, a staple material in writing workshop, in this first-grade classroom:

- stories are recorded on paper daily; they might be drawn but preferably are written;
- paper is used for writing, drawing, and occasionally for cutting, folding or stapling to make books;
- all papers are stored in individual writing folders, in labeled bins on low accessible shelves;

- stories are regularly shared with peers who listen quietly so everyone can hear and make positive comments;
- in whole-group sharing sessions, about fifty children sit in a circle and look at the speaker; drawings are difficult to see if shown at all.

When we unpack these routines, we can see how they support the following valued School Literacy practices:

- writing independently, quietly and continuously to fill pages of paper and create books;
- retelling by talking about drawings, reading own writings and elaborating stories through talk;
- commenting on literature but primarily listening to others' stories by taking turns in whole-group sharing.

Some of these practices are more highly valued than others in the School Literacy nexus; writing, listening, and talking are positioned as more important than drawing. We can also see this when drawings must be transmediated—translated from one mode into another—from the mode of image into the preferred verbal modes of speech and print. That is, images must be explained verbally before they 'count' and can be understood as texts within the School Literacy nexus. Drawn images are usually illustrations that accompany and enrich a written or spoken text rather than being understood as stand-alone artwork that conveys meanings visually.

It is clear that some children thrive in this kind of classroom environment, particularly those 'good students' who

- can produce pages and pages of text;
- can wait patiently for a turn to speak (or not);
- can sit still and write or listen easily for long periods of time.

However, it is also clear that this approach constricts literacy to a single verbocentric pathway that disadvantages many children. It leaves little room for children to experience stories by viewing, acting, crafting, singing, building, dancing or playing with friends—diversified pathways that allow many more children to easily engage in storying (Gallas, 1994; Gregory, Long, & Volk, 2004).

CHANGING THE NEXUS

Changing the School Literacy nexus means imagining otherwise. The filmmaking and toy-making practices in literacy playshops (Wohlwend et al., 2013) align with an emerging nexus of New Media Literacies (Jenkins, Clinton, Purushotma, Robinson, & Weigel, 2006) in early-childhood education (Alper, 2013). Importantly, in nexus analysis, the power to transform sedimented practices in any nexus of practice comes from identifying and transforming a small but key practice along with the related modes and materials that anchor restrictive expectations. In the School Literacy nexus, we identified *writing independently* as the key practice and *paper and pencil* as key materials that anchored expectations for individual production of a written text and that privileged speech and print over other modes. What happens when we shift the expectation that children must write their stories on paper to acknowledge and value other materials that children naturally use in play? How might we change the School Literacy nexus by accepting cameras and toys as valid literacy tools?

EXPANDING STORYING IN THE SCHOOL LITERACY NEXUS

In this early-childhood classroom full of books and paper for making books, there were no toys. However, once children began making films, they spontaneously repurposed paper to create artifacts: the puppets, toys and scenery needed for filming their play. In this section, we share examples of the kinds of artifacts that children produced when allowed to expand the idea of storying to include toy making and filmmaking. Specifically, we look at two child-made films as examples of expanded storying: (1) flat paper puppets bouncing left to right across a paper backdrop and (2) a 2-foot paper Godzilla and paper pterodactyls crashing into paper buildings. Following each vignette and transcript, we first highlight how these printless texts meet School Literacy nexus expectations for verbocentric storytelling. We then revisit the vignettes, looking closely at the paper toys and films through a New Media Literacies lens, to detail what we can see when we switch the nexus and change our expectations for what counts as story.

Horse and Dinosaur's Day—A Filmed Puppet Show with Paper Puppets

Five first-grade girls collaborate in the corner of the classroom, filming a puppet show that follows an unusual cast of characters from sunrise to sunset. The final film grew out of the multiple Popsicle-stick puppets, pieces of scenery and envisioned plot lines that the girls developed independently and merged once the classroom teachers encouraged collective storytelling. The puppets starring in the final film include two brightly colored dinosaurs that are siblings (Fred and Lily), a turkey that crows like a rooster (Mr. Turkey), a cowgirl (Anna) and her horse (Mayley) and a dog (Cocoa). The girls move these puppets around on top of and parallel to the background that has been placed on the ground. The camera films the ensuing action from a bird's-eye view.

Partial Transcript and Summary of Horse and Dinosaur's Day

The 2-minute film opens with the sound of the puppets snoring in unison: "So-me-me-me-me. So-me-me-me-me." Mr. Turkey wakes up the other characters with a loud 'cock-a-doodle-doo.' Anna, a brown-haired cowgirl, comes out from underneath her house and asks, "Hey guys, wanna have breakfast in the forest?" From here, the puppets move between playing in the barn and eating lunch and dinner in the forest. The most unexpected part of the story occurs after lunch (about a minute into the film). The puppets are saying hello to the 'birdy' in the tree, when Anna suddenly adds:

Anna:	Oh, I almost forgot . . . she's pregnant! She had one egg, but I've got to call the doctor because it looks like she's sore and needs help. [Anna gets off Mayley and goes underneath the house to call doctor.] Bop-boop-beep-beep-beep. Ah, I'll be right over. [Anna appears on the the roof again, this time as the doctor.] The doctor is here. Let me put on my gloves. Eeeeeeeeeee [attempting to pull out egg/chick]. I've got it. And here are her baby chicks [puts two yellow chicks in the nest]. One already hatched, that's why it is taller.
Mr. Turkey:	Oh.
Anna:	And there are your chickies.
Fred:	Cute little chickies.
Lily:	Let's see if they can fly.
Anna:	Yeah, let's make them fly to the rainbow.

Surprisingly, the newborn chicks can fly up to the rainbow. Everyone jumps around for a few seconds before Anna says that it's time to go back. The chicks return to the nest, and Anna tells everyone it's time to go eat dinner in the forest. Lucy soon observes that "it's getting dark" and suggests that "it's time to go home." The film ends with the puppets saying goodnight.

We can see that *Horse and Dinosaur's Day* offers the audience a clear and predictable chronological sequence (sunrise to sunset) and thus an identifiable beginning, middle and end. These story elements reflect first-grade writing expectations in the School Literacy nexus. Story structure was heavily emphasised by teachers during the filmmaking unit in order to address state writing standards, which dictated students should be able to 'recount two or more appropriately sequenced events, include some details regarding what happened, use temporal words to signal event order, and provide some sense of closure' (CCSS, 2012, Writing 1.3). The girls' film offers an easy-to-follow plot line that marks it as 'good writing' in this classroom. Teachers found that crafting an ending with a 'sense of closure' was especially difficult for young students; their films—like their writing—would often be long lists of events that were abruptly cut off with the phrase 'the end'. However, in this film, the young female filmmakers set up a story arc by articulating a problem (the pregnant bird), a resolution (the doctor arriving) and a closing scene (everyone saying goodnight). There is a sense of closure even without the telltale marker of 'the end'.

Lery vs. Godzilla and a Pterodactyl— A Live-Action Film with Paper Toys

In a small nook at the back of the classroom, Ezra dangled a paper robot from one hand while holding the camera in the other as he filmed, narrated and animated the main character. His 3-minute film featured a villain's monologue and a rampage by Lery (pronounced Larry), a giant robot who battles an equally large Godzilla, crushes a building and finally retreats after he is carried away and dropped into the ocean by a pterodactyl.

Transcript of Lery vs. Godzilla and a Pterodactyl

Hahahahahahahaha
I will DESTROY you Godzilla! [*Close-up of robot's face*]
You know why? Because.
Because once I destroy you, the people of Earth will bow down to me.
And then, they will do my biddings.
I want to be supreme ruler of Earth
And to do that, I just have to get rid of YOU.
RRRRRR-AW-YEEEEE [*Shot of Lery attacking Godzilla, drawn on a Popsicle-stick frame.*]
Laser punch. Pshhhh Pshhhh.
Rrraoww. Pssh pshhh pshhh.
Uh oh. He's going to blow fire on me.
He blew fire on me!
Curse you Godzilla! Curse you!
But I can still do some bad stuff.
Like crushing this building. Pshhhhh. [*Cutaway shot to crumpled paper bag building*]
See what happened when I'M done with it.
Hahahahahaha. [*Close-up of robot's face*]
Errrryahhhh. He blowed fire on me again.
Curse that Godzilla.
Rrrrow raaah raaah [*Shot of flying pterodactyl*]
(The pterodactyl's new.)
He's on Godzilla's team? You gotta be kidding me!
Aw—You gotta be kidding me. He's picking me up! [*Shot of pterodactyl carrying robot*]

Wha—He blew fire on me again. You gotta be kidding me. [*Shot of robot, sprawled on floor*]

Finally, the moment has come for me to destroy you. [*Shot of upright robot, resuming attack*]

Hey, wait. I just noticed something.

I am in the Oceanaut and I'm in a robotic suit.

I'm standing in the middle of the ocean. How did the building even get there? Huh.

I   don't   know.   Well,   anyways,   I'm   really   trying   to DAAAAAAZZZZZZZEWWW

[Lower pitch to indicate Godzilla is speaking] Ok, ok. I'm going back to the ocean.

[*Closeup of pterodactyl*] Dum dum da dum dum. That's all, folks.

We can see much in this film that exceeds first-grade writing expectations in the School Literacy nexus. In fact, the storytelling meets the third-grade benchmarks outlined in the Common Core State Standards, albeit for written text rather than film:

Write narratives to develop real or imagined experiences or events using effective technique, descriptive details, and clear event sequences.

  a. Establish a situation and introduce a narrator and/or characters; organise an event sequence that unfolds naturally.
  b. Use dialogue and descriptions of actions, thoughts, and feelings to develop experiences and events or show the response of characters to situations.
  c. Use temporal words and phrases to signal event order.
  d. Provide a sense of closure.

Common Core State Standards, Writing 3.2a–d
(National Governors Association, 2012)

The archetypical maniacal laugh that opens the villain's monologue reflects its strong character development: 'Hahahahahahahaha! I will DESTROY you Godzilla! You know why? Because. Because once I destroy you, the people of Earth will bow down to me. And then, they will do my biddings [sic]. I want to be supreme ruler of Earth.' The script is filled with expressive and descriptive vocabulary (e.g., destroy, bow down, my biddings, people of Earth, supreme ruler, pterodactyl, robotic, the moment has come). Further, the story arc is sequential and logical. The introduction sets up the conflict between Godzilla and Lery, establishes Lery as the antagonist, and explains the reason for their conflict. The dramatic conflict that escalates with the surprise addition of the pterodactyl as another defender of Earth is resolved when the pterodactyl wins after knocking down the propped-up Godzilla 'DAAAAAAZZZZZZZEWWW', who retreats into the ocean. The pterodactyl closes the film with Warner Brothers' classic cartoon wrap-up 'That's all, folks'.

EXPANDING STORYING IN THE NEW MEDIA LITERACIES NEXUS

A second look at these vignettes from a New Media Literacies perspective allows us to see valued practices that are overlooked from a School Literacy perspective. In a School Literacy nexus that values print on paper and talk about print and encourages primarily booklike texts, we might worry about the time children spent making toys or working out who stands where. But a New Media Literacies nexus values action with artifacts and encourages multimodal storying with expanded forms of recording with digital cameras and all the available materials, including paper. During filmmaking, children focus on capturing action texts, writing only as needed to anchor their play roles or previously negotiated pretend meanings. Accordingly, in this section, we also rely on image, through photographs of the child-made paper puppets and toys that reveal children's inventive use of materials and modes.

Storying through Filmmaking

In the New Media Literacies nexus, texts are reinvented from moment to moment, with each change subject to player negotiation and agreement. As children play together, they negotiate who plays which character but also whether their individually proposed scenes cohere and make sense within their shared story. Similarly, filmmaking requires children to cooperate to distribute camerawork and character roles as they interact with each other and with materials. In this way, a New Media Literacies nexus expects and values texts that are interactive and fluidly multilinear, similar to digital literacy texts such as video games and virtual worlds that have seemingly limitless paths and endings.

The negotiation and collaboration needed to orchestrate the play expanded the classroom norm of sequential turn taking and multiplied the ways that children could simultaneously participate. (Of course it is important to recognise that teacher mediation is often necessary to manage the challenges of equitable turn taking.) In the film *Horse and Dinosaur's Day*, the girls initially planned to use a tripod to hold the camera so they could each manipulate their own puppets within the story. However, after a few trial runs, one of the group members volunteered to be the camera person, 'because if we just had a tripod the characters moved around a lot so [the camera] would just look at something blank'. The necessity for a camera person complicates traditional expectations of collaborative writing and accountability in schools where children are expected to equally contribute to a project/story. The tensions were also evident in the distribution of materials within the film: Of the eight puppets appearing in the film, five were controlled by Amanda, while the other three group members each handled a single puppet. Amanda, as Anna the cowgirl, also initiated almost every transition in the storyline (e.g., 'let's go have lunch; 'let's go have a hay fight inside my barn'). The messiness of collective authorship opens up opportunities for classrooms to serve as places for teachers and children to explore what equitable social relations look like when they are engaging with and producing new media.

When multiple players contribute to a shared story, they must also bring their multiple ideas of the story line together; when this produces tangents or story loops, the result is multilinearity. Although the girl filmmakers had to negotiate and merge a diverse collection of puppets, scenery and story lines, their final *Horse and Dinosaur's Day* film was fairly linear. However, there was one identifiable moment of invention that expanded the linearity of the story. This rupture was initiated by Amanda's sudden recollection (as cowgirl Anna) that: 'Oh, I almost forgot . . . [the bird's] pregnant! She had one egg, but I've got to call the doctor because it looks like she's sore and needs help'. This introduces a pressing conflict to the story line that had been missing up until this point as well as an immediate sense of tension. Anna proceeds to move between a series of different roles as she calls the doctor ('bop-boop-beep-beep-beep') and moments later appears as the doctor ready to help pull out the stuck egg/chick from the mother. Sound effects are a key modal element here in building tension, as the doctor arrives and pulls the egg/chick out of the mother chick; it is Amanda's extended 'Eeeeeeeeeee' that conveys the struggle and strain of the moment far more richly than what can be represented visually on paper.

Children also negotiate the meaning of the story and attend to the ways inventions and added ideas interact within a cohesive text. A rupture in cohesive meaning-making and its close connection to improvisation are apparent in the Godzilla film when Lery suddenly realises that the improvised move to the ocean now makes the crumpled skyscraper incongruous in the ocean fight scene. 'Hey, wait. I just noticed something. I am in the Oceanaut and I'm in a robotic suit. I'm standing in the middle of the ocean. How did the building even get there? Huh'. In this rupture of the story line, Ezra attends to the constraining expectation to produce a cohesive text but quickly decides to move ahead to keep the film's action going.

Storying through Toy Making

Importantly, a New Media Literacies perspective also values the improvisation that produces novel uses of ubiquitous materials such as writing paper. As children played, they colored, cut, folded, rolled, taped, crumpled, and tore paper to make their own toys, puppets and scenery, enriched with a variety of modes (e.g., speech, sound effects, gestures, movement, etc.) to create modally complex meanings, not to compensate for their emergent language but because they intended to convey the richest meanings possible (Kress, 1997).

While the girls created flat, traditional Popsicle-stick puppets for *Horse and Dinosaur's Day*, there were subtle details in their construction that expanded opportunities for interactivity between the characters and their surroundings. The most obvious example of this was the design of Anna and her horse Mayley. The brown- and white-spotted horse had a detailed saddle that was taped rather than glued, making it removable. The barn even had a small saddle rack where the saddle could hang when it was not needed; however, the girls rarely took the saddle off 'because sometimes it rips'—referring to the limitations of making things with paper. The saddle was also designed in such a way that Anna (on a Popsicle stick) could slide into the saddle and essentially 'ride' the horse (Figure 3.1). This allowed the creator to control both Anna and Mayley with one hand, freeing up a second hand to operate additional puppets. These design features gave the flat puppets a more toylike feel, suggestive of action figures and dolls sold with accessories that can be added or taken off depending on the desires of the child. Elements of the scenery were also designed to give puppets opportunities to interact with their surroundings. The hay ball hanging in the barn was taped only at the top so that puppets could physically 'swing' the ball around during a hay fight scene. And Mr. Turkey's wreathlike nest on top of the blue house (Figure 3.1) had a slit cut on the left side so that the puppet could slide into the nest easily, thus appearing to sit inside the nest rather than floating on top of it.

In addition to interactivity, there are signs that the girls began to think in three dimensions despite the apparent flatness of the scenery. Anna's house, the blue- and pink-striped building on the left, appears to have a tree 'floating in thin air' with the chicks' nest, but the girls were eager to point out that 'if you fold the roof over you can see the tree' *behind* the house (Figure 3.2). Young children often do not represent depth relationships between objects in their drawings; thus it might be expected that the tree would be drawn *next to* the house. However, here the girls experimented with layering paper in order to give the audience the impression of depth within the scene. For example, Amanda attempted to convey depth when she moved her puppet underneath the scenery to indicate when Anna was inside the house. The children's various puppet-handling practices also reflected expanded three-dimensional thinking. While all of the puppets moved with an archetypical bouncing motion, a closer look at the girls' divergent holding and handling strategies in relation to the set and other puppets reflected conflicting responses to implicit questions like: Should puppets face the scenery, each other, or the camera? Should the puppets move parallel or perpendicular to the flat scenery? These questions speak to the limitations of working in a two-dimensional representational story world while thinking about action as embodied and interactive.

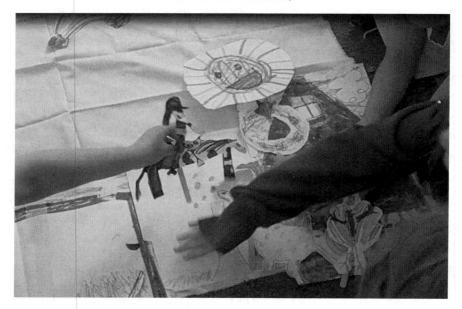

Figure 3.1   Interactivity: Cowgirl Anna rides on her horse Mayley.

Figure 3.2   Thinking in three-dimensions: Anna 'inside' (underneath) her house.

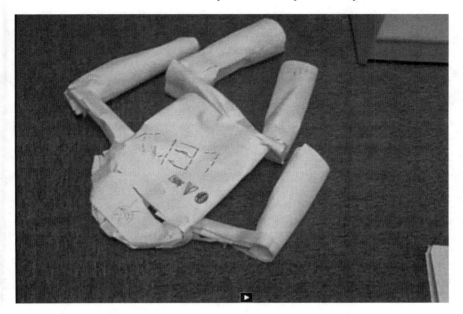

Figure 3.3   Lery (villain).

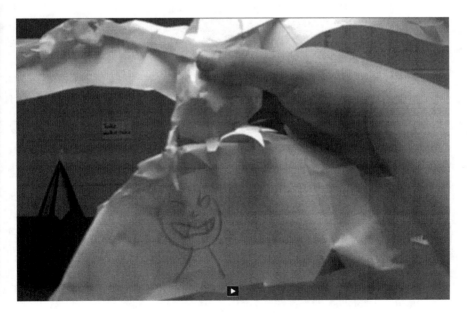

Figure 3.4   Interactivity: Pterodactyl flying away with Lery.

In the dinosaur story, the girls adhered more closely to teacher directions for drawing and cutting out characters, aligning with the School Literacy expectation for two-dimensional characters who progressed in a more or less orderly fashion across a flat scene. Popsicle sticks were provided by the teachers, who anticipated that children would make stick puppets. Across the room, however, the boisterous fight scenes in the Godzilla film were enabled by a set of paper toys that had substance and texture. Ezra's group repurposed paper and Popsicle sticks from flat images to three-dimensional artifacts by rolling tubes, crumpling paper to create mass and taping sticks and parts together. These characters were 2 to 3 feet tall, too unwieldy for popsicle stick handles and not intended to be puppets; these were clearly toys with movable and interactive parts. Godzilla was drawn on a 3-foot piece of paper and stretched on a frame made of taped-together Popsicle sticks, which was propped up by a cardboard stand. Lery, the 2-foot robot with moveable legs and arms, was constructed of paper tubes connected with masking tape (Figure 3.3). The pterodactyl was the most identifiable toy, with its framework of Popsicle sticks and crumpled paper to support its wings (Figure 3.4). Its claws provided the necessary interactivity to snatch and carry Lery. Children treated these as toys, handling them like dolls rather than bouncing them across a set like puppets. Godzilla, Lery, and the pterodactyl were examples of the unexpected making and repurposing of materials that occurred when teachers allowed the children to make toys.

USING FILMMAKING AND TOYS TO CHANGE THE NEXUS OF SCHOOL LITERACY

Overall in this classroom, children expanded the range of story production as they blended live action with animation of hand-drawn, constructed paper characters and paper scenery. Children recorded story ideas by:

- drawing storyboards;
- writing cast lists;
- constructing paper toys, puppets, props and three-dimensional sets;
- digitising films and capturing play through video, voice recording.

Storying takes various forms in the New Media Literacies nexus: *action texts* such as live-action play or animation videos, *image texts* such as storyboards, and *print texts* such as scripts. Additionally, toys are key *artifacts* that children use to anchor story meanings (Wohlwend, 2009). Table 3.1 summarises the contrast in expectations, materials and modes in School Literacy nexus and New Media Literacies nexus.

In this classroom, the goal of expanding the nexus of School Literacy and changing the nexus to New Media Literacies expectations hinged on putting cameras in the hands of children. The provision of cameras and expectation that children would make films provided the key element of

Table 3.1   Contrasting Expectations, Modes and Materials in School Literacy
Nexus and New Media Literacies Nexus

	School Literacy Nexus	*New Media Literacies Nexus*
Key practices	Writing	Playing Toymaking Filmmaking
Expectations	Single reader/writer	Multiple players
	Working	Playing
	On an original text	In a shared scene
	Using print to craft	Using action to interact
	Personal narrative	Embodied activity
	Individual production	Sustained collaboration
Available modes	Verbal: print, speech	Verbal: speech, sound effects

	Image: illustration reflects text	Image and Dimension: Toy design
		  reflects 3D character or artifact
		Scenery (backdrop)
		Camerawork (framing, zooming)
		
		Movement and proximity
		Interactivity
		Toy handling (front/back, vertical/
		  horizontal)

Key materials	Paper with pencils/markers Books	Paper with scissors, tape Toys and puppets Digital cameras

change, because suddenly it was not enough to write scripts and plan storyboards. Children needed puppets, toys and sets to film. A School Literacy
nexus supports paper products: books and even the scripts and storyboards
of preproduction filmmaking. But once the camera is turned on, there must
be action and there must be something to see. We found that when children
do not have the materials they need, such as toys or interactive sets, they
make them to fill that void.

It is important to recognise that shifting our expectations and changing
nexus takes time. At first, teachers asked children to write down their plans
for films on storyboards, requiring them to transfer their play or animated
popular media to paper. In this transmediation, rich meanings that children conveyed by action, movement and sound effects were reduced to a
few words on a page. Similarly, the children's engagement in playing stories
shriveled to quiet compliance as they filled paper sheets with scripts and
cartooned storyboards. Even when children did record plans in writing,
stories changed radically when they picked up the camera to film. Later,

when the teachers discussed this in study groups, we talked about alternate ways to record play meanings that could move beyond print. We envisioned children recording stories in film and using the camera to create video clips or screen shots that could be cropped into digital puppets or printed out to create photo sequences to use as storyboards. Children had their own ideas, of course, and quickly turned to the material they knew best, paper. The following year, when Karen revisited this classroom, teachers had provided children with a bin of found materials (e.g., cereal boxes, corrugated tubing, fabric, containers of all sorts) for making costumes, props and toys.

Finally, understanding the literate potential of toys and the active storying that play uniquely provides is key to reestablishing play spaces in early-childhood classrooms. During this study, children met School Literacy nexus expectations for storytelling and exceeded these when allowed to play and make films in the New Media Literacies Nexus through an approach that built on their strengths. They easily played and storied together when teachers recognised multiple pathways to literacy beyond print. Filmmaking and toy making offered a range of modes to notice and a rich array of materials to explore.

ACKNOWLEDGMENT

This research was made possible by a grant from the Maris M. Proffitt and Mary Higgins Proffitt Endowment, Indiana University, Bloomington.

EDITORS' COMMENTARY

Wohlwend and Buchholz's proposal for a 'new media nexus' places literacies amidst a broader network of communicative practices. It acknowledges and values children's meaning-making across a wide range of media and, in doing so, opens up new possibilities for children to design, compose and play. Whilst digital technology is used alongside other resources typically found in early-years settings, Wohlwend and Buchholz argue that the introduction of cameras prompted children to make diverse modal choices and generate rich narratives that may have been neglected in conventional school literacy. In their work, there is the same kind of shifting between technologies, texts and embodied play that we see in other studies of children's media production, such as Parry's analysis of the 'socially negotiated and evolving narratives' that older children produced in creating animations (Parry, 2011).

Importantly the process of producing texts is foregrounded in the New Media Literacies Nexus, and this highlights how on-screen creativity is embedded within and inseparable from material interactions and engagements. Wohlwend and Buchholz highlight the central role of play as 'productive literacy', noting how 'texts are reinvented from moment to moment'.

Rather than developing through a planned process of design, creativity derives from ongoing improvisation. This process is, as Wohlwend and Buchholz suggest, 'interactive and fluidly multilinear' as children take up different resources and explore what they can do with them. This happens on and off screen, through bodies, sounds and crafting as well as written and spoken words. These different media offer different kinds of possibilities for story making, so that the improvisation works in different directions—through drawing, moving, writing and making and in relation to plot, character, setting and dialogue.

In Wohlwend and Buchholz's chapter, we see an eclectic shifting between modes and media in which improvisations in different media enrich the narrative in different directions. This contrasts with the linear process often associated with a more ordered and structured approach to filmmaking (through storyboarding, making, scripting, rehearsing to filming). Multimodality matters here not just in terms of modal choice but also because experiments in different modes drive meaning-making in different ways. This can generate tensions as the potentially expansive and divergent urge to improvise can conflict with the reductive and convergent urge for coherence. However, as we see in the pterodactyl episode, the desire for a meaningful product may balance the desire to keep playing.

If, as this chapter demonstrates, modal choice allows the production of richer texts that draw on a broad range of communicative resources, it would seem important for us to support learners in understanding the affordances of different forms. The focus on improvisation perhaps raises questions about how we might best do this. In much literacy teaching, for example, learning is often scaffolded by bounding literacy learning in terms of objectives or steps towards achieving a particular outcome. Encouraging the kinds of productive improvisations enabled here would require a more open-ended approach to planning literacy tasks. It would prompt us to reexamine some established pedagogical practices and engage with important questions about the role of the teacher. It also raises questions about how we respond to the different kinds of texts learners produce, such as the 'collaborative, hybrid and transgressive texts' (Parry, 2011) that may result from these playful opportunities for creativity.

In the next chapter we see another example of the improvisational quality of meaning-making in Burnett and Bailey's study of children's use of *MinecraftEdu* (Teacher Gaming, 2013) during a school lunchtime club in the UK. Burnett and Bailey describe what happened as children moved across and within the hybrid spaces of Minecraft Club. Like Wohlwend and Buchholz, they focus particularly on how children played together; their analysis arrives at some important considerations for how we conceive and plan for collaboration during on- and offscreen activities.

4 Conceptualising Collaboration in Hybrid Sites

Playing *Minecraft* Together and Apart in a Primary Classroom

Cathy Burnett and Chris Bailey

INTRODUCTION

Bringing digital resources into the classroom is not a simple matter. Associated practices can disrupt classroom routines and sit uncomfortably with literacy curricula focused on individual attainment, measured using fixed paper-based outcomes (Burnett, 2011a). And institutional practices, in turn, may be significant to how digital environments are taken up (Wohlwend et al., 2011). Such disruption, however, can provide an important opportunity to look again at the process of meaning-making in educational contexts. How is the classroom context significant to the kind of meaning-making that happens around digital resources? And how might we view the classroom context differently in the light of what we notice about what's going on? Paying close attention to disruptions can make an important contribution to literacies research, as it can lead us to reexamine some of the foundations of established literacy pedagogy and practice.

In this chapter, we consider some of the disruptions that occurred when one class of 10- and 11-year-olds used a version of the sandbox world-building game, *Minecraft*, during a lunchtime club in a primary classroom in England. There is strong support amongst educators for using virtual environments—such as virtual worlds and games like *Minecraft*—to generate opportunities for learners to create, solve problems, and play together in digital spaces (Beavis et al., 2013; Gee, 2007; Merchant et al., 2013) and we know that many children find such opportunities engaging in their lives outside school (Marsh, 2010). In order to better understand the possibilities for using these resources in school, however, we need to recognise the complex ways in which what happens onscreen intersects with what happens off it. This, we suggest, means looking at their use in terms of hybrid on/offscreen sites.

Below we draw on the notion of 'fractionality' (Law, 2004) and ideas about '(im)materiality' (Burnett et al., 2014; Burnett, forthcoming) to explore what happened in the hybrid site of Minecraft Club. We focus particularly on how children played together (and apart) and use this to revisit ways of thinking about collaboration. References to the value of collaborative learning are prevalent in much contemporary pedagogical discourse. However, in primary schools, at least, there has been little discussion about what this might look like when children work across hybrid physical/virtual sites. Adding to such debates and drawing on our study of Minecraft Club, we highlight five dimensions of being together that we suggest are significant to children's meaning-making in virtual environments in school settings. We emphasise the importance of seeing collaboration as fluid, operating on and off screen through different modes and intersecting with practices and identities associated with other locations. We argue that these dimensions are not just relevant to learning in digital environments but have implications for how children work together (and apart) on other literacy tasks, too.

LITERACIES IN HYBRID ON/OFFSCREEN SITES

Literacy researchers in the NLS have increasingly 'located' literacies within complex networks, exploring how actions in one location relate to what happens elsewhere, and highlighting the complex entanglements that occur as different practices interweave to generate ways of making meaning (Brandt & Clinton, 2002; Kell, 2011). In elucidating these entanglements, there has been a growing interest in the reflexive relationships between the material (the physically present stuff that is part of literacy practices such as bodies, texts, artifacts, architecture) and the immaterial (feelings, purposes, memories and thoughts). These (im)material relations have been seen as related both to our subjective experience of texts and textual practices and to broader historical, economic, political and cultural flows (Burnett et al., 2014; Pahl & Rowsell, 2010). Rather than seeing the material and immaterial in terms of binary distinctions between on/offscreen or on/offline, we can see these relationships in terms of 'mesh' or a 'great evolving horizontal web of interweaving practices' (Schatzki, 2002: 154).

(Im)material relationships have particular implications for the use of digital technologies, where individuals' actions and intentions materialise 'virtually' on screen but of course are always enabled and experienced in physical locations. Specifically, researchers have explored relationships between people's actions and identities in and out of virtual environments (Hine, 2000; Leander & McKim, 2003) and challenged the notion that gaming occurs within a 'magic circle of play' (Weber & Dixon 2007:253). Experience in virtual environments is not, as the popular media might suggest, one of complete immersion but of 'multiplicity of presence' (Martin et al., 2012:222) as players/users are simultaneously on/offline and on/offscreen (Burnett, 2011b). Being in one location, the identities and possibilities associated with that location mingle with ways of being in other locations as what we do on/offline and on/offscreen intersects (Burnett et al., 2014; Burnett & Merchant, 2014).

These intersections play out in particular ways when virtual environments are used within educational settings. Schools and classrooms are patterned by complex practices, discourses and histories that shape possibilities for meaning-making. They are 'an intersection in social space, a knot in a web of practices that stretch into complex systems beginning and ending outside the school' (Nespor, 1997: xiii). In conceptualising what happens as children work together across fluid hybrid on/offscreen classroom/digital sites, we therefore draw on the idea of 'fractionality'—of 'being more than one and less than many' (Law, 2004: 62). For Law, this notion provides an important way of conceptualising complexity and acknowledging multiplicities in our account of social life. In this chapter, it provides a way of holding together what are often seen as binaries —home/school, on/offline, on/offscreen. It facilitates an examination of what this means for how we conceptualise meaning-making and, in this case, specifically how we understand the significance of being together and consequently collaboration.

INVESTIGATING MINECRAFT IN THE CLASSROOM

The work described here comes from a nine-month study of 10- and 11-year-old children's use of digital technologies in a classroom in a small rural primary (elementary) school in northern England. At the time of the study, one of us (Chris) was the class teacher whilst the other (Cathy) was a university researcher. All but three of the children in the class (eight girls and ten boys) had been together throughout their seven years in primary school, with Chris as their teacher for four of those years. The study aimed to investigate how children took up available resources as they interacted with and around a range of digital technologies in the classroom. We understood resources to include what was available on screen but also other children, objects, locations, and immaterial resources such as memories, preferences and prior experiences. During the year, all children were invited to attend a lunchtime Minecraft Club, to play *MinecraftEdu* (Teacher Gaming, 2013), a version of *Minecraft* designed for educational use; this work provides the focus for this chapter.

Minecraft (https://minecraft.net/) is an independently produced 'sandbox' videogame, available across multiple platforms. Players construct landscapes using blocks representing materials with different properties. For example, players can build using wood or stone. Fire and virtual TNT can be used to destroy structures or clear areas. Items such as doors, ladders or teleportation blocks enable movement between different parts of the game's landscape. Blocks can also be combined and manipulated to create new objects, including tools, plants and other entities. There are two modes of play: survival and creative. Survival mode involves the player, as a standardised avatar, arriving on—or 'spawning' onto—a randomly generated island full of trees, hills and other structures. The player starts the game with nothing and must collect objects to enable him or her to survive the night, when monsters arrive. Creative mode offers a similar experience but without the threat: the player inhabits the world with very little danger. The game can be played in single or multiplayer scenarios and players communicate using an online chat function. *MinecraftEdu* (http://minecraftedu.com/page/) is a modified version of the game made for school use. The main difference is that it can be easily controlled by the teacher, who decides on the range of resources and options available. *MinecraftEdu* enables a server to be run in the classroom so that all class members can access the same world.

Chris introduced Minecraft Club because several of the children had talked enthusiastically about the game and Chris wanted to explore the possibilities for using it in school, particularly given the potential to create a virtual environment as well as act within it. Whilst children's prior experience of *Minecraft* varied, all attended Minecraft Club, although some more regularly than others. At home, keen players played *Minecraft* in survival mode. In school, Chris limited play in *MinecraftEdu* to creative mode, so that children, theoretically at least, could only build (rather than fight, kill or destroy). Presented with an infinite expanse of flat, green, virtual land, the children were invited to collaborate to 'create a community'. They set about building a town, which they later named Bradborough (see Figure 4.1).

In order to investigate the entwined nature of on/offscreen activity (Hine, 2000), we used a variety of methods. We conducted group interviews

Figure 4.1 Bradborough by night.

to gain insights into how children's *Minecraft* play drew on friendships and experiences from elsewhere and to gather children's perspectives on Minecraft Club. We also talked to children as they played and instigated child-led in-world tours. We noticed, however, that these methods changed children's play; children slowed down and shifted into teaching mode as they guided us (perceived quite correctly as inexpert adults) around and explained what they had done and why they did it. This stopped them from talking with others in the class, interrupting the kind of collaboration we were interested in observing. For this reason we relied heavily on observation. We used a combination of video and field notes to capture actions and interactions at different scales: video to record the detail of children's interactions with others and the stuff on/offscreen around them and field notes to respond rapidly to changing patterns of interactions that cut across the whole class. In analysing relationships between the material and the immaterial, we juxtaposed our data in different ways. We identified different trajectories, identifying changes over time on/offscreen (in Bradborough and the classroom) and ways in which experiences and events from other times and places seemed to play out in Minecraft Club. We also looked for relationships between what was happening at different scales, between what happened close up (revealed through fine-grained analysis of video data) and broader movements and perspectives evident from field notes and interview data.

PLAYING TOGETHER IN MINECRAFT CLUB

Minecraft Club was not like school. Children decided what they would do and who they would do it with. It was also noisy and, to a casual observer, may have lacked the quiet order often typical of a class of 10- and 11-year-olds. But then it was not like *Minecraft* either. Minecraft Club was a hybrid between *Minecraft,* the classroom and Bradborough; and of course *Minecraft*, the classroom and Bradborough were each hybrid, too (Burnett, 2013). In what follows, we look across the screen and classroom to examine how children played alongside each other and what collaboration looked like in this hybrid site. We begin by describing how what they did converged and diverged as they worked out how to play *Minecraft* in Minecraft Club; then we explore the improvisational nature of their play. Next we describe the complex intersection between their on/offscreen actions, suggesting that this was often more about 'being together' than 'doing together'. Finally, we consider how the children seemed to work across multiple communities as they drew from available resources, and we consider some of the challenges in doing this. These moves combine to present the process of playing together across the hybrid site as complex and fractional. This, we suggest, has implications for how we conceive and plan for collaboration.

Building Bradborough Together and Apart
(Im)Materially: Convergence and Divergence

Like others who have studied of children's use of virtual environments in institutional settings (Fields & Kafai, 2010; Wohlwend et al., 2012), we noted that being in one room enabled children to learn how to play and what was possible from each other. In contrast to conventional patterns of classroom organisation, children sometimes worked together in Bradborough but in separate classroom locations. They shouted instructions or invitations across the room, using repeating phrases—'Look at this, look at this, look at this' or repeated deictic gestures (pointing towards the screen with both hands)—to draw others' attention in the busy classroom. Sometimes they did not physically turn but shouted to others as if *through* their screens. Whilst children did not necessarily set out to guide or support one another, the less experienced became familiar with the language and affordances of *Minecraft* as they heard others shout about what they were doing and looked across at their screens or searched for similar things on their own screens. This learning did not come from structured collaboration but from physical proximity and the 'thingness' of laptops; once children saw or heard what was possible, they found ways of achieving it. The fluid golden blocks on screen, for example, were only recognisable as 'lava' when experienced children had named them as such; once they had been seen and named, others started using lava too. In many ways we could see these children as operating within an emerging community of practice, with newcomers apprenticed into established practices and moving from peripheral to complete participation (Lave & Wenger, 1991). However, this does not quite account for what happened. Whilst some children were apprenticed in how to do *MinecraftEdu*, all were working out how to play *Minecraft* as enmeshed with the classroom site. As they built, they generated new possibilities for play, and this influenced what Bradborough became.

Possibilities were of course framed partly by what Chris made available, and available resources may have prefigured certain kinds of play. The children, however, recruited *Minecraft* resources in different ways. Some seemed to build for the pleasure of building, continuing to adapt or rework constructions over several weeks, developing aesthetics or functionality. Others built in response to the changing environment in Bradborough: when Chris introduced animals, for example, some children built aquariums and farms to keep them in. Others created venues for specific events—two girls, for example, built a theatre, where they staged *Mamma Mia* (Lloyd, 2008). Others built places to play. As in Marsh's (2010) study of children's interactions in *Club Penguin* (http://www.clubpenguin.com/), this play took different forms, including fantasy play, such as restaging *The Hunger Games* (http://www.thehungergames.co.uk/), and sociodramatic play associated with everyday settings. Some children rarely built but toured through the Bradborough landscape or played with things they found.

These different responses are reminiscent of the contrasts between 'patterners' and 'dramatists' that Gura (1992) describes in her analysis of children's block play; some children enjoyed creating the text of *Minecraft*, whilst others played within it. However, creating the text of Bradborough itself involved storying, translating the blank world into a particular kind of place (hotel, theatre, farm, etc.), often drawing extensively on popular media, as we explore more fully later. Sometimes, for example, buildings were constructed to play an active role in other players' *Minecraft* lives. This happened, for example, when experienced players subverted resources to play as if in survival mode. *MinecraftEdu* contains blocks that cannot be destroyed, which allow users to create permanent structures. Some children used these to play pranks, trapping friends within permanent walls. Once, a spa was created with a sign inviting visitors to use the amenities, only for unwitting players to find that the jacuzzi was a bottomless death trap. In a similar move, a deep pit was dug next to a teleportation destination, again resulting in others plummeting unexpectedly to their deaths. As they built, the children set precedents for what others might build, and as some started playing in survival mode, others did too. Practices across the class converged as children caught onto what others were doing.

At the same time, there were sometimes clashes as different kinds of play materialised onscreen in Bradborough. For example, some of the least experienced players spent time exploring. This tourism caused tensions when, unsure how to navigate *Minecraft*, children unintentionally destroyed others' buildings. In one case, a child was trapped in a hotel so had to smash a wall to escape. Annoyed, the hotel builder placed pressure pads in the doorway that activated the intruder's ejection from Bradborough. Such clashes led to changes in where children built. The most confident initially built in the centre—large high buildings that dominated the skyline. Others built smaller cottages at the edge of town. As the year progressed, the more experienced players moved out of town, often travelling long distances to find sites where others would not find them.

The quality of the hybrid Minecraft Club site—how children played and what they built—evolved as different practices knocked up against each other and children worked out how to be together. During the year, their play became increasingly aligned with the values established through their shared history of being together in the class—linked to responsibility, mutual respect and nonviolence. Many stopped playing in survival mode and settled to the more 'appropriate' practice of creating buildings. There was increased dissatisfaction about others acting in destructive ways. Experienced players told us they enjoyed these acts of destruction when playing at home, but at school they complained. There was also less shouting out and screen displaying; children worked increasingly as individuals or in groups, although these groupings were fluid, some sustaining for the year, others shifting as friendships grew and waned. Importantly, however, whilst modes of play variously converged and diverged, their physical proximity continued to be significant to what and how they created in Bradborough. This rarely involved the planning and negotiation we might typically associate with school collaborative tasks. Instead, their creations seemed to emerge through spontaneous improvisation that progressed through spoken and embodied interactions with each other and objects on/offscreen. We examine this in more detail in the two sections that follow.

Creativity and Emergence

Sometimes children came with clear plans of what to build or wanted to continue existing projects. Luke, for example, rushed in one day and started building straightaway. He told Cathy he had built a rollercoaster in *Minecraft* at home and was now trying to recreate this in Bradborough. Once started, however, the pleasures of creation seemed to take over. Children rarely spent time discussing what to do but simply started building and improvised from there; repeated clicking and selection led to the intensely rapid production of blocks or digging of cavernous pits, and choices about colour, tool and material were made quickly and rarely discussed. Ideas were generated through the momentum of building and design was playful, not planned. As one girl commented, 'basically you just start doing something and then it looks like something else and suddenly you get an idea of something and end up doing something by accident.'

Leander and Boldt (2013) draw on Deleuze and Guattari's (1987) notion of 'emergence' to describe this kind of in-the-moment improvisation and argue that this has been sidelined in some accounts of literacies. They explore the 'affective intensities' (p. 36) associated with text creation and its relationships with a whole range of other generative acts. Improvisations wove through Minecraft Club in different ways, associated with:

- aesthetics, e.g., playing with material, colour, texture, size and shape;
- location, e.g., moving to different sites;
- timeframe, e.g., continuing a project or responding contemporaneously;
- storying, e.g., generating events or locations around or through their buildings;
- acting on other players, e.g., playing tricks;
- drawing on, or perhaps showcasing, intertextual references, e.g., associated with popular media.

We see these different improvisations as focused on different *concerns*, foregrounded differently at different moments for different children; at times children were concerned with aesthetics, for example, and then moved on to a concern with something else, such as location. We can draw a parallel here with improvised drama in which spoken utterances or actions are seen as 'offers', invitations to others to respond; the drama develops as participants accept and build on others' offers (Johnstone,

1981). In Minecraft Club, children's 'offers' sometimes worked to focus or refocus on a particular concern: as one started building something massive and dominating (foregrounding aesthetics), for example, others did too. These concerns coalesced. All play was spatially and temporally located, had social purposes, and had aesthetic, intertextual and narrative qualities. This fractionality meant that improvisations veered off in new directions as new concerns took over. In each case, it seemed that children were driven by the inherent pleasure of generating onscreen content through building or moving through the textual world. In Leander and Boldt's words, their play could be seen as, "living its life in the ongoing present, forming relations and connections across signs, objects, and bodies in often unexpected ways. Such activity is created by the ongoing flow of affective intensities that are different from the rational control of meanings and forms" (Leander & Boldt, 2013: 36).

In the next section we zoom in to take a closer look at how being together was significant to how this happened and how relationships between materiality and immateriality were significant to how 'being together' played out.

Being Together in Bradborough

These children did not always work together on shared projects. More often, they played in parallel, nearby each other in Bradborough and sometimes in the classroom, but engaged in different tasks. In many ways, 'being together' seemed more important than 'working together'. We see this in the following vignette:

Working on laptops next to each other, Fran and Sophie are also next to each other in Bradborough. Sophie is finalising the squid aquarium while Fran is 'shaving' (shearing) sheep. She repeatedly comments on this: 'There's my two shaved sheep . . . all the shaved sheep are mine . . . still shaving sheep'. Each sometimes looks to see what the other is doing. Occasionally, Sophie uses Fran's keyboard to make something appear on Fran's screen. At one point, Fran notices some wolves which another child has generated —and comments that her sheep are in danger. Sophie reaches across and puts leads on the wolves so that the sheep are safe. Neither comments on this. Later, Fran spots a pig. Still looking at the screen, she comments 'There's a pig with a saddle on'. She turns to Sophie and reminds her that they had tried riding pigs before (perhaps inspired by the Baby Monkey Riding on a Pig Youtube video http://www.youtube.com/watch?v=5_sfnQDr1-o): 'Remember when we got on and couldn't get off'. She decides to switch from shearing sheep to riding pigs: 'I'm going to ride a pig and go off'. She gets on. Whilst she stays sitting next to Sophie, she moves away from her in Bradborough.

These two girls are not playing/working together in the conventional sense by 'collaborating' on a single project: Sophie constructs the world while Fran plays within it. This is not discussed but the running commentaries ('still shaving sheep') and proximity of screens mean that each follows what the other does and they seem to maintain a sense of togetherness, which allows them to move in and out of each other's onscreen worlds: Sophie breaks off what she is doing to 'interfere' with Fran's projects, reaching across to sort the wolf problem. The children seem to revel in both the pleasures of in-world play and the delights of sharing what they are doing. Whilst their parallel play would hardly count as collaborative in the conventional sense, being together and pleasing each other seemed central to what they did. It is worth emphasising the different ways in which the materiality of the laptop was significant. At times the screen worked as a wall, enclosing their play by separating them from the rest of the class. At other times, the girls were positioned by each other (and the screen) as viewers and the screen became a 'site for display' (Jewitt, 2008). At others, they acted 'in' the onscreen world, shifting their focus to look through the screen which mediates the virtual environment.

A second example allows us to look in even more detail at how their on/offscreen actions articulated with each other and see how being together was significant to what they did, and how what they did reinforced their being together. Table 1 is a transcription of a sixty-second excerpt from a later interaction. By this point, Fran's enthusiasm for pig riding was well established, but on this occasion she was unable to find any pigs to ride. The transcript distinguishes between what happened onscreen, offscreen (actions, posture, proxemics, facial expression), and speech. Reading across and then down, we can see how their interaction worked as a 'multimodal ensemble' (Kress et al., 2001; Taylor, 2012) through an intermingling of on/offscreen activity. We can see the fractionality here in different ways: Fran and Sophie are both together and apart, both watchers and doers, both on and off screen.

We see how Fran and Sophie mostly defer embodied action to the screen (Hayles, 2005). They adopt a posture that reflects this liminality: eyes fixed to the screen and fingers poised over keyboards. Their tiny physical movements—of specific keys and mouse—materialise Bradborough in different ways linked to their own preferences and concerns. As in the previous example, each was ostensibly playing by themselves; the small amount of speech concerns commentary not negotiation. We can see a range of offers, some taken up and some ignored, that help to progress their play. These offers flutter in and out of world, drawing on gestures, onscreen actions, onscreen chat and proxemics. They drive each other on, both in what they do and the resources they use. Sophie knows about Fran's lack of pigs due to Fran's running commentary, and responds by spawning pigs onscreen. Fran responds to Sophie's

Table 4.1 Fran and Sophie

Line	S On-screen	S Off-screen	S Speech	F On-screen	F Off-screen	F Speech
1	S's avatar is on ground next to the skyscraper; pink rectangular blocks are appearing in front of her (pigs).	S sitting forward, looking at her screen, fingers on keyboard.		F's avatar is flying high over the city and moving fast (looking for pigs). We can see the holy butter pyramid, a skyscraper in the distance.	F is leaning forward, eyes fixed to screen, fingers on keys to move her avatar around Bradborough.	
2						
3						
4						
5		S points at her screen.				
6			'Fran,'			
7		She reaches across S's screen and points at a pink block in the distance just by the skyscraper.				
8					F leans forward even further, fingers on keyboard.	'Pigs!' (elongated squeal)
9						
10				F moves rapidly towards the pigs by the skyscraper.		
11		S lifts her hands together in parallel (like a magician's 'reveal' gesture).				
12						
13						

	S avatar	S action	S speech	F avatar/action	F nonverbal	F speech
14	S's avatar is still on ground with pigs.			F's avatar is still moving towards pigs.		
15		S leans back in her chair, looks at her screen. then turns to F & points her finger towards F.				
16			'which.... what you don't know....'			
17						
18		Withdraws finger, then repeats pointing gesture.				
19			'is that I spawned them.'	F arrives at the pigs.		
20					F's eyes are fixed on screen, fingers on keyboard.	'Pigs'
21						
22		S turns to me, away from F. She uses her hand to shield her mouth.		F's avatar is now riding a pig.		'Yes!'
23			'What she don't know is I just spawned them.'			
24						
25						'I'm on top of a pig,'
26		S turns to F			F leans back from the screen and clenches both fists in triumph.	
27			'What you don't know is I just spawned them.'			'I'm on top of a pig'
28		S looks at her screen, using keyboard.			She turns to S.	

(continued)

Table 4.1   (continued)

Line	S On-screen	S Off-screen	S Speech	F On-screen	F Off-screen	F Speech
29	Pink blocks ('pigs') are rapidly appearing on S's screen as she continues to spawn 4 more pigs (approx 1 per second).					
30		She shakes her head from side to side as the pigs appear.			F looks back at screen, brings up chatscreen and starts typing.	
31						
32				F's words appear at the bottom of the screen 'Hallulejuh . . .' (rest is too indistinct to read)		
33					F points at own screen, then reaches across S and points with her left hand at S's screen and smiles, indicating what she has just written.	'I don't know how to spell Hallelujah.'
34						
35						
36						
37		S turns back to her screen, reads, laughs, then starts typing.		F continues riding a pig.	She looks at the chat on S's screen and shakes her head.	
38						
39	Her words appear on the chatscreen (indistinct).					'pig, pig, pig, pig pig, pig pig, pig , pig, pig, pig . . . (rapidly)
40		She reaches across F and points with her right hand at what she has just written (now appearing on F's screen).				
41						
42					F turns back to her screen. She starts typing a new entry into chatscreen.	
43						
44						
45						

gift of pigs not by thanking her but by indicating the chat screen where she had shared her excitement. Sophie takes up this offer and joins the chat too.

What they do onscreen is interlaced with what they do off it; they act in each other's screen worlds and use out-of-world gesture to draw each other's attention to what they have done. In the busy world of Bradborough, these tiny acts of friendship could be easily missed. However, this combination of on/offscreen action allows them to mark certain actions and events out from the ongoing play. This happens for example through repetition—of words, deictic gestures and onscreen actions (e.g. column 3, lines 14–16 and 18–19; column 4, lines 15–20, 23–24 and 27–28)—and mirroring physical move-ments (e.g. shaking heads in column 3, lines 30–31 and column 6 , 37–38, or turning to the screen in column 3, lines 37–38 and column 6, 42–43). As in Marsh's analysis of the social order of *Club Penguin* (2011), these patterned interactions seem to carve out what seems—for brief moments at least—to be a shared on/offscreen space in the noisy and apparently chaotic classroom. But in Minecraft Club, this patterning happens both on screen and off. Interest-ingly however, the girls maintain the separateness of their play. When they want to draw the other's attention to something, they do not point at their own screens, inviting each other into their visual space, but reach across and point at what they have done in the other's onscreen space. This in turn gener-ates momentary shifts in the location of play: Sophie's gesture, for example, prompts Fran to stop playing *in* the world and look *at* it. They engage in a complex fractional dance, drawing on and enabled by the fluid materiality of the laptop as it shifts from object to surface to window.

We can see how playing next to each other helps to propel their play. Looking at one another's screens, they gain different perspectives which prompt subsequent actions. Their actions interrupt or disrupt each other's individual 'walks' through Bradborough. Just as their togetherness prompts their actions, so their actions reinforce their togetherness. Recently liter-acy researchers have argued that the role of affect has been underplayed in social accounts of literacy practices. Vass (2007), for example, argues that 'emotion-driven thinking' is central to children's collaborative com-position, whilst Maybin (2013) argues that it is emotional commitment—desire, hilarity, shock, and so on—that drives children's engagement with texts. In Minecraft Club—as in Vass's and Maybin's examples—we see the affective dimension of creating alongside peers in the immediate sur-roundings of the classroom. Sophie and Fran act separately in the textual world of Bradborough, but their in-world actions work to consolidate their friendship. Their collaboration was not just about working together but being together. Their actions in Minecraft Club sat within the much longer trajectory of their friendship.

This meshing of Minecraft Club practices and friendship practices also needs, however, to be seen in relation to a host of other meshes and entan-glements. As explored below, collaborations seemed to work in relation to the histories of multiple communities. We can see this by zooming out again to consider the resources they drew on as they played.

Playing across Multiple Histories and Communities

Earlier we noted how play evolved over the course of the year. It would be misleading to suggest that this was a purely linear progression. In Bradborough, the past lived alongside the present as in any town. Whilst buildings were frequently abandoned, sometimes half-built, they remained in the textual world of Bradborough and often evoked memories; as children moved through, they passed these buildings and often commented on them, as if looking through old photographs or touring a familiar city: 'Do you remember when we . . . ', 'I made that with . . . '. The semiotic work buildings were doing seemed to shift as they changed from projects to places to landmarks. Sometimes meanings shifted back and buildings were reincorporated into play. Old buildings, for example, became the focus for new activity as children torched them—as they revelled in the joy of doing so, acts of deletion were framed as destruction.

Other resources were associated with different contexts, often linked to broader constellations of literacy practices (Steinkuehler, 2007). Friends sometimes had experience of playing *Minecraft* together out of school and drew on this in the classroom, inviting each other to recreate parts of buildings they had created before. All children spoke of using YouTube and other popular media as inspiration for building, particularly the vast number of *Minecraft*-related fan websites. Whilst, as explored above, children often worked individually or in subgroups, some patterns of activities worked across the whole group. Memes spread virally across the classroom. Once, for example, everyone started wearing pumpkin heads and another time placed cakes on top of all the buildings. Many of these fads lasted briefly, then faded. This remixing and reincorporation reflected findings from other studies of intertextuality in children's play (Willet et al., 2013).

Importantly, Minecraft Club practices reached out to other sites. Like Pahl (2006), who traced the recurrence of themes in children's texts over time, we noticed that certain themes repeatedly surfaced in children's creations in Bradborough and crossed into lessons. We first noticed Luke's use of 'butter', for example, when he was working with Joe to program an animation using Scratch (http://scratch.mit.edu/): he created a 'butter god', which flew across the sky and crashed into an aeroplane. Butter then started to appear in *Minecraft*: a holy butter pyramid was created and avatars started wearing butter armour. Luke explained that the butter fad originated with a YouTube machinima—a spoof 'Sky Does *Minecraft*' featuring butter. As the children, starting with Luke, imported this to their *Minecraft* play, butter became an ongoing visual and oral/aural joke—'butter, butter butter' (in an 'American' accent—'butter/budder/budder')—was sometimes chanted when butter was being used. The butter theme gathered momentum as it crossed sites, was celebrated through classroom banter, and took on a new life as situated within this class. Like other memes, butter was appropriated and reworked in different ways (Knobel & Lankshear, 2007), and the way it was used helped to define the hybrid Minecraft Club site. As children took up and ran with these memes, they both reflected and reinforced their being together. Memes circulated because children shared the on/offscreen site, and their use helped to establish or reinforce the centrality of humour. In this class, humour was high stakes; making people laugh generated social capital. Building was often about creating visual jokes or, as one child told us, 'funny ideas or like silly ideas or things that people like'. As in our earlier exploration of emergence, again the emphasis was on pleasing and amusing themselves and others, not planned production for future audiences. We could see their *Minecraft* practices, then, as working to uphold the Minecraft Club community but also existing within and inflected by multiple communities of known and unknown others. In addition to the intimate interactions described in the previous sections, their activities drew from and worked to reinforce broader communities across and beyond the class.

Positioning amongst Hybrid Communities

A focus on emergence is liberating. It shifts us away from products to processes allowing us to consider the ephemeral and apparently inconsequential. It highlights how being together in the moment was significant to what children did. However, when they talked about what they did, they often drew on discourses that represented structured ways of seeing the world. They suggested that the ability to take up opportunities in Minecraft Club was linked to how they were positioned, or positioned themselves, across intersecting communities. There are many dimensions here but two contrasting examples serve to illustrate the point.

The first relates to gender, a recurrent theme during interviews. Whilst few girls played *Minecraft* at home, all came to Minecraft Club. They spoke, however, of being unable to admit to playing *Minecraft* for fear of being branded 'geeks' and 'nerds'. Together in the classroom, they legitimised each other's play; girls could act as builders and makers in ways they felt criticised for in other contexts. We would be reluctant, however, to see Minecraft Club as a 'third space' (Guitierrez, 2008). The girls' comments suggest that they still positioned themselves and felt positioned by others in ways that limited what they could do and how they could play. In describing this they recruited discourses of gender. As one commented, 'normally boys they like to build things like zombie traps like shooting and stuff and they think when girls go on they might just make like a little butterfly house with flowers'. Larger, high status buildings in Bradborough were all built by boys (although not all boys built such buildings). It seemed that girls were excluded, or self-excluded, from some kinds of building practices. Girls'

Minecraft practices, like girls' practices in other digital environments, were by no means 'stable or predictable' (Pelletier, 2007); they held coffee mornings and staged musicals but also created traps. However, unlike girls playing anonymously online, these girls played with children they knew and saw regularly. Whilst Minecraft Club may have opened up new possibilities for play, these were overlaid with other expectations; as in other studies of girls as gamers (e.g., Beavis and Charles, 2007) identities constructed around Minecraft Club intersected with other perceived norms and how they positioned themselves in relation to these.

For others, part of the challenge of positioning in relation to Minecraft Club seemed to be about successfully straddling different communities. Our second example illustrates this:

> Towards the end of the session, Joe finishes building an apartment block and invites everyone inside. Once they are all there, he fills the apartment with lava and they're all killed. (Or at least returned to re-spawn again into the game.) The others lean back in their chairs (thrown out of the game, the invisible link to the screen is broken) and many exchange glances—knowing glances that seem to recognise what Joe's just achieved. Others stare at Joe; one comments, 'that was evil,' but the accusation seems mixed with awe. Joe has a look of pride as he absorbs their reactions.
>
> Later, in the plenary at the end of the session, Chris asks the class what they think they have learned through playing *MinecraftEdu*. The discussion turns to working together. Joe comments, 'There's an extra level of friendship with people you've helped through the game'. This prompts further exchanged glances between others in the room—they haven't missed the irony here and one child glances at Joe, seeming to register the unfairness of what he did and how he has just framed it in his official comment. No one comments on this out loud.

Joe seems to straddle at least three communities here. Within the community of experienced *Minecraft* players, he skilfully draws on available resources to play in line with the joyfully destructive possibilities of *Minecraft* in survival mode. His re-framing during the plenary suggests he knows his actions do not align with the 'official' class community, where his actions could be seen as 'griefing' or wilful destruction of others' creations. He seems to play to more 'acceptable' classroom identities as a good team member and collaborator. At the same time his reframing works ironically to help him take 'the stage in the peer world' (Dyson, 1993: 71); his transgressive play perhaps gains renewed impact given the audacity of his reframing. Joe seems to switch between being: skilled, strategic *Minecraft* player; responsible, sensitive class member; and amusing if infuriating friend.

As children built Bradborough, and worked out how to play *Minecraft-Edu* in the classroom, they had to find ways of positioning themselves.

These positionings, however, happened across multiple communities. In terms of fractionality, they were simultaneously on/offscreen; 'now' and 'then'; friend and pupil; in school and elsewhere. Negotiating this fractional experience at times opened up new opportunities. At other times, intersections seemed to work to limit what children felt able to do.

DISCUSSION: RETHINKING COLLABORATION AS FRACTIONAL

Tracing some of the threads that joined classroom practices to other practices and identifying trajectories that worked across temporal and spatial boundaries helps us see collaboration as complex and multilayered. Of course our study is a partial representatiom. By focusing on observable behaviours and verbal accounts, we were unable to fully trace this complex web (if indeed this were possible). In particular, our analysis did not explore the multiple economic, cultural, historical and political movements that played through available resources (material and immaterial) and inflected the classroom where Minecraft Club took place. The significance of adults too (not least ourselves) is also written out of our account. However, by focusing broadly on how children took up resources in this classroom and the kinds of resources they used, we were able to identify some important dimensions of using virtual environments within classroom settings.

It is worth noting that Minecraft Club generated opportunities that were closed to some children outside school and allowed others to draw on and perhaps develop their extensive expertise. As Bradborough became entangled with the classroom (and the stuff, individuals and practices associated with it), it provided a site where children could play/work together on projects they found compelling. The inclusive principle underpinning Minecraft Club—that everyone gets to have a go—was important here, as was the fact that the children were together in one classroom and gathered around screens. In some ways their collaborations were similar to those achieved through affinity spaces (Gee, 2004), with individuals and pairs often working on unconnected projects but coming together to share expertise and support one another as necessary. Like Black and Reich (2013), we noted the significance of social interaction to how children were inducted by others into new ways of doing things. The open-ended task enabled them to contribute in different ways, and they often devoted considerable concentration and effort to their creations. In many ways, this work demonstrates how, in developing collaborative work around virtual environments in school settings, we might capitalise on the potential for children to work face to face and support them to play and create together in new ways.

In addition to these general points, however, we want to emphasise some dimensions of the way children worked together and separately, which we feel prompt us to see collaboration as a rather slippery phenomenon. These observations are highlighted by considering children's actions and interactions in terms of fractionality. We could see their play as fractional in a number of ways as they acted both on and off screen; simultaneously belonged to different communities; at once played as individuals, groups and a whole class; and operated across different time frames. Children also interacted with fractional objects—both on and off screen—which were taken up in different ways at different times. In the light of this, we suggest that five interconnected dimensions of being together in this hybrid site that may prompt us to think differently about collaboration:

1. The enactment of collaboration: Children in Minecraft Club worked across planes of meaning-making. Collaboration occurred through a range of on/offscreen moves: multiple modes and embodied interactions within the material environment were entangled with speech and onscreen action.
2. The boundlessness of collaboration in time and space: Collaboration occurred within long trajectories rather than fitting neatly into lessons. Children moved in and out of groupings, working sometimes individually and sometimes together. Often they collaborated on tasks that spanned multiple Minecraft Clubs or crossed home/school boundaries.
3. The meshing of communities: On/offscreen activity within and beyond the classroom (e.g., linked to gender, schooling, popular culture or gaming) seemed to shape emerging practices in *Minecraft*, and different realities intersected. These crystallised differently for different individuals at different moments with different implications for social capital. At times the whole class community was foregrounded, but this was overlaid by the formation and dissolution of other communities within or beyond the class. Moments of collaboration were related rhizomatically to events and experiences in other sites. Sometimes this was generative, at other times it was stultifying or frustrating.
4. The significance of being together: Whilst resources may originate from widely dispersed locations, their use coalesces in single moments. Collaborative meaning-making happens, then, as children improvise together with shared resources (material and immaterial) available through multiple communities.
5. 'Being together' as an end in itself: Emotional ties often seemed to matter more than negotiated exploration, and children's onscreen actions were often about amusing or supporting each other in the moment rather than working towards a shared outcome. Children used each other as instant audiences, and creations emerged to please themselves and their friends. The children were not just creating texts but creating friendships. Similarly, negative reactions—irritation, frustration—were often the drivers for on/offscreen activity.

These five points prompt us to see collaboration as fluid and spontaneous. Collaboration, from this perspective, is about improvisation in the moment and inflected by a multitude of flows. This apparently paradoxical perspective explodes bounded and organised notions of collaboration and helps us see working/playing together as complex and multiply framed. This is important, as it highlights the vast range of directions children may move in and through as they work and play together. And this, in turn, perhaps leads us to consider new ways in which being together may be significant to learning. As Law (2004: 66) argues, 'the discovery of fractionality opens up the possibility that realities may be otherwise'. At the same time, these dimensions highlight the significance of community—of being together—both within and beyond the class. Whilst the diversity and ephemerality of children's play seemed at odds with more established notions of communities of practice, the idea of community seems important. *Community*, perhaps seen as more fluid than commonly conceptualised, captures the emotional resonance that *collaboration* misses and implies long-term commitment that puts relationships into the frame.

Whilst this project foregrounded these dimensions of being together in relation to virtual environments, we might also see them as applicable to all literacy activities. Thus literacy activities *always* map onto communities within classrooms—whether or not these are the same as the imagined communities (Anderson, 1983; Richards, 2012) assumed by groupings of 'class' or 'school'. Whilst the verbal realm may dominate discourses around pedagogy (Kamler, 1997), children will *always* draw on a range of (im) material resources in different ways as they interact with one another and recruit schooled activities to their own purposes. They will *always* move between different communities, and the children who are most successful—both socially and in terms of schooled achievements—are likely to be those who are resourced to recognise and navigate the norms of different communities. Finally, what happens in school will *always* matter to children, and affective dimensions—linked to working together and creating stuff—will always be significant, whether this is boredom, rejection, hilarity, companionship or the generative pleasure of making stuff happen on screen. Our five dimensions of collaboration, then, may be useful in helping us look differently at how children engage with *all* kinds of texts in classrooms. We could also argue that all sites, not just those associated with virtual environments, are hybrid.

CONCLUDING COMMENTS

This research did not attempt to document exactly what children were learning as they engaged in *MinecraftEdu* together or arrive at evaluations of the effectiveness of their collaboration. That would have needed a different kind of study. Tentatively, however, we raise questions that may be worthy of future pedagogical research. Framed by an accountability agenda that rests on children's acquisition of specific literacy skills, much schooled literacy in England and elsewhere generates outcomes for unknown or deferred audiences. Collaborative work is often directed towards predetermined ends and managed within fixed groupings and defined spaces and times. Working from the perspective that all sites are hybrid, we ask whether it would be more appropriate to consider literacies as communal process: collaborative, provisional, negotiated and lateral. It is worth emphasising here that we are not suggesting that collaboration—around and in virtual environments or not—always has positive outcomes. As the examples above illustrate, being together may suppress as well as enable and distract rather than enrich. We argue that this way of conceptualising collaboration offers new insights, gives traction to our analysis of being together and leads us to foreground different priorities as we plan for schooled literacy in and around virtual environments or not.

Considering literacies as communal processes—and paying attention to the five dimensions of collaboration explored above—might involve prioritising considerations that are often sidelined in official accounts of schooled literacy as individualised and linked to the production of fixed outcomes. Considering literacies as communal processes might involve more flexible planning for collaboration, with fluid groupings, allowed to develop over time and informed by understandings about friendships and how different individuals may be positioned. Children would be encouraged to draw on a variety of physical and virtual resources, not least those gathered through experiences within and beyond school. Activities would not just be about designing outcomes for future audiences but be inherently pleasurable; the process of creation would be valued as well as the product. And the significance of 'community' would be foregrounded, both in terms of the classroom community and in recognising how play operates across communities. In such classrooms, 'being together' would be given status alongside 'learning together'.

EDITORS' COMMENTARY

As in the previous chapter, Burnett and Bailey explore how playful creativity involves taking up available resources and repurposing, repackaging or adapting them. This focus on improvisation helps us to see literacies in relation to a broad range of material and immaterial resources and the meanings that emerge as we draw on these from moment to moment. It highlights, we suggest, a material reality and affective dimension that has been underplayed in previous accounts of literacy. From this perspective, modal choice is not just about selection from a range of options but is associated with what we feel, what has just happened and who we are with, as well as what we want to mean. Importantly though these improvisations arise from, and help to reinforce, social ties. The joint endeavour—and fun —of creating for and with peers can be deeply felt.

There is a growing body of research into learning and teaching in virtual worlds, but less is known about the intricacies of collaboration across actual and virtual spaces. In describing 'being together' in Minecraft Club, Burnett and Bailey discuss the shifting nature of space as children move fluidly between the virtual world and the classroom. Burnett and Bailey observe the complexities of interaction when virtual contexts mesh with physical contexts. Screen-based text-making seems to leach into other spaces so that the sense of position in relation to others becomes slippery. In Minecraft Club, the children conducted themselves in new ways recognising the hybridity of the space and adjusting their interactions to accommodate a more provisional, improvised space for learning. This was a space where children became agentive; they learned from their peers and they explored in ways their teacher could not have predicted.

It is worth noting that, to carry out this work, the teacher established a lunchtime club, a semiformal context that was unconstrained by curricular requirements. The children were nevertheless gaining valuable experiences, developing tactics for gathering resources, making sense of materials and texts and creating digital multimodal artefacts for a range of purposes. This project represents a challenge to policymakers; the challenge to move such work into the curriculum proper where game playing is valued and where children can contribute in different ways. At the same time, we see how what happens in a particular location is framed by and helps construct different identities, variously legitimised as children play together.

Importantly, the chapter makes a further contribution to our understanding of literacies as 'placed resources' (Prinsloo, 2005) by exploring how the uncertain and fuzzy boundaries between contexts impact on identities as children operate across settings—where bodies in the classroom are simultaneously tied to virtual presence. Working as a class in a virtual world the children were excited and engaged and moved from conversations within world, to interactions about the world, across the space of the classroom. They learned by stealth; overhearing what others were doing, drawing conclusions and acting through peer to peer interaction and using all resources available. We witness how the children were able to gather information, learn codes of behaviour and make decisions about what might be appropriate. Thus while boundaries seemed fluid, and while collaboration was impacted on by diverse presentations of identity, provisional across contexts, some aspects of identity remained 'anchored' as opposed to 'transient' (Merchant, 2006), unaffected by the shifting boundaries of *Minecraft* in the classroom.

In the following chapter, Davies expands on this theme of identity, describing research on identity performance and the Facebook practices of four female hairdressers. Like Burnett and Bailey, Davies draws our attention to the spontaneous meaning-making that happens moment by moment across hybrid on/offline spaces. Notions of context become destabilised and online and offline spaces blur as what happens online shapes what happens offline and vice versa in complex and multiple ways.

5 (Im)material Girls Living in (Im)material Worlds

Identity Curation through Time and Space

Julia Davies

INTRODUCTION

This chapter draws on research about Facebook and the role it plays in the lives of a group of hairdressers living in a city in the north of England. The research has an ethnographic texture, where I, the researcher, shared in the young women's Facebook spaces and took part in their conversations. They washed, cut and dyed my hair; they had lunch with me and we talked about Facebook. These women, my 'Facebook Friends', were aged between 17 and 19 and were taking an advanced hairdressing course at a local college. They were neither confident about nor interested in academic reading or writing; their preoccupations were fashion and beauty and trying to acquire financial independence at a time when jobs were scarce and the cost of living high. They invested substantial amounts of time reading and writing within Facebook using their phones—which they carried with them all the time—like the young people Williams describes in Chapter 9. None of them owned a laptop or desktop computer and they used their mobiles with dexterity. These literacy practices were an essential part of my Friends' social and working lives; Facebook was used to make social and work arrangements, to advertise their hairdressing skills, to find out information, to debrief after social events, to display aspects of the events in their lives. Sometimes Facebook interactions constituted social events in themselves (Davies, 2013). This latter was instantiated by such things as online word play or other games that might later be referred to in face-to-face interaction, then taking on the status of a key happening in the Friends' lives. Thus Facebook sometimes mediated and sometimes constituted social acts, becoming, alongside text messaging, part of the fabric of everyday life. As the project was closing, all the women had also adopted Twitter and Instagram and later still some were using Snapchat alongside Facebook.

Much of the 'social work' (Eggins & Slade, 1997) which the women performed through their interactions within and around Facebook concentrated upon crafting presentations of the self and their connections with each other. Their textual identity performances both reflected but also affected how they saw themselves, their world and their place within it. Many spaces became embedded within Facebook—and vice versa; the boundedness of different spaces seemed porous, as images of bedrooms, nightclubs and bars, the salon and the college were displayed in online albums. The online context seemed to bring these spaces closer, blending the private and the public and flexing any boundaries between them. The very materiality of the young women's lives was drawn into and reflected within digital spaces, so that they often regarded themselves on a moment-by-moment basis, within the ever-evolving 'glass cabinet' of the online world, being at once within and 'looking out', but also materially rooted without while 'looking in'. The girls often used their mobiles to keep abreast of events while we were together; they showed images to each other and sometimes commented on each others' pages, so that they interacted both 'online and offline' at the same time.

I saw how the world of digital text and the material world have a synergy, blending together. I argue that this dynamic gives rise to complex interactions and relationships bringing about new ways of performing and understanding the self. Before moving on to exemplify this, I outline aspects of my theoretical framework, which arises from work from the New Literacy Studies.

THE NEW LITERACY STUDIES

The social turn in literacy (Barton, 2007; Barton & Hamilton, 1998; Cope & Kalantzis, 1999; Street, 1984) has been reflected in the increasing number of ethnographic studies in the field (see Heath & Street, 2007). Ethnography has become prominent in the NLS, although it is not an exclusive methodology (Street, 2001; Barton et al 2007; Tusting 2013), through concerns to see literacy not just as a set of skills, where readers decode and encode alphabetised text, but also to regard literacy as something people 'do' in their lives (Barton & Hamilton, 1998). Researchers have keenly shown literacy as practiced within contexts, adapting to relational, geographical and sociocultural circumstances (Prinsloo, 2005). The literacy event and practice have been key concepts, where events are the enactments of the more abstract practices, which have been identified as observable and located in specific contexts. The NLS created a space for studies that examined literacy beyond the formal academic practices valued within educational institutions and which reflected on the myriad ways that literacy is embedded in everyday life. More recently, explorations of digital text-making practices have helped theorists recognise the problems related to the situatedness of literacy in specific contexts, and I discuss this in relation to the concept of (im)materiality (Burnett et al., 2014) below.

STUFF: (IM)MATERIALITY

Kell (2011: 606) argues that we need to pay attention not just to meanings within contexts but also *across* contexts; she explains that we need to move from a focus 'on the production and interpretation of meanings within contexts towards a focus on the projection of meanings across contexts'. Thus understanding that meaning-making requires attention to flows and processes across spaces, especially given contemporary 'intensified mobility . . . of people, objects and information' (Kell, 2011: 606). Kell shows that it is difficult to make sense of a literacy 'event' (Barton & Hamilton, 1998) when we consider it in relation to the multitudinal instances of digital communication across time and space of the present day.

Burnett et al. (2014), also remind us that literacy practices often 'span different domains' (p. 2), and that these can 'evoke a variety of contexts in different ways' (p. 2). Thus we can present aspects of our identity across textual spaces, including the simultaneous occupation of real and virtual networks. Moreover, as other writers have started to identify, the material aspects of literacy practices significantly impact on meaning-making (Leander & Boldt, 2012; Leander & Sheehy, 2004; Mackey, 2011; Pahl & Rowsell, 2010). The material dimension of our experiences, including our own embodiment, are inextricably entwined with the meaning-making process. Burnett et al. explain, 'how the material constantly conjures the immaterial which in turn relies on material experience for its salience. It is this reflexive and recursive relationship between the material and the immaterial that we refer to as (im)materiality' (Burnett et al., 2014: 93).

Drawing on Lefebvre (1991), Leander and Sheehy in *Spaitializing Literacy Research* (2004) consider how literacy produces space. They argue that 'Because discursive practices are located in space, and because discursive practices actually produce space 'they disrupt notions of how literacies are 'situated' (Leander and Sheehy, 2004: 1). This is a disruption of the idea of context as a stable entity and instead advances the notion of context as an 'ongoing process' of creation (Leander and Sheehy, 2004: 1). Leander and Sheehy suggest that there is an 'interpretive loss' when literacy events and practices are conceptualised as occurring *in* fixed spaces. Perhaps this unsettling aspect of space is part of what makes the Internet so seductive; it feels at once familiar and yet 'uncanny' (Carrington, 2005). Spaces of uncertainty in their shifting malleability may seem more beguiling, liberating, offering a sense of agency—even a place where risk taking and experiments with identity and relationships seem appropriate/more possible. Yet conversely there is a sense in which space created through digital text making is mundane. Metaphors referring to websites predominantly conjure resonances of physical space, such as 'chat*rooms*', '*home* pages', 'cafes', 'walls' and even 'worlds'. The metaphors extend to users of websites, with words such as 'guests', 'lurkers', 'surfers', 'visitors' and so on, reinforcing ideas of bodily presence within spaces. Lakoff and Johnson (1975) point out that 'the metaphors we live by' are strongly influential in the way we perceive our world; these metaphors reinforce the conceptualisation of online spaces as reified social venues. Spaces and our sense of the spaces we inhabit are articulated then, by our experiences, the discourses they are produced by and that are produced 'in' them and are therefore constantly shifting.

So we can understand space as produced through our own discourses. In this way my Facebook space is coconstructed through the combined discourses of myself and my Friends. This space is reinvented on a moment-by-moment basis and its dimensions are beyond descriptive capture—the space of Facebook exists within the screen but also beyond in the spaces where it is being constructed and shared by its users. Facebook is not just a single, monolithic online site; it is dynamic, multifarious and continually reconstituted. Further, participants not only construct the Facebook space but jointly construct versions of themselves that in turn affect the way in which they regard their own identities and ways of being in the world. Yet as I suggest below, whilst writers/speakers who use/create Facebook are agentive, their presentations of self are interpellated through Facebook. Self evidently, Facebook provides a template that members cannot bypass; this template is the substance of Facebook and you are not 'in it' unless you use it; to join Facebook is to access the template. This template prioritises certain information, encourages particular gestures (such as 'liking' and 'poking'); it categorises and organises users' texts in particular ways (such as in a time line or photos in albums). Moreover, whilst users present themselves to others in ways they *can* control, they simultaneously create large volumes of data about themselves to those who invest financially. The aggregation of 'big data' about demography, topography, consumer habits, and so on is automated and continual and arguably invisible to users. Yet this also is a huge domain created by users for investors, something of which my Friends seemed only peripherally aware.

In a theoretically exploratory paper, Leander and Boldt (2013) consider embodiment in literacy activities; that is to say the ways in which literacy practices are embedded in real-world social action, so that 'literacy-related activity' is 'not as projected toward some textual end point but as living its life in the ongoing present, forming relations and connections across signs, objects, and bodies in often unexpected ways' (Leander & Boldt, 2013: 23).

They continue to explain that 'Such activity is saturated with affect and emotion; it creates and is fed by an ongoing series of affective intensities' (Leander & Boldt, 2013: 23). Their analysis of a 10-year-old boy's interaction with *Manga* and *Manga*-related play shows him reading the text and playing with the story and related artifacts across a day's activities on his own and with others. Leander and Boldt argue that researchers need to acknowledge nontextual aspects of practice because 'Literacy is unbounded. Unless as researchers we begin traveling in the unbounded circles that literacy travels in, we will miss literacy's ability to participate in unruly ways because we only see its proprieties' (Leander & Boldt, 2013: 42).

Like Burnett et al. (2014), who explore the ideas around the shifting nature of domains and spaces, Leander and Boldt's paper puzzles around the same kinds of difficulties and tensions in seeing how literacies are situated as Burnett et al.'s interest in the *(im)material*. And they explain the term as signaling a challenge of 'the binaries between the material and the immaterial, and crucially, do so in a relationship to practice' (Burnett et al., 2014: 91).

So to briefly summarise this section, I argue that we can understand space as something that is produced through our own discourses and that each space is defined in relational ways—that relationships mediated by multimodal interaction amongst people and things concurrently produce the space or domain of practice. Thus Facebook can be understood as a domain of practice that is constructed through the combined discourses of its participants, and this space is reinvented on a moment-by-moment basis as interactions ebb and flow. Facebook is not just one monolithic online space; it is dynamic, multifarious and constantly reconstituted. This means not only that participants' discourses construct the Facebook space but that the discursive space may go beyond Facebook; the digital discourse may have its roots in the materiality of the salon, the local bar or in a home—or even in all of these. Thus whilst the uncanny may be a feature of Facebook interaction, at the same time there is a sense of the mundane, where interactions are also often connected to specific geographical spaces; these spaces may be represented multimodally through maps, images and even representations of local patterns of language use, including accents and dialect in the written form. Exemplifications of these processes are shown below, but I first mention my positionality in relation to the work.

FACEBOOK FRIENDS

Drawing on the work of Stirling (2009, 2014), I capitalise the word *Friends* when I refer in particular to those who are my research participants and with whom I met to discuss the data. These young women were recruited to my project face to face at the college where they were doing their hairdressing course. Following established ethical protocols, including the right to withdraw at any time (BERA, 2012), I was thus able to describe my project to them and share my research notes with them. They were able to elaborate on what was happening in their online interactions and to share details as needed. We had reciprocal access to each other's Facebook pages and, as time went on, made occasional comments or would add 'likes' to each other's pages. When the project finished, I remained Facebook Friends with all the young women and continued to have my hair cut by them. Subsequently I have gained consent to become involved with one of them on a further project but would not use data from any of the others without further consent being acquired. At the request of two of my Facebook Friends, I use their real names, while the rest are pseudonyms.

SNIPPETS FROM THE DATA

For the purpose of this chapter I focus on my Friends' online activities, which provide succinct instantiations of (im)materiality with minimal requirement for contextual detail.

A Night Out with the Girls

The first example focuses on a social evening—a night out after work. As mentioned in the introduction, as well as following my Friends on Facebook, I met them regularly in order to explore the meanings and contingencies that were involved in the production of the text. I also sought to understand the materialities involved in each Facebook update and ensuing interactions.

Having not managed to get a hairdressing job after training to be a hairdresser and even specialising in 'bridal hair' and 'updos', Josie now works in a local Discount Store. One of her college friends, similarly unable to get salon work, also works in the same store and also attends the social event in question. Below I describe a series of 'digital engagements' that occurred across an evening, having pieced together the sequence by reading across a number of Facebook pages as well as by referring to Josie for explanations and to check my understandings. Methodologically, this raised an issue akin to that described by Burnett and Merchant (2014) around the difficulty in isolating a literacy event as 'a framing concept' (2014: 4). For ease of reference, in the data presentation below, rather than trying to define events, I itemise a series of key 'technology and text' or 'digital engagement' points in the evening where Facebook/Twitter or SMS (Short Message Service—or mobile phone texting) interaction took place.

1. At work Josie enters a status on Facebook: '"So excited . Going out with the girls for drinks'. (Facebook software also automatically adds to her text the note, 'via mobile', to signify the device Josie used.)
2. Josie's friend adds an update in which she also tags Josie and two of her other friends. The update includes a map (Figure 5.1) showing the location and name of the bar.

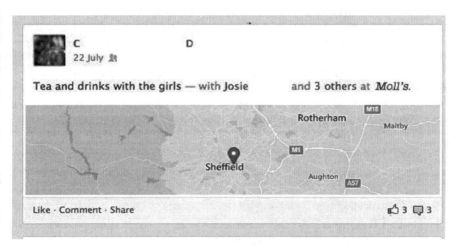

Figure 5.1 Location of venue and participants.

Figure 5.2   At the bar.

3. As Josie leaves her workplace, she uses her mobile phone to help her find the bar (pseudonym: Moll's), constantly checking her location as she navigates her way.
4. On arrival Josie updates her status to say she is at the bar and tags the bar (via mobile).
5. As all the friends arrive at the bar, they take photos of each other using their mobiles. Some of these are deleted, some put on Instagram (a photo-sharing site), and others are uploaded to Facebook.
6. Josie's mobile runs out of power and she uses a friend's charger to recharge it.
7. One of the images captures one of the women using her mobile (Figure 5.2).
8. Some of those in the party make comments while one participant, Mark, who is not at Moll's, also comments from his phone. Below is the interaction transposed from Facebook (I use Josie's real name but the other names are pseudonyms):

Josie: Omg my ears look huge	Monday at 21.12
Sara Louise: LOOL!!	Monday at 21:17 via mobile
Mark Scadden: Who U messagin Miss Lake	Monday at 21:32
Suzie Lake: U ov's	Monday as 21:32
Sara Louise: was gunna say the same Suze ;)	Monday at 21:39 via mobile
Mark Scadden: Hope u r bein a good girl	Monday at 21.46

9. That evening many of the friends use Twitter and interact with others not present as well as 'retweeting' (quoting) the tweets (comments) made by celebrities.
10. During this time Josie texts another friend, using simple SMS messaging, and arranges to meet her later in another bar in town.
11. In the early hours of the next morning, another photo appears on Josie's Facebook. She and her friend are standing in a fountain, up to their knees in water. Josie captioned the image 'This happen'd'.

Commencing this evening's itinerary as outlined here, we see Josie announcing to all her Facebook friends that she will be going out. In doing so she tags the friends with whom she is going to share her evening. This enables those 'accompanying friends' to see that she has published the occasion online and further allows her Facebook friends to click on the hyperlinked names and look at the public profile of her friends. In this way Josie affirms to those she will be going out with that this is a significant appointment; she is looking forward to it, so this is an act of friendship endorsement. Further, Josie provides a gateway to access the Facebook spaces of those with whom she is connected. In tagging her friends, she opens out the space for others to share, but readers reach the space via Josie's page and thus are encountered in relation to her. Josie's action, her tagging, is a kind of commendation of their pages, their profiles, their online identities, but they are also regarded through the lens of her own network, so there is a sense in which Josie's identity accrues meanings through association. Josie's Facebook space accommodates that of her friends; the discursive practice of tagging creates a larger domain of practice through which their identities are presented.

Danath and boyd (2004) have talked about online 'displays of connection' where social networking sites allow individuals to accrue reputation through their associations with others, and we see this in action here with the way tagging is used in this series of events across the evening. boyd (2006) has also discussed how the boundaries of online spaces are defined by one's friends; so the more friends one has, the larger the space. Thus in being mentioned by Josie, the friends are viewed by a network defined by Josie's friend list. The tags are part of the discourse that defines the space.

In item (2), Josie's friend (CD) invokes the venue for the night by locating it on a map. Here we see how one text (Bing maps) is embedded into another (Facebook) but also that the hyperlink to the venue itself brings in a wider domain of reference, the corporate world of business, which advertises through friends' social networking. As well as being able to geographically locate the social event via a map, we see here the broader structural forces of capitalism as a part of the domain, framing the local practices. The use of a range of applications, the naming of corporations and as we saw earlier, the identification of device brand names, all contribute to an invisible larger narrative of big data sets collected by others. These forces are further exemplified in Facebook's software, which identifies the medium of interaction 'via mobile' wherever possible, and in other updates that evening I saw 'via Blackberry' as an endorsement of a specific trademark. In this way the friends' interactions are framed by global corporate interest. But it is not that these young women are unaware of it. 'It's like, well, we like our phones and you wouldn't use it if it put a crap name online next to your name would you? It's good if you can get "iPhone" next to your name', Jodie told me. This articulation expresses clearly that the young women were aware of the ways in which brand names can be read off by others as part of a reading of themselves. They seemed comfortable with this idea and did not look further than wishing (or not) to be associated with particular brands.

At points (3) and (6) there is a strong sense of materiality in Josie's digital activities. She uses her digital device to negotiate her way through the physical world, from work to Moll's. In charging her phone while at Moll's, we get a sense of the limitations of the physical device and the reliance Josie has on it; while Josie uses her smartphone to transcend aspects of the physical world, she is at the same time bound to it. One of my Facebook Friends talked to me about how 'lame' it is if your phone is not always charged and that you shouldn't have to charge it in front of people. It seemed this was backstage work and that only fully functioning, 'fit to go' smartphones are part of the image of the slick set. As Hannah had told me before (Davies, 2013: 18), your phone is all part of your image: 'We plan every detail. It's details that count. Even your nails and your mobile phone. They have to match. You have to think about your phone and '"do I look good using my phone?"'

At points (7) and (8) the girls' Facebook friends are able to see a photograph of them in the location of Moll's and involved in a social happening. The girls view the image at the same time, so that Josie is able to evaluate the representation it gives of her: 'Omg my ears look huge', while her friend, who is present, represents her own laughter on the screen 'LOOL'. Indeed Josie reported that her friend did actually 'Laugh Out Loud' while sitting in Moll's and viewing the image. Yet her choice to also represent this, to transpose this into written form, is akin to ventriloquism (Bakhtin, 1981; 1986) where she attempts to represent her audible reaction for others to 'hear', and makes accessible the social occasion to those who are not in the bar. In doing so, she plays with the now conventional 'LOL', suggesting an elongated sound ('LOOL') for emphasis or comic effect. They play with the affordances offered by Facebook showing a dexterity and an enjoyment of exploring what is possible. It is very clear at this point that the young women are attempting inclusivity, to involve a wider audience in what is happening in the physical space of the bar, so that the domain of practice is at once on and offline, (im)material. Around fifteen minutes after this a 'voice' from beyond the physical location of Moll's asks, 'Who U messagin Miss Lake'. Far from reflecting a total opening out of the location, therefore, a sharing of the domain, the question emphasises spatial separateness; it seems that in seeing the uploaded photo, Mark feels excluded, not included. Mark sees the image of his girlfriend texting and wants to know what is happening, but he cannot see or control events as clearly as he wishes. There is only a partial revelation of what is happening and he is aware of the possibility of a back channel. The immediate but apparently ironic (as was revealed to me) reply, 'U ov's' (You, obviously), meant that Mark was not told whom Suzie was texting. If Suzie had been texting Mark, he would of course have received the text and not asked his question; he knew he was not being told the truth. Thus while Mark was included in part of the activity, he was disempowered by it—he was being teased. In this way the girls manipulated the context to their advantage and gained the upper hand in the power dynamic of the exchange. Here we see how the girls' interactions with each other reach beyond their physical placement and that they make choices as to how and when they mediate their discourse and the parameters of the spaces they create. Inhabitance of space is not always reciprocal; when one person is unable to access all the resources available to others, he has unequal access to the space they have produced. The domain shifts on a moment-by-moment basis as participants filter voices in and out, closing and opening channels, swopping between apps and modes (as we see next), alerting some friends through tags, but not others.

The move to a new platform later in the evening, through the switch to Twitter (9), means that the words of celebrities enter the conversations of the cocreated textual space the girls inhabit and that new sets of friends, now also from Twitter, become part of the space. The mixing of the young women's voices with the voices of those whom they admire or whose lives they like to follow are blended into their own world in Moll's bar. The discourse of celebrity becomes entwined with the discourses of the young women, and they become involved in the dramatic disputes played out in the public sphere by famous people. The young women are thus able to appropriate a range of voices in a complex domain where they operate on the fringes of celebrity worlds, which they incorporate into the bricolage of their text-making practices.

Josie uses a back channel, using the SMS text facility on her Smartphone, privately organising a new event for herself where no one is tagged and where the domain of Facebook and Moll's is closed out. She narrows the field by using a direct and private messaging system; after she meets her friend elsewhere in the city, the phone stays in her bag for a few hours. In this way she chooses to maintain some privacy, a social occasion she does not wish to mediate to others—time, she told me, with her best friend. That is, until the early hours of the morning, when she takes a photograph to make people laugh—a selfie of her and her friend, saturated in the fountain and looking comedic after too much to drink. This is the kind of image that the young are often warned against sharing; where the 'wrong' people might see—an employer for example. Yet from seeing the range of applications that the young women used throughout the evening, we see them exercising choice and being judicious about how they open out the discursive domain, frequently altering the parameters of the context and filtering some people in and some people out.

Hannah and Her Pictures

One of my other Friends has mainly images on her Facebook, with just small captions and comments to follow; this is not exclusively the case but predominantly so. A large number of these were taken on the occasion of her 'high school prom'; there are also a great number of images of herself and her friends getting ready to attend and then actually attending a Hallowe'en party. Finally there are also a large number of images taken at the salon where she works.

The images of Hannah in her prom dress show her wearing a silken and voluminous pink ball gown; the outfit looks very similar to those in Disney Princess images, dreamlike and photogenic. She is seen in many different poses, both individually and with her friends, similarly dressed at the 'prom' itself. The idea of the high school prom is now a fixed occasion in many UK school calendars but is a relatively new phenomenon, having been influenced by American high school television series and other media 'imports' that have been the staple diet of teenagers in the UK over a number of years. In this way the gowns, the stretch limousines and the occasion of dancing at grand local venues are all discursive artifacts of a global phenomenon and seem to index a rite of passage—the end of compulsory schooling. In Hannah's Facebook page we see this interpreted locally via her images of herself with friends in gardens, standing against the terraced housing, caravans parked in drives and abandoned vehicles on roads.

The images of Hannah and her friends in the house on Hallowe'en show her opening out the private space of the bedroom to her Facebook friends. We see them gradually preparing themselves, applying makeup, wearing outfits made through the binding of bandages, with fake bloodstains around their bodies. Yet the young women are not trying to make themselves look grotesque; their interpretation is akin to the glamorous images of popular culture Goth TV series, films and books, such as *Buffy the Vampire Slayer* and *True Blood*. They draw on an uncanny discourse of femininity depicted in such films and stories, where, as Martin (2013) argues, females are represented as 'other', partly as victim, partly as terrifying. Further, as has been suggested by Griffin Wolff (1979: 98), the genre often uses female characters to express the 'dilemmas of feminine sexuality'. The Hallowe'en theme is therefore a popular culture phenomenon, residing in the domain of globalised TV and film. In the meantime the girls interpret this locally in their bedrooms, standing in poses of friendship as they take each other's pictures, encapsulating the undercurrent themes from the TV series they have seen. In some images, Hannah and her friends have copied the hair and makeup of celebrities they admire, meticulously following instructions from YouTube videos and creating outfits customised from cheaper items they saved to afford. The improvisations and ventriloquising of postures and gestures, something Taylor (2010) refers to as 'postural intertextuality', brings wider domains through to the local. The luxurious discourses are transformed into commodities that can be afforded by Hannah and her friends and which present an online identity that they enjoy curating (Potter, 2012). There is a sense here of DIY Media (Knobel & Lankshear, 2010), where the young women are creating and producing a range of digital texts. These are not the people who make YouTube videos (Willett, 2008) or complex machinima (Ito, 2011), but yet these young women use the resources at their disposal to publish images of themselves online that they can reflect upon immediately and for time to come. These activities enrich their lives; this is play, experimentation and the projection of the self into domains beyond the immediate—opening out the boundaries of their locality. Through designing their costumes and makeup, repeated taking of photographs, editing and deleting, tagging and comments, the Friends adopt discursive positions that take them into the realm of fantasy. In looking back at themselves, they see representations that comprise the shared online spaces of celebrities and fantasy characters who adopt the same poses and wear similar costumes. These are the material girls that Madonna sings about, but unlike in the 1980s, they are able to project images of themselves that blend the local and the global in a cocreation of (im)material worlds.

The hairdressers told me that they often spent time culling their Facebook pages, deleting references to themselves so that particular images would then disappear from their 'walls'. There is a sense in which they live their lives in anticipation of being on Facebook—and moreover that not having an online presence is to be viewed as absent from the social scene entirely, with presence therefore being (im)materially perceived. 'Pictures are everything. I can't wear the same thing twice because of all the photos on Facebook. Even if you are going out with different groups of people—it could be social suicide (laughs). No you don't want people to think you've not got many clothes.'

The Hallowe'en night images taken in Hannah's house, number in their hundreds and Hannah told me even though they spent hours getting ready, they never ended up going out that evening as they had such fun taking photographs and posing. The channelling of popular culture horror stories, of the high school prom and of girl bands are all enacted through the physical body. These are shared in the discursive space of Facebook and where the images are seen side by side with images from the salon, from college and even family holidays. The events seem to merge together within the photograph albums online, and readers can click on tags that open the spaces out further in ever-changing tessellations, where friends can be traced through from one Facebook page to the next.

One of Hannah's interactions involved a map, similar to the one shown in Figure 5.1. The map shows the location of a Christmas celebration where the owner of the salon, Ann, for whom Hannah worked, was taking her staff out for a meal. Ann had uploaded the map, had identified the restaurant where they were, tagged the Facebook page of her salon, and also tagged the young women who were with her. In this way, the employees and their boss were all drawn into the same physical space whilst also being represented in the restaurant yet still affiliated to the salon. In addition to tagging the places and the people, Ann also commented, 'Treating my fabulous staff to dinner. Love my girlies—with Hannah and Toni and Liz and Soo'. As with the interaction with Josie and her friends, this act seems to add an additional layer of complexity to the space, so that Ann communicates (face to face and in Facebook) not only to those with whom she is physically present but also those who might read her Facebook and (through tagging) the Facebooks of her staff. Further, while she is communicating face to face with her 'fabulous staff', she is also communicating in a way that brings them to acknowledge what she says *about* them. While still at the restaurant, the 'girlies' each 'liked' the comment by clicking on the 'like' feature in Facebook; they clearly had their phones with them, which will have buzzed and signaled a new update when Ann had uploaded her comment. In one sense this was a back channel, because the update was about those present; but nevertheless because the girls 'liked' the comment, they showed that they were aware of it. The (im)material discourse was subsumed within the face to face, so that there was a kind of endorsement of their friendship that was at once articulated yet not spoken out loud. By using a different mode, the materiality of the gathering was suffused with another layer of digital meaning-making. This was also amplified because Ann placed this comment where her Facebook friends as well as her customers could see; the space was opened out as if the meal were taking place in front of others. The friendship was doubly endorsed by the opening out of the (im)material domain. The efficacy of this was seen in the multiple likes that followed and in the long list of comments wishing them all a Happy Christmas, 'Have a great time', and so on.

FINAL COMMENTS

The title of this paper invokes the words of Madonna's 1984 song 'Material Girl', whose lyrics celebrate the joy of possessions: 'I am a material girl, living in a material world' (Madonna, 1984). The character of the girl depicted in the song embodies an identity associated with high fashion, and Madonna's video performance is highly salient in popular culture. The young women in my study, like Madonna's character for the song, carefully styled themselves and enjoyed doing so. They sought opportunities to pose for photos and to take photos of themselves against chic and fashionable backdrops; they curated (Potter, 2012) these images and captioned them. Sometimes these activities would seem to be events in themselves—the curation of images to put on Facebook in order to reflect a lifestyle. The creation of such images required them to gather at particular locations, to source the right artifacts and fashion items, to put together the right styles of hair and makeup, and even to pose in the right ways—in ways that evoked celebrity discourses and lifestyles. This process will be familiar to many readers and is not necessarily associated with the digital age; however, the recording of images digitally and the rapid and abundant dissemination of these brings a new dimension into the present material world—that of the active audience. My Facebook Friends used digital tools to source materials through which they could participate in local interpretations of fashion. Digital devices thus serviced their complex and iterative performances of gender flowing across and through on/offline spaces. I have described how these hairdressers performed identity in this way in greater detail in Davies (2013), describing it as an example of a gendered community of (literacy) practice, where localised practices are often linked to broader globalised dscourses and where young women are often influenced by others even in oppressive ways. Digital tools facilitate the monitoring of others' behavior, so that individuals and groups often feel coerced into following group norms. It has become usual to talk about being 'online' or 'offline' as material and discrete dimensions; on/offline spaces are referred to as if geographically located in relation to each other. Sometimes we hear about the permeability of online and offline borders, which—while recognising a porosity between such spaces—nevertheless endorses the notion of boundary crossing and thereby assumes the presence of boundaries. In this chapter I have problematised the idea of boundaries and their placement. My data have shown that these can be present, absent, moved and immutable over short periods of time as participants and their artifacts interact.

I have also been interested in how materiality becomes problematised specifically in Facebook, where users recursively move their interactions within and without (even through) Facebook in some instances. There is a sense in which their existence in the real space is authenticated by their Facebook interactions and, moreover, that their material presence is affected by what is happening through the medium of Facebook. It is for this reason, to trace meanings across spaces, that I have used a connected approach (Leander & McKim, 2003) tracing meanings, continuities and discontinuities across spaces. As I reported elsewhere (Davies, 2013), Facebook can sometimes act as a kind of 'anchorage' for groups of people, drawing them into a particular space for particular purposes, but here I have developed the idea that this anchorage can be ephemeral.

Burnett and Merchant (2014) have explored how the notion of literacy events invites further investigation; the uses of literacy mediated by digital technologies seem to expose tensions and uncertainties in the concepts encapsulated by the NLS of discrete events within bounded contexts. Context is not so much a 'static container' (Burgess, 2010: 19) but something more dynamic.

The examples I have discussed in this chapter show a kind of kaleidoscoping effect of space and time within many of the interactions that take place using Facebook. As Burnett et al. (2014: 91) have argued, 'Individuals' lived literacy practices . . . often span different domains or evoke a variety of contexts that intersect in multiple ways.' Aberton (2012) describes how we live in a materially complex world and talks about 'a mixing up of things and people in processes' (Aberton, 2012: 114).

Because individuals move with their mobile devices and use these devices to help them perform social acts, and those acts are embedded within literacy and vice versa, the domain of literacy practice becomes multilayered with meanings from multiple 'real' spaces, virtual sites and different combinations of participants. It is the discourse itself that creates space, and our understandings of the complexity of this is crucial for us to manage our increasingly complex lives.

EDITORS' COMMENTARY

In Chapter 5, Davies explores the nuances of mobility, of porous global forces, of performed identities and, like Burnett and Bailey, invites the reader to recognise how disparate meanings gain purchase across context, calling into question dominant conceptualisations of context as static and stratified. Her work problematises our understandings of contexts for learning and contexts for literacy. It implies that we need to interrogate more closely the notion that contexts have boundaries within which literacy events occur. In her study some key distinctions between the local and the global, the public and the private and online and offline networks begin to dissolve as these young women interact and document their movements and activities on Facebook.

One facet of this work is the circulation and uptake of global, corporate ideologies in digital spaces. Wittingly or unwittingly, individuals constantly support, reinforce and promulgate brands and corporations when they communicate and interact on a daily basis—whether that takes the form of a Blackberry signature in a text message or advertising for a restaurant embedded in Bing maps (Fuchs, 2007). Davies's chapter displays how global forces bleed into local, personal lives in practical but also rhetorical and ideological ways. This raises questions about how corporate ideologies hijack meanings and the ways in which they are taken up in online communities.

As these young women use their mobiles, they draw on transnational discourses—such as those associated with the status of products, celebrity lifestyles, school proms and fashion. These discourses, however, are locally textured, mixed in with vernacular idioms and experienced in specific locations—and they work to sustain social relationships between a close-knit group of friends. Here we see what Davies describes as 'complex iterative performance of gender flowing across and through on/offline spaces'. These gendered practices generate a very different translocal assemblage to those described by Lemphane and Prinsloo (Chapter 2), but they serve to under-line how the taking up of digital resources is both personally meaningful and inflected by a range of social, economic and cultural influences—the instantiations of ideology and power. Importantly, Davies shows us that these meaning-making practices are not just localised but themselves work to produce local social spaces. As these hairdressers reappropriate digi-tal resources through Facebook, they produce spaces where they can be together. This raises questions about how digital resources get reappropri-ated in school settings. In education, the local is often erased in favour of the universal goals and expectations. Curricula tend to iron out local dif-ferences, setting out generalised teaching objectives or specifying common curriculum content. We argue that the local is just as relevant in individual schools as it is in these hairdressers' lives.

In the next chapter, Beavis considers how a curriculum can respond to and build on students' meaning-making practices. Beavis explores how video games can be seen as new forms of narrative, and shows how their incorporation in the curriculum not only draws on students' out-of-school experience of digital texts but also provides opportunities to explore aes-thetic and literary dimensions of these complex multimodal texts. Beavis explores the ways in which video games involve active and critical read-ing and position children and young people as producers and consumers of transmedia narratives. We can read her chapter as an example of how educational institutions can support students in appropriating translocal resources in ways that are creative, critical and personally meaningful.

6 Literature, Imagination and Computer Games
Videogames and the English/Literature Curriculum

Catherine Beavis

LITERATURE, IMAGINATION AND COMPUTER GAMES

This is an exciting time for literature, imagination, storytelling and children's digital lives. Literature has always been an important presence in the English and literacy curriculum, sometimes hovering in the sidelines, sometimes dominating other dimensions, or sometimes working in an integrated partnership with literacy and language. In a time when digital texts and stories are a vivid and pervasive part of young people's worlds, the opportunity is here for literature that includes digital texts to take its place alongside other forms—picture books, novels, poems, plays and the like—to be an integral part of curriculum; that is, to be approached in ways that enhance and deepen pleasure and appreciation, children's understandings of texts and how they work, and their understandings of the nature of reading, of themselves, and of the world. Working with literary texts creates opportunities for imagination, creativity and play, and there is no good reason why this should not include games.

The recognition of texts in a wide and diverse range of forms, including digital, that might be considered 'aesthetic', or in other ways 'literary', as part of English, provides opportunities to bridge between students' in and out of school worlds in powerful ways. It enables a study of literature that includes but extends beyond traditional classic print and oral forms to comprise visual, multimodal and digital forms, and it encourages the incorporation of literature from a wide range of cultures, reflective of the diversity of students in contemporary communities. It enables an approach that recognises diverse and multiple communicative forms and the need for students to be critical, capable and creative users of digital and multimodal forms of literacy alongside the traditional print curriculum.

Children have always come to text and story through a diversity of modes—through songs and spoken myths and narratives, stories, images and symbolic objects, stained glass windows, artifacts, picture books; dramatic and imaginative play. In the digital age, this range of ways in which stories—and other forms of literature—are made and told, created and experienced, broadens dramatically. We are seeing changes in the patterns of children's reading, in children's experience of texts, and in their exposure to imaginative textual worlds. It is not that children's literature as we knew it has disappeared, but there are changes under way. Digital forms of narrative sit alongside print, oral and picture book genres. As Marsh and Richards (2013) note, 'children are immersed in "mediascapes" (Appadurai,1996) of contemporary media digital cultures and their "ruling passions" (Barton & Hamilton 1998), often related to particular media characters, texts and artefacts, seep into all aspects of their lives from a young age' (Hodge & Tripp, 1986; Marsh et al: 12).

'Transmedia' stories flow across different forms and platforms, with 'transmedia navigation'—'the ability to follow the flow of stories and information across multiple modalities'—a key 'new' skill for meeting the challenges of Participatory Culture (Jenkins et al. 2009: 15).

What does this mean, for children and for classrooms? What does it tell us about what children's experience of 'literature' and the world of text and story might be? What does it suggest about the kinds of texts schools might approach as literature in the classroom, how they might be taught, and how teachers and students might work with them? These are pressing questions for English teaching that incorporates digital texts as part of the spectrum of 'literature' explored and created in school.

What Kinds and Forms of Text?

Traditional forms of literary texts, where language is used in creative and imaginative ways, clearly remain central to the study of literature. To argue for the inclusion of a broader range of texts alongside traditional forms is not to deride the value of those forms. Rather, it is to recognise the diversity of children's experience of finely shaped imaginative worlds and the ways in which new possibilities for meaning-making are creating new textual forms. There is a place for both traditional and contemporary forms. New forms of narrative, new ways of positioning readers, and new forms of participation and engagement are emerging; these warrant attention alongside more familiar forms. The digital 'revolution' has enabled the development of a range of cultural forms, including e-literature and videogames, which reward close study and are a significant part of many students' lives.

What Kinds of Experience?

In their out-of-school worlds and their experience of texts before they even come to school, children's experience of literature is increasingly multimodal. It is also increasingly participatory. In Participatory Culture, young people expect to be actively involved in the textual, digital world, as both consumers and producers as well as readers/viewers/players and creators (Jenkins et al., 2009). There are two foci here then: (1) the ways in which children's experience of textual worlds, which crosses many forms, and

(2) the active nature of participation and creation, beyond that of 'active reading' to the production of new stories, new games, new commentaries and communications that springboard from the original text(s) to become something related but new.

Narratives and other literary forms have always called on other stories, older versions, generic conventions and the like and recreated them, making them their own. In addition, we now have forms of connection, where narratives cross media platforms and tie in products and marketing. In this way children do not simply read about Harry Potter and Hogwarts; they can also become part of that world more actively, through reading the books or seeing the films but also through listening to Stephen Fry's reading; playing one of the related computer games; owning socks, lunch boxes or Harry Potter pencils; visiting the costume and Harry Potter world exhibition or participating in many of the Harry Potter websites and fanfiction sites.

At the next remove, they might also follow the battles over ownership of the Harry Potter 'brand' and the way it is represented, between J. K. Rowling and commercial interests. They might follow the post-Harry Potter film lives of key actors from the films and reflect, perhaps, on parallels with their own trajectories from childhood to adolescence and beyond—a reflection of the ways in which literary characters become part of our lives, and the intricate dance of association, distance and closeness with which we bring significant stories and images into our lives. Such moves are consistent with how we call on real and imaginary characters, and on literature and other narrative forms in the ways we imagine, understand and negotiate our interior and exterior worlds.

Important, too, is the active nature of participation. For children and young people at ease in the digital age, production is a central part of participation in the online world, with options for making and creating in relation to texts and narratives from within and outside the digital world. Children are expert in watching and listening to television programs and video downloads, playing on iPads, manipulating digital devices such as cameras and mobile phones, playing games on small hand held consoles such as the DS (Nintendo dual screen console) or PSP (Play Station Portables) and other technologies, playing digital games, and incorporating digital stories and digital culture into their everyday play. Examples abound of observations of young children's out-of-school early play that crosses readily between on/offline worlds, in stark contrast, often, to the more formal parameters and restraints they meet in school. O'Mara and Laidlaw, for example, describe their observations of their own primary and preschool children's home-based digital play, in Australia and Canada respectively, as they access the 'tween cartoon series *Monster High* (Mattel, 2010) online or enjoy a '21st-century tea party' mixing an iPod game, stuffed toys, plastic tea sets and digital cakes and tea. Of interest here are the children's expectations about, and experience of, texts, technologies and play—both in relation to the active nature of the play, which includes making things happen through accessing and activating various technologies—and in the easy integration between on and offline activities and worlds of imaginative play (O'Mara & Laidlaw, 2011).

What Kinds of Qualities?

What makes something 'literature' or 'literary'? This has always been a problematic question. Central however, is a focus on the richness and aesthetic values of the text, the care taken in its shaping and the capacity of the text to enlarge understandings and enrich readers' (viewers', listeners') lives. So too are the ways in which such texts offer nuanced and multiple meanings that resonate differently with successive readings. Attempts to identify the kinds of qualities that 'literary' texts provide include close attention to shaping and a consideration of the kinds of attention they promote. Linguistic definitions include forms of writing where the patterning of language is over and above what is required for basic meaning. Kress (2002) talks differently, about 'salient' texts rather than 'Literature'—that is, texts that have a particular significance or cultural meaning that is highly valued in individual communities—an important step forward in recognising ethnic and cultural diversity while also paving the way for the study of texts in nonprint forms. Misson and Morgan (2006) argue that we need a different term than *Literature*, a different way of thinking about literary texts to avoid some of 'baggage' that comes with assuming that *Literature* refers only to classic and canonical print-based forms. They argue for the concept of the 'aesthetic', for the place of literary (creative, imaginative) texts within a critical literacy curriculum and for a teaching approach that allows the exploration of how imaginative inner and creative forms of engagement may also be critical and social (Misson & Morgan, 2006).

What Kinds of Attention?

Pedagogically, the kinds of attention paid to texts should include a focus, first of all, on the readers' experience of the text—the pleasures and enjoyment they found, what they liked, what puzzled them, points of connection, points of disagreement, surprise or worry. Questions of how meaning is made and how elements contribute to the whole follow and are at the heart of the close study of texts—attention to the nuances of values and meaning created for example by the particular choice of words or images, the juxtaposition of one element with another, the ways in which values and ideologies are conveyed, assumptions made about readers/viewers/players and the values they hold, or that the text would like to persuade them to share. Discussion might also attend to the cultural salience of the text—why this text has been thought to be important, what its significance might be; whether, perhaps that is justified and from whose perspective.

THE PERVASIVENESS OF GAMES

Digital texts and imaginary worlds are part of the everyday stuff of children's imagining, woven in and out of 'real world' play and part of that bigger exploration of self and the world that texts of all kinds enable and are used for by different readers in different ways. Just as Laidlaw and O'Mara's children incorporated TV shows and websites, iPad technology and laptops into their everyday play, so too do children make use of videogames as part of the 'stuff' of their imaginative lives and sense of who they are. Hannaford (2012), for example, documented the ways in which play with games linked in with children's explorations of being 'a certain kind of person' (2012: 31) in the after-school computer club she ran for her primary school students. Children included Caitlyn, an avid reader with a preference for fantasy texts, who 'mainly liked Internet dress-up games especially those featuring rock star and princess characters' (2012: 27); Kimberley, who did not fit easily in the world of school but took great pleasure in her mastery of the mechanics of game play—being able to 'do' things with *Tipton Trouble*, her game of choice; and Edward, one of the best football players in his year, who wanted to make sure that his puffle in *Club Penguin* had the chance to escape the igloo, to 'get fresh air and run around . . . if it doesn't, it gets het up in the igloo and gets very bored' (2012: 29). Amongst older students, links between game play, pleasure, imagination and identity have similarly been explored.

Computer games and games played on consoles and mobile devices such as mobile phones are now a mainstream part of children's lives, particularly in the Western and industrialised 'First World'. The *Digital Australia 2012* Report (interactive Games and Entertainment Association, 2012) gives the following snapshot of game play in Australian families. Amongst other things, the figures are interesting in the picture they provide of the moderate amount of time spent on games by children within this age range and the generally positive attitudes and involvement of families in supporting or participating in game play:

- in 2012, 92% of Australian households have a device for playing computer games, up from 88% in late 2008 as mobile gaming has become mainstream;
- 95% of homes with children under the age of 18 have a device for playing computer games;
- 94% aged 6 to 15 years play video games;
- Playing habits are moderate, with 59% playing for up to an hour at one sitting;
- 83% of parents with children aged under 18 living with them play computer games;
- of these, 88% play with their children;
- 90% of parents who play computer games themselves use them to help educate their children;

- family games accounted for 19% of all unit game sales in 2012, followed by Action (18%), First Person Shooters (15%), and Sports and Racing games (9%).

Not all games are narrative in orientation, but all require players to be able to interpret and interact with images and symbols on the screen. Children's immersion in narrative and textual worlds online may be characterised by features such as the existence of prestructured story schema within which they nonetheless experience agency, the need to interpret and act on symbols and information presented in multimodal form, the need to take action to precipitate what happens next, complex positioning within the game provided by the player's avatar and the player's relationship with the avatar; if this is the case, it is likely that the expectations children bring to literary texts encountered in school will be coloured by experiences such as these.

ENGLISH CURRICULUM AND COMPUTER GAMES

As hybrid cultural forms, games call on a range of reading and interaction skills and knowledge to make them work—in effect, multimodal literacy practices. Gee's 'design' and 'semiotic' principles encapsulate this relationship. In the 'design principle', 'learning about and coming to appreciate design and design principles is core to the learning experience'. In the 'semiotic' principle, 'learning about and coming to appreciate interrelations within and across multiple sign systems (images, words, actions, symbols, artefacts, etc.) as a complex system is core to the learning experience' (Gee, 2007: 41–42).

While the degree to which computer games might be regarded as text is problematic—games quintessentially entail both text and action (Apperley & Beavis, 2013; Beavis 2013)—a design-based view of literacy, which includes images, sound, gesture etc. alongside print based forms (New London Group, 1996), constructs a powerful argument for the inclusion of computer games as objects of study within the English curriculum. There are a number of reasons why computer games, as specific kinds of digital/textual forms, might play a part in the English curriculum.

Games as Hybrid Narrative Form

First, games present new or 'remediated' (Bolter & Grusin, 2000) forms of narrative construction, organisation and experience. For many children, some of their most satisfying and engaging experiences of narrative and of the making and playing of stories come through computer games and/or their playful involvement with others in online virtual worlds. Narrative-based games, such as quest-based role-play games, for example, draw on older traditions of telling and making stories and build on familiar genres and forms. Players need to know a significant amount about stories and about games in order to play. They may need to remember the back-story, for example, know what sort of action and scenarios to expect, to have a fair idea of what different characters are typically like and what they do. They need to call on generic and intertextual experience, including knowledge about this game and about games and stories that are similar. As forms of narrative, games entail a mix of old and new ways of creating meaning, new forms of narrative or argument, using traditional literacies and 'new' literacies, positioning the reader/player in complex ways, and relying on considerable intertextual and generic knowledge both of similar narratives in games and other forms. Features include a shift from narrative to spectacle, a reliance on intertextual referencing, a 'remediation' of older forms, a mix of first, second and third person address and a shift from print to multimodal forms of literacy. Bradford (2010) describes games as

> hybrid products which incorporate narrative and game elements while engaging players in energetic action and (in many cases) interpersonal and social processes. . . . Like all cultural forms. . . . video games reflect aspects of the society in which they are produced; they also shape players' perceptions and promote values both implicitly and explicitly. . . . As complex, evolving forms, they invite analytical strategies which take account of the multifarious ways in which they produce meaning and create subject positions for players. (Bradford, 2010: 54)

A Combination of Text and Action

Second, games comprise a unique mix of text and action. Games resemble other storytelling forms, such as literature or film. But there are significant differences too. Central here is the role of action as integral to the enactment of game play. Players need to *do* something in order to make the game happen, in interaction with the algorithm of the game and the machine. To read games as primarily narrative is to mistake the nature of games and to superimpose inappropriate frameworks for the analysis and understanding of games. Games are not (merely) textual forms. Games work as 'both object and process [they] . . . can't be read as texts or listened to as music, they must be played' (Aarseth, 2001: n.p.). Galloway (2006: 3) argues that 'Their foundation is not in looking and reading but in the instigation of material change through action—the action of the change through action—the action of the machine is just as important as the action of the operator.'

If games are studied or in other ways incorporated into English as digital textual forms, the action-driven nature of games and game play must be recognised.

Multimodal Literacies

Third, computer games call on multiple elements to make meaning—sound, images, words, actions, symbols, colour and the like—singly or in combination. As such, they provide rich and attractive exemplars of multimodal texts. To make sense of computer games, players need to recognise how all these different elements combine. Understanding the ways combinations work is key: 'learning about and coming to appreciate interrelations within and across multiple sign systems . . . as a complex system is core to the learning' (Gee, 2007: 42). Features may include split screens, where information is provided in several places at once as well as in several forms. Maps in one corner, for example, may show where the main play is taking place in the games world. Panels on the side or below the 'main' action may show clothes, weapons and the like to buy, use, combine, add or in other ways take into account. Different combinations of characters, qualities and weapons will have different effects and results. Working with computer games as part of English provides opportunities for students to explore multimodal literacies and how many elements work together to create the overall design.

Literacy Practices, Situated Play

Fourth, game play is very much socially situated and grounded in 'real world' time, place and activity. Game play takes place in real-world contexts and online. As they play computer games, alone or with other players, young people are involved in a rich range of literacy practices, from reading information in print and digital form, discussing play with friends, working out strategies, reflecting on what happened and why, negotiating for their next turn, solving problems and so on. Games exemplify social and participatory forms of engagement with texts typical of many contemporary forms. They teach and require collaborative literacy practices and the capacity to weave between on/offline information, action and decision making with others and alone.

Becoming Critical

Fifth, the introduction of games into the curriculum provides a space for developing critical perspectives on games. The development of critical perspectives is a central concern in English and literacy curriculum. Understanding how texts work includes identifying the values and assumptions in the text and the ways in which different elements work together to create the overall meaning in combination with what the reader brings. Helping students understand more about the richness of games they enjoy (or their dissatisfaction with games they don't) and how that experience is created is as important in relation to digital texts as it is with respect to texts of more traditional kinds, such as poetry or children's literature. So too is becoming more aware of the ways in which texts contribute to how students understand themselves and the world. Attention to values and assumptions and how these are created and conveyed in multimodal form is important here. The three-dimensional model of l(IT)eracy, (Green 1999; Durrant & Green 2000; Green & Beavis, 2012), where teaching and learning combines critical, cultural and operational dimensions, provides an excellent framework for this aspect of English particularly.

Creating Texts

Sixth, many games provide tools and contexts for students to create texts of their own, within or around the game. Production and creativity are important parts of the English and literacy curriculum. As Marsh and Richards (2013: 12) note, 'many children are located within a digital nexus in which play and creativity are central to multimodal, multimedia meaning-making practices' (Willett et al., 2009). Whether they imagine what a new character or layer in the game might be through drawing, print or multimodal forms, physically create their own avatar or use game-making software or options for making small animations provided by some games (machinima) to create a new episode, create digital stories or act out a subplot or new adventure in improvised or scripted drama, video games provide rich opportunities for this 'productive' dimension of English and literacy.

GAMES IN THE ENGLISH CLASSROOM

There have been a number of approaches to bringing computer games into the English classroom in ways that respond to the subject's traditional foci and concerns while also recognising games' qualities and affordances as specific cultural forms. Rylands, for example, introduced *Myst III: Exile* (Presto Studios, 2001) as a springboard for developing descriptive writing with upper primary school children, capitalising on the narrative and visual parameters of this very literary game to build bridges between students' out-of-school digital experiences of videogames and play and their in-school world of the formal study and development of written language (Rylands, n.d.).

More literary approaches include the use of existing virtual worlds or the creation of new ones as a context for the study of literature. Dick (2012), for example, documents the creation of the *Pied Piper Literary World* with 350 college students across five subjects and two years as part of the *Virtual Worlds* project (Webb, 2012). The *Pied Piper* project

> encouraged textual intervention on a large scale. Class after class of students were encouraged to invent the lives of the Hamelin townspeople,

and create and recreate everything about the location as well as the story line. Fostering research skills and critical thinking, and locating stories, people and objects in historical contexts were important objectives in all of my classes. In this case, the end product of our work was the creation of a medieval town full of people and activity—a virtual version of Hamelin, Germany. (Dick, 2012: 98)

Approaches such as these use games or virtual worlds as a context for print-based literacy and literary work, seen as core business for English. Other research-based classroom studies directly address the specific properties and affordances of games (Carr, Buckingham, Burn, & Schott, 2006; Beavis, O'Mara, & MacNeice, 2012). Pelletier's account of 'the uses of literacy' in analysis and creation of games in middle-years English and media (Pelletier, 2005), for example, centres on the game-making aspect of students' work. Berger and McDougall (2013) by contrast, describe the formal study of games as 'authorless text' in senior literature. Amongst detractors, computer games are seen as directly antithetical to the traditional literary English curriculum. Yet as Berger and McDougall's (2013) account of A-level students' study of *LA Noire* (Rockstar Games, 2011) suggests, this need not necessarily be so.

In the case of 15-year-old Erin, the expansive view of literature provided by her teacher Jen enabled her to initially to demonstrate her understanding of classic literary devices by analysing their presence and workings in the computer game *Assassin's Creed II* (Ubisoft Montreal, 2009) while also recognising the significantly different nature of games and literature and the action-driven, embodied nature of game play. The opportunity to work within and across both spaces enabled Erin to develop complex insights into the structure and organisation of each form, comprising a detailed and nuanced understanding of the ways in which aesthetic elements worked and to what effect. It let her enhance her capacity to use both language and formal elements of game-making to construct sophisticated critical and creative outcomes and analysis.

In her year-10 English unit dealing with literary texts and literary meta-language, South Australian teacher Jennifer Russell encouraged students to build explicit connections between school texts and a wide range of texts of their own choosing provided that these texts were sufficiently robust to allow students to achieve the levels of understanding at the core of her curriculum (Russell & Beavis, 2012). A prerequisite to students working with texts of various kinds of their own choice was that they thoroughly understood the elements and classical terminology of literary analysis, explored initially through classic, school-based texts. Texts chosen by students ranged across films, TV programs, cartoons, novels and computer games.

In 2011, the course included a classic text study, a metalanguage unit covering many diverse texts or text segments, the study of a visual narrative text, the study of *Romeo + Juliet,* a Shakespearean film text (Luhrmann, 1996), and a connected text study that began with a compulsory novel—selected from a set text list and negotiated according to students' choice —which then connected with a second text with a thematic connection, which could be a novel, film, poetry, play or multimodal text of another kind.

For the first task, students were required to show their understanding of a literary theory term ('metalanguage') and the contribution made by the selected element to the effectiveness of the text identified. Erin focused on *Assassin's Creed II* (Ubisoft Montreal, 2009), set in Renaissance Florence. She created a compilation of relevant cut scenes and information segments from the game and of herself playing Ezio,the protagonist, and showed this to the class. The literary metalanguage she chose included pathos, sound, symbol and historical context. She discussed these with reference to the game in a voice-over monologue describing each element and its effect as it occurred in the context of play. In relation to rhythm, for example, she explains:

> Throughout *Assassin's Creed*, the designers used rhythm which is defined as 'the combination of syllables in the way words are presented to form a set pattern or create an effect'.
>
> As shown in the previous clip, the creators expressed rhythm through the music and sound effects rather than a poem or lyric. In applying this technique, the developers used, for example, different instruments that would be used in a horror film—the sharp piercing sound of violins, the strong pounding of drums and the gradual crescendo as the scene escalates.
>
> In the next scene, Ezio is running from the guards while a drumming pattern is played. The drum represents a heartbeat which stimulates the heart of the player causing an adrenaline rush. The player feels aroused by this rush causing a slight anxiety to escape. This emotion also stimulates an uncertainty but curiosity in the player as mentioned before.

Erin's analysis attends to both textual and action-driven dimensions of game play and to the embodied experience of play, which resembles but differs significantly from that entailed in reading print-based forms. Her exploration allowed her to link formal school curriculum with her already considerable expertise with games to make new connections and develop new insights in quite daring ways about the ways in which the techniques studied operated in the computer game form. That is, she had the enthusiasm, interest and confidence to break new ground in making her own analysis in a context where there was considerable energy and commitment from most members of the class in drawing their own conclusions, analysing in depth and presenting texts of their own choosing to the class. The grounding in the formal study of metalanguage, coupled with Jen's openness to opportunities for students to apply their knowledge in innovative and cognitively demanding ways, meant that Erin and her classmates were encouraged to explore the affordances of their chosen genre fearlessly in a context where there was genuine interest in what each person did and found.

As Erin explained, she chose *Assassin's Creed* as her multimodal text

> because I find it easier to relate to games where I am playing as the character as one would when reading from a narrator or character's point of view. I am able to not only emotionally but physically participate in a series of events throughout the text. I wanted to creatively express my perspective in another form of multimodal texts so others could also appreciate this growing part of today's media.
>
> *Assassin's Creed* appealed to me because of its huge historical reference and realistic setting. It contains a variety of techniques, such as symbolism and effective pathos which I wanted to use as an exciting variation made easy by its close relation to literary metalanguage and techniques. I also discovered various auditory techniques used such as sound effects and music (rhythm) which are not expressed in traditional texts. I wanted to use *Assassin's Creed* to compare similarities and differences between two texts of novels and games. Not only was I able to grasp a better understanding of literary metalanguage and techniques, but I was able to understand and discover a new language with new techniques which are presented in the gaming world.

In subsequent tasks she created a four-person narrative within *Runescape* (Jagex Studios, 2001) as a creative response to Tracey Moffatt's photographic nonlinear narrative *Laudanum* (1999) exhibited at the Adelaide Gallery, and a *Minecraft* (Mojang, 2010) chapel laden with symbolism speaking back to *Romeo + Juliet* in rich and metaphoric ways. In both instances this entailed creating new narratives/architecture of her own. Her work in this unit was completed with a formal literary essay comparing the novel *Lord of the Flies* (Golding, 1954) with the games *inFamous* and *inFamous 2* (Sucker Punch, 2009, 2011).

Erin's analytic and creative work with computer games was one aspect of a course that was thoroughly literary and multimodal at the same time. The course exemplified ways in which schools might address a number of the concerns about English articulated by Ellis, Fox and Street (2007: 4): 'a disjuncture between the 'cultural meaning-making practices of children and young people and their lives outside school and subject English as it is enacted in [the] classroom'; 'a marginalisation of the aesthetic as a uniquely important way of knowing that draws its power from the integration of the cognitive and the affective' and 'the way in which the ideological content of subject English—that which has the capacity to engage students and give it a socially critical purpose—has become so easy and in some cases necessary to avoid'. For Jen, Erin's teacher, the answer lay in empowering students, setting challenging tasks and linking English to the contemporary world.

IMPLICATIONS

The incorporation of multimodal texts, including digital games, into literature and the recognition of close links between children's experiences of narrative across a range of mediums and modes makes much possible. A broad range of texts, options to explore how stories are made and told in different ways and in different modes and media, and the opportunity to link classic and contemporary texts to students' worlds provide for a 21st-century English curriculum in which literature, narrative, creativity and imagination are highly valued and fundamental. A curriculum that connects with and builds on the knowledge students bring with them helps them actively engage with a wide range of texts, enhances their understandings of key elements and their effects and of how texts work, what they like or dislike and why, and encourages them to become powerful and reflective in doing so. It supports students to be readers/viewers/players and makers of texts, to take pleasure in texts, and to critically reflect on the values and structures of texts and on themselves as readers.

English as a subject is in a challenging position currently in relation to literature and literacy and its own purposes and identity. In a subject traditionally concerned with the workings of written and spoken language, the place of written literary texts and the affordances of spoken and written language continue to be core. At the same time, however, the expansion of contemporary literacy to include the multimodal provides the opportunity for students to gain deep understandings of contemporary literacies, and of aesthetic narrative texts in many forms. It provides opportunities for an enlarged and expansive body of texts to be available, building on children's experience of digital culture and providing engaging and relevant material, together with opportunities students to take pleasure in texts, to reflect critically on the values and structures of texts and on themselves as readers. What is needed is a curriculum in which classic, traditional and contemporary literary texts, and the strengths and affordances of verbal and written literature, are recognised for what they offer but do not stand alone or in isolation from related multimodal aesthetic forms. It is not yet clear how this balance will be achieved. What is clear is that we need to make sure that we maintain a focus on literacies both traditional and new, on aesthetic literary texts however defined, and a place for imagination, creativity and play.

EDITORS' COMMENTARY

This chapter stresses the importance of drawing on students' cultural meaning-making practices in addressing and developing textual study in the classroom. It provides a persuasive argument for a particular focus on gaming in the Australian curriculum—a focus that will be relevant to students in many other localities too. In any location, however, paying attention to students' cultural capital must be a priority, and in any location we need to pay attention to both cognitive and aesthetic dimensions of meaning-making.

Cognitive and aesthetic responses to texts contribute to ways of knowing that connect to established traditions of working on literary fiction and textual analysis. Children and young people's encounters with new textual forms must be understood in the context of the pleasure and engagement that they experience. Their engagement with videogames brings with it considerable challenges in description, since their responses often involve them in 'playing the text' (Mackey, 2002), producing meaning through both text and embodied action in ways that draw on narratives and themes in other forms and on other platforms.

It has been argued that the aesthetic is a distinctive 'way of knowing' that integrates the cognitive and the affective (Ellis et al., 2007); in schools, this has traditionally been the province of literature study in the English curriculum. As a result, literary fiction has, over the years, occupied a central position in the liberal arts curriculum, but until recently less attention has been given to newer forms of narrative. Beavis's work, following on previous contributions that analyse videogames (e.g., Carr et al., 2006; Gee, 2003; Steinkuehler, 2008), illustrates their rich potential to contribute to aesthetic and critical understanding in classroom contexts. Beavis persuades us that many videogames are carefully crafted, offering multiple readings and reading paths (Kress, 2003); in so doing they provoke our puzzlement and surprise as well as our pleasure and enjoyment. In the case of Erin, we see the development of a narrative appreciation of game aesthetics and how this connects with and expands more familiar forms of textual engagement through the metalanguage she uses.

Beavis's chapter reminds us that children's experience of narrative, although always multimodal in nature, is increasingly diverse, encompassing multimedia digital products, new textual formations, and transmedia stories that 'flow across different forms and platforms' (Jenkins et al,, 2006). Classrooms, it is argued, would benefit from including a wider range of texts that reflect children's experience of new media as well as their cultural diversity (Merchant, 2013). There is an imperative for helping students to become what Beavis describes as 'critical, capable and creative users of digital and multimodal forms of literacy alongside traditional print curriculum'. Here the emphasis is placed on understanding how various forms of mediated texts achieve their effect, how they relate to other similar texts and the kinds of response, reflection and action that are engendered (Littau, 2006). In building on the knowledge of videogames that students bring to the classroom as producers and consumers of these texts, teachers can legitimise their playful and pleasurable engagement with digital culture and support them in reflecting critically on the values and structures of texts and on themselves as readers, players and producers of digital texts (see, for example, Bazalgette, 2010; Burn & Parker, 2003). The chapter suggests that there is an important element of the English curriculum that continues to have relevance and can be seen as the site for significant innovation. The tradition of encouraging creative responses to literary fiction—itself a bedrock of the liberal arts curriculum— can be enriched by allowing children and young people to draw on elements of digital culture such as videogames in the classroom context. Central here is the notion that students should be encouraged to work with texts and materials of various kinds of their own choice in a way that creates subtle but meaningful connections with texts that are part of a prescribed syllabus.

The focus on aesthetics foregrounds the importance of understanding the design principles that lie behind multimodal text production and how we respond to these. The following chapter explores the significance of multimodal performance to the everyday Facebook practices of young English language learners in Canada. Rowsell and Burgess explore how social networking sites provide rich opportunities for young people to perform identity online and demonstrate how, in their creative acts of multimodal composition, they are able to explore their connection with others as well as their orientation to wider social and cultural issues. This chapter presents the significant and nuanced work of young people who perform their 'diasporic identities' through Facebook, weaving together singular embodied and emotive personal histories with wider social forces that circulate through the global mediascape. The chapter illustrates what occurs at the intersection between new literacies and language learning in the context of 'superdiversity'.

7 A Tale of Multiple Selves
Im/materialising Identities on Facebook

Jennifer Rowsell and Julianne Burgess

A multitude of people and yet a solitude . . .

A Tale of Two Cities (Dickens, 1859: 77)

INTRODUCTION

One summer's evening Jennifer observed three 12-year-olds playing *Saints Row* (Voliton Inc., 2006), a popular PlayStation video game, on their PS3. It took an hour for them to create avatars for each other, and this was done amidst critique, discussions, raucous laughter, revisions, more laughter, subtle shifts in body parts and facial expressions, a variety of skin colours and genders. They eventually played the game for ten minutes and then shifted over to a DVD to watch *Dinner for Schmucks* (Roach, 2010). The brief scene threw into relief a strong theme in the book and in this chapter, which is a liminal space that transpires when corporeal, material bodies vaporise into cybernetic immaterial systems. Cybernetics is a process through which a human becomes digitised into an avatar or online character. It is a way of separating the physical from the mental—moving from materialities into immaterialities. The naturalised practice of taking a physical form and transforming it into an ephemeral, vaporised self is fairly commonplace and is the focus of this chapter, which follows the way in which four individuals materialise self in immaterial spaces.

Watching three tweens play with their identities online is fairly commonplace, yet this keen interest in playing and improvising in material and immaterial spaces is absent from the kind of thinking work that students do at school. In this chapter we present an interview-based research study of young adults ranging in age from 18 to 27 and their creation of different selves on Facebook. Working with young people newly arrived to Canada, it became clear to Julianne, their teacher, that there was something intriguing about how her twenty-something students designed and invested time in their Facebook accounts to depict their diasporic identities.

The chapter sits in four parts: the first two sections extrapolate notions of immaterial and material literacies and provide details on the research and the second two draw out implications and ways forward to leverage diasporic media practices for language and literacy students.

SETTING OUT TERMS

According to Foucault (1982), identity can be viewed as a social construct, as individuals take on a range of characteristics based on the cultural constraints in a given point in time. Individuals who engage in self-formation, or 'act upon themselves', are not completely free to do so; they are bound by the resources available to them (Foucault,1988: 18). Identity construction through text is not a recent phenomenon. The evolution of the Internet, however, has brought new avenues for identity negotiation and self-presentation; rapidly evolving technologies allow content to flow across media, and individuals are able to interact with media easily, offering new opportunities to create and manipulate the presentation of the self in online spaces.

As with so much research, the term *identity* looms large in this study. Building on Rowsell and Pahl's theorising of *sedimented identities* in texts (Rowsell & Pahl, 2007), we situate 'identity' within the chapter as performing and materialising agency through representational and communicational choices. Taking up Raymond Williams belief that 'cultural is ordinary' (Williams, 1990), we view the everyday practices and choices that individuals make about how to represent their agency in terms of *sedimentation*. 'Sedimented identities' derives from Kress's notion of 'motivated sign', which is 'the combination of form and meaning' motivated by humans (Kress, 1997: 93) and Bourdieu's notion of habitus (as histories and dispositions in practice) performed in the everyday (Bourdieu, 1990). Sedimenting identity happens all of the time, from wardrobe choices to iPhone home screens, and these choices signal ways in which we all perform a desired identity. Texts, like clothes and iPhone home screens, then function as artifacts that display histories and dispositions and where, in Bourdieusian terms, habitus can be discerned. Habitus can be observed playing in texts as an 'unfolding of dispositions' (Bourdieu, 1990). Within the chapter, we view Facebook pages as instantiations of habitus (Bourdieu,1990). Speaking with individuals about how and in what ways they represent themselves on Facebook, we expose ways in which a certain population sediments identities through diasporic media practices. Through photographs and writing, our research participants materialise immaterial parts of their identities and sediment them in concrete, vivid and couched ways.

To conduct the research, we examined how individuals in the same college language class use Facebook to materialise and sediment parts of their identities in social media. We found that many of them sedimented a feeling of displacement and spoke about their migration from one part of the world to another. To help us extrapolate themes of migration, diversity and mobility (which were recurrent in interview data), we drew on Blommaert and Rampton's (2011) work on superdiversity. In an introduction to a special issue on the topic, Blommaert and Rampton begin their article with a text, a notice in a window with two forms of Chinese on it and a phone number. As they unpack the seemingly mundane text, what unfolds is a theory about how *superdiversity* operates; we would add sediments within communicational events. They talk about texts as having two different styles of voice—that of the producer and that of the addressee—and the mix of script suggests that their styles are not identical. One form of Chinese is 'a simplified script' from the People's Republic of China, whereas the other one is more formal and traditional. The text exemplifies the type of everyday text that people see in store windows, which would not necessarily elicit a second thought. Yet for Blommaert and Rampton, 'the text bears the traces of worldwide migration flows and their specific demographic social and cultural dynamics' (2011: 2). Admitting that linguistics alone is not enough to thoroughly analyse such semiotically dense texts, they suggest that multimodality offers a way of deepening how people apprehend meanings.

Texts, therefore, especially texts that signal or enact diversity, should be seen as ideological artifacts that carry with them mobility, histories and political dynamics that are sedimented as outlined above. Blommaert and Rampton (2011) discuss how researchers should consider registers, styles, genres, modal referencing, visuals and embodiment as part and parcel of heteroglossic texts. In particular, diasporic media like Facebook leverage the rhetorical power of visual, animated and linguistic modes to materialise and sediment such notions as diversity or mobility. As ideological artifacts, Facebook pages align with what Blommaert and Rampton describe as texts exhibiting superdiversity through these stages: (1) recontextualised histories and political views embedded in textual choices within text like Facebook pages; (2) mobility affects texts and interpretive work; (3) then, these very same texts and interpretive practices get embedded into new contexts (Blommaert & Rampton, 2011: 9). They maintain that, 'it is worth turning to language and discourse to understand how categories and identities get circulated, taken up, and reproduced in textual representations and communicative encounters' (Blommaert & Rampton, 2011: 10). They talk about how such language and discourse circulates in different modes of articulation. Much of the time diasporic media practices on Facebook go unnoticed as such and are rendered instead as mere updates on everyday life. But in this chapter we insist that Facebook users *are* exerting identity and agency through their placement of visual, linguistic code switching, and these acts of identity mediation are ideological. As ideological practices, they call on thoughts, intellect, emotions and affect. People like the language learners in this chapter invest in them and, as a result, these ideological practices represent valuable material for teaching and learning. The key point here is that participants in our study struggle with their English language skills (they said so in interviews) and accessing and building on such naturalised and ideological practices as sedimenting their identities and materialising a certain kind of preferred identity in social media should be a part of their learning and thinking.

THE MATERIAL AND THE IMMATERIAL

Conducting research in and out of physical and virtual spaces made it difficult for us to capture the materiality of modes with the ephemeral nature of habitus. Sitting with the language learners in a college classroom and observing them edit a documentary about their move from their host country to Canada made us pause to think more about what these kinds of choices signal and how they relate to identity, and sedimented identity in texts specifically. There is something important, sophisticated and undertheorised within education about the naturalised practice of taking a physical form and transforming it into a vaporised self. The process of breaking down identity into fractal parts tied to linguistic systems, cultural practices, social class and aesthetic preferences and then materialising these very same

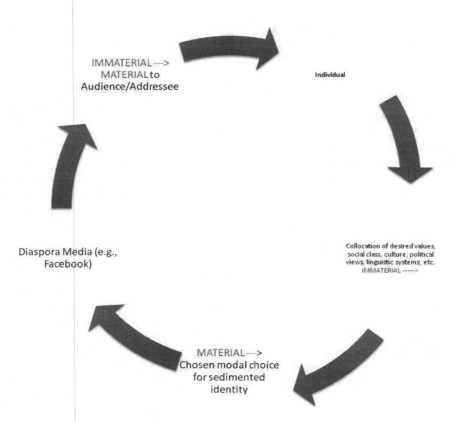

Figure 7.1 Moving in and out of (im)material.

ideologically laden constructs into aesthetic, physical features *is* sophisticated in ways that we do not think are properly understood . . . yet.

Within this research and other studies (Pahl & Rowsell, 2011; Rowsell, 2013), individuals perform either identities or ideas through physical choices and this is the process of sedimentation referred to earlier. To be clear, moving from the immaterial to the material is not moving from nondigital to digital—it is more about exerting self to an audience—it is about being heard and about knowing how to be heard through modal choice.

Figure 7.1 shows the process of moving in and out of im/material worlds, and this process is iterative and cyclical. People move in and out of different kinds of spaces (e.g., digital/nondigital, personal/professional/ institutional, public/private, etc.); with all of this to-ing and fro-ing, they are constantly gathering parts of self and performed agency, materialising them in some way or manner, using a channel to do so, then materialising it to speak to an addressee/audience and then the cycle repeats itself. Successful communicators are likely to be those who use available resources in ways that are recognised by different communities.

MATERIALISING SELF ON FACEBOOK

Facebook, in facilitating diasporic media practices, offers a variety of ways to perform self and to interact with others (Rowsell, 2009). After signing up, users build their own profile, a personal web page where other users regularly update photos, post notes, links and videos to share with their 'friends' more specifically—those who are connected to their online network. Facebook users create albums of photos, list their friends, and groups (social networks), describe their personal activities, interests and hobbies. They create a personal news feed, share music with online friends, use Facebook Chat to instant message online friends in real time. Graph Search, a new feature in Facebook allows individuals to access an archive of information and photos that they or their friends have shared on the site in the past (Facebook Newsroom, 2013).

RESEARCH BACKGROUND

The research study grew from a common interest we share in how individuals materialise themselves in digital spaces. The focal population of our research is young adults who invest much of their time materialising self on Facebook. The young adults featured in the chapter are students at a community college in Ontario who are completing a program in English as an additional language called LINC—Language Instruction for Newcomers to Canada. Julianne teaches learners in the LINC program, and she has noticed over the years a gap between LINC students' basic language and literacy skills and their sophisticated practices with communication systems. Together, we set out to examine how LINC students materialise self on Facebook. To conduct the research, we interviewed four students and asked them to talk through their choices and decisions about how they designed their pages. Data collection involved Julianne's in-person interviews and Jennifer's visits to the class, where she spoke informally with case study participants. The other data generated from the research included multimodal analysis, combined with phenomenology as a framework, of Facebook pages. Before each interview, case study participants logged on to their Facebook sites on Julianne's laptop for Julianne to look at and refer to. Later, Julianne and I met with case study participants to clarify aspects of their Facebook pages. During discussions about Facebook pages, participants pointed out specific parts of their Facebook pages, such as photographs and written text, that were germane to interview dialogues and to the theme of sedimenting identity in texts. Phenomenology played a role in highlighting affect, emotional essence and embodiment within Facebook pages. For data analyses, we applied the im/material conceptual framework that we established earlier in the chapter as a way to isolating and extrapolating themes in the interview data.

CASE STUDY PARTICIPANTS

There were four case study participants: Melissa, Lionel, Sam and Narmin (pseudonyms are used for all participants). Melissa is a 21-year-old student from Vietnam. She has been in Canada for two years. Melissa is an only child; she immigrated to Canada with her parents; they are a close-knit family. She is especially close to her mother. Melissa maintains close ties with her friends in Vietnam and spends a lot of time on Vietnamese websites, shopping and chatting with friends. Melissa feels proud of her country in spite of its economic difficulties. She feels that Vietnamese women in particular show strength and resilience in their society—that they have fought for equality at home, in school and in the workplace. Melissa revealed these characteristics in her classroom life.

Melissa had a constant smile in class, and although she did not often volunteer answers or opinions in large group discussions, she demonstrated strong academic skills and worked enthusiastically with other students on class projects. Melissa says she prefers the Canadian education system to that of Vietnam because she feels freer to express her ideas. Melissa has kept a diary since childhood. She originally used it to record her own invented short stories, only sharing them with her mother. Now her diary records all of her life experiences. She rereads her entries often. In her class journal, Melissa explained that her diary helps her to process all of the things that are happening in her life: 'It looks like a short film about my life and I see myself being stronger day by day'. After she finishes the ESL college entry program, Melissa plans to continue her studies in business accounting.

Lionel's sense of humour made him stand out in the class. He is quick with a quip, which is an indicator of his lively personality as well as his comfort and competence in English. Lionel is originally from Iraq but his family left the country when he was only 3 years of age. He has lived in Libya, Jordan and Oman, and although he has no memories of his place of birth, he feels a strong tie with Iraq and being Iraqi. He is Muslim but prefers not to discuss religion. He is interested in politics and social issues; he shared his thoughts openly in class and showed an interest in other students' opinions. He is outgoing and was very popular with his classmates; at the time of the study, Lionel was often consulted for his computer expertise and invited to join groups to work on assignments. As a 19-year-old, Lionel has a high school diploma from Oman, and his goal is to study mechanical engineering at a Canadian university. His parents are both teachers (his mother has a Ph.D. in mathematics from a British university). Lionel's parents chose to move to Canada because they felt their two sons' educational opportunities as well as their own prospects for work were better in Canada than in the Middle East. Lionel is comfortable with all aspects of technology and spends a great deal of his free time online. He feels that his English has improved from using English sites on the Internet. He enjoys playing games and has explored a number of social networking sites as they have become available. However his ruling passion is without question soccer. His favourite club is Barcelona; his enthusiasm is uncontained when he describes the team's progress, the players' lives and details about the club's history.

Sam is a soft-spoken young man who has faced many struggles in his life and has, at times, felt marginalised in different environments, yet he remains an idealist and a romantic; according to Sam, his music and faith sustain him. Sam identifies as Burmese, although his family is ethnically Chinese, having escaped the war in China in the 1960s. At the age of 16, after a violent encounter with the Burmese military, Sam was forced to flee Burma for Malaysia by himself. He lived with relatives in Malaysia and worked while studying network engineering. He completed his program but was refused a diploma because he was not a Malaysian citizen. At the age of 23, Sam left Malaysia and came to Canada on his own. He shares a basement apartment with a friend who is also Burmese. He is currently studying in an ESL college preparation program and plans to continue postsecondary studies at the college. Although he has a quiet demeanor, Sam has made friends easily. He is multilingual—speaking Burmese, Chinese and Malay. As well, Sam is a dedicated musician and dreams of being a musician and composer as a profession. His preferred instrument is the guitar, and he writes love songs in Burmese and English. He brought his guitar to class often for various celebrations, and he plays his own music with intensity and emotion. Sam changed religions after leaving his homeland, converting from Buddhism to Christianity. His Christian identity is reflected in the large cross he wears around his neck and in his online presence. He is an avid Facebook user and uses the social networking site to keep in touch with friends in several countries and to share his music. Although he faces many challenges as a newcomer, Sam is comfortable with his life in Canada.

Narmin is a 26-year-old aspiring filmmaker from Iraq. She is a story-teller and believes film is an ideal medium for exploring challenging issues and communicating ideas to a worldwide audience. Her family moved frequently before settling in Canada because of the volatility in the Middle East. They left Iraq when she was 6 years old, settled in different locations in Iran, and then moved to Azerbaijan. The difficulties of adapting to new countries, frequently changing schools, trying to fit in and make friends, have left a mark on Narmin's identity; she does not feel Iraqi, she feels a deep sense of rootlessness. Narmin recognises the advantages of having lived in numerous cultures. She says she does not have a sense of limits or barriers between herself and others because of differences such as race, religion or culture. She speaks, reads and writes Arabic, Persian and Azeri fluently and is also able to communicate with Dari, Turkish and Russian speakers. In the classroom, it appeared as though she could speak with almost everyone in his or her home language. Narmin is an avid reader and an activist who enjoys tackling feminist and religious issues. Her father introduced her to philosophy when she was 14. She initiated her own self-study programme, exploring Marxism, existentialism and nihilism. She noted in her class journal, 'I am a human now made by books. You know, Julianne, if there is a god I hope his heaven to be like [Jorge Luis Borges's] *Library of Babel*'. In addition to keeping in touch with friends scattered across the world, Narmin's interests in literature and philosophy are also reflected in her Facebook practices. After completing a radio and television programme at a local community college, Narmin hopes to attend a film studies course at a Canadian university.

MATERIALISING THE IMMATERIAL

Everyday creativity such as choosing an original avatar calls to mind the kind of 'sensuous human activity' that Willis described in his ethnographies of the British working class. In *Common Culture*, Willis details how messages are not just 'sent' or 'received'; rather, they are communicated in reception (1990: 135). Within our study, participants constructed self as dialogic—that is, to be thought about and rendered meaningful by communicating with an audience. This is where sedimented identities in texts comes into play—creating avatars or visualising and performing self on Facebook represent acts of sedimentation during text production. To consider what happens conceptually when materialising self on a screen, we draw on three different theoretical frameworks: multimodality for the sign making and social design; phenomenology for the sensual and embodied engagement and dialogic and ventriloquising work for communicating across audiences.

To think about the multimodal piece, everyday creativity involves some understanding and application of design principles and aesthetics. Styles of photographs, fonts, wording, colour schemes and image placement on a screen affect how messages are received. All four case study participants talked about characteristics of self that they wanted to foreground to tell their story. This is reminiscent of Kress's description of a young child's selection of characteristics and features to foreground in drawings or representations of self. As Kress suggests, 'those characteristics which he regards as most important for him in the thing he wants to represent, and finds the best possible means for expressing them' (1997: 93). These kinds of choices rely on *analogy*—as they signify an emotion, feeling and thought.

During discussions with her students, Julianne recognised that there is something sophisticated about social media practices. What was unique about her population of students was how they often constructed multiple selves in different Facebook accounts. That is, her students created different Facebook accounts to speak to different audiences, creating an account for each part of their lives. Narmin, for example, on her Facebook page, put a great deal of thought into an image that would capture her struggles with religion and spirituality and her sense of rootlessness in Canada. Figure 7.2 below shows how she materialised her feelings.

She described choosing the image for her Facebook page as follows:

> this one is me, alone, close to the sea, because, I think, I don't know, but the best place for me is the sea because when I am close to the water, I feel like I'm a child, I want to play and laugh, and forget all my suffering. And that's it. But this is sad image because I took it when I, when we left Bacu. April 2013.

Narmin discussed feeling unsettled in Canada and what this rootlessness brought out in her that she wanted to portray on her page. Motivated by emotions, philosophy and politics, Narmin designs her Facebook page for her new Canadian friends and some friends back home. Returning to Kress's notion of motivated signs, Narmin's multimodal work has a double motivation: one deriving from 'who the sign-maker is, and what her or his history has been' and the other from what she assesses to be 'the communicational environment' (Kress, 1997: 93). Black and white photos, hair flying in the air, a dramatic scene of an ocean, Narmin framed her Facebook to show and tell her sense of ambivalence about place and identity.

To theorise the case study participants' movement from material spaces to immaterial spaces, we need to have a way of extrapolating not only the design process but also affect and ways of representing affect,

Figure 7.2   Narmin's visual mediation of self.

embodiment and felt emotions. To do this, we refer to the work of phenomenologists such as Husserl (1913) and Merleau-Ponty (1962). Husserl (1913) talked about how phenomenology investigates essences or meanings underlying appearance. Often analysing emotions, perceptions and embodiment, Husserl looked at phenomenon in the moment, as it is lived. He explored intentional and nonintentional acts and experiences. For him, humans constantly move in and out of conscious and unconscious worlds.

A different and later phenomenological thinker, Merleau-Ponty (1962) focused on sense perceptions. Rather than isolating and analyzing the object to be perceived, Merleau-Ponty looked at how someone perceives and experiences an object. Describing the moment when we perceive something, Merleau-Ponty talks about our participation as bodies in the 'flesh of the world'. There is a reciprocal relationship between objects and landscapes, and it is in this reciprocity that we develop and hone our subjectivities. Merleau-Ponty talked about the roots of the mind being 'in its body and in its world, going against doctrines which treat perception as a simple result of the action of external things on our body' (Merleau-Ponty, 1962: 3). In his work, Merleau-Ponty concentrates instead on the text as 'a spectacle that is sufficient unto itself.' The world of perception is filled with in-the-moment sensations garnered from the details of material worlds.

Bringing together Husserl's focus on the binary, which we experience through objects of intentionality of matter and the nonintentional nature of matter, with Merleau-Ponty's focus on the essence of our experiences with texts, we argue that the movement from a part of self, such as religion, can be materialised and therefore sedimented in modes such as words, images, colours, music, etc. Using the example of Narmin again, she struggles with her religious beliefs, as she has for most of her life. Having grown up with a father who is a professor of philosophy and a mother who is a devout Muslim and reads voraciously across disciplines and topics, she was reared to be polemical and call all things and issues into question. Narmin has intentional immaterial messages that she foregrounds on her Facebook pages, and most of these images are affective and driven by emotions and embodiment. In Figure 7.3, there is another image from Narmin's Facebook page that manifests the dismantling of old concepts of gender roles and the empowerment of women through social media.

Finally there is Bakhtin (1999), who has been helpful in pushing our thinking about ventriloquising across im/material communities. What

Figure 7.3   Photo to capture the essence of activism on social media.

is evident in all of the case study participants' activities is the way in which multiple layers of knowing, learning, believing become materialised through the orchestration of space and visuals. Facebook pages are almost like stages that the user walks across, where he or she may take on many roles whilst maintaining one self. Bakhtin explores the polyphony of voices in literature, such as works by Dostoevsky, whose major heroes speak in many voices with their own respective histories:

> What unfolds in his works is not a multitude of characters and fates in a single objective world, illuminated by a single authorial consciousness; rather a plurality of consciousness, with equal rights and each with its own world, combined but not merged in the unity of the event. Dostoevsky's major heroes are, by the very nature of his creative design, not only objects of authorial discourse but also subjects of their own directly signifying discourse. (Bakhtin, 1999: 6–7)

Thinking about Facebook profiles, individuals like Narmin concentrate on images and words that may sit in different worlds but that create a collective, singular authorial voice. The use of different languages represents one way in which Narmin manages to combine plural voices. At times she will inject Persian into her Facebook comments and, more often, Arabic; even more frequently English will be her chosen language, and these different linguistic systems bring her different communities together into one. As Narmin articulates it, 'like with my friends, we mix all languages'. Narmin has lived in Iraq, Azerbaijan, and Iran—she has a diaspsoric sense of language and of sense-making—and she imprints these different selves into her Facebook page.

FACEBOOK AND MATERIALISING SELF

Social media sites are commonly believed to be liberating spaces where individuals are free to construct new identities—a notion that has been interrogated in a number of studies (Bouvier, 2012; Rodogno, 2012; Zhao, Grasmuck & Martin, 2008). According to Zhao et al. (2008: 211), Facebook provides a venue for self-construction in a 'nonymous' (rather than anonymous) environment, anchored in real-life relationships. Exploring ways in which identity is constructed, the authors found that Facebook users generally present the self indirectly rather than through explicitly narrated identity claims. The visual self is constructed through the extensive display of personal and peer photographs uploaded by users themselves, collections of photo albums and pictures with comments posted to users' accounts by friends (wall posts). The visual images are designed to demonstrate the depth and extent of the member's social connections.

Returning to Bakhtin (1999) and his belief in communicating across polyphonic voices, case study participants spoke extensively about speaking across friends—understanding them through friends, family and associations—and, showing beliefs, thoughts and ideas rather than telling them. Sometimes materialised self on Facebook is actual self, whilst at other times it might be an idealised self. Lionel, for instance, objectifies idealised parts of self. In Figure 7.4 we offer a page from one of his Facebook accounts where he projects both his love of the Barcelona soccer team and his desire to play for the team, idealising self as linked to the team and inflecting his own identity in with the ethos of the sports team. In Julianne's interview with him, he said,

> When I was a kid I used to love this club so much, and this club actually is not just for soccer, ummm its big organisation that support children all over the world. And they tried, are trying hard, for peace between Israel and Palestine. Yeah so (J—the soccer club is doing that?) Yeah the soccer club, it's like more than a club, you know? Yeah this is the logo for this club, more than a club shows it.

Here Lionel lifts out multiple ideologies inherent to what he sees as the Barcelona team (i.e., the club itself and the players) and their work to forge peace between Israel and Palestine as well as their pursuit of excellence, which contribute to an overall sense of who Lionel is and how he can depict this self to his Facebook community. There is something more to the Barcelona logo than meets the eye (i.e., more than simply a devotion to a team). Barcelona and the values and ethos it represents aligns with how Lionel likes to depict himself in his world. In this way, the Barcelona team sediments part of his identity and who he is and wishes to be in the world.

Figure 7.4   Lionel's idealised self.

Figure 7.5   Lionel hanging out in Toronto.

At the same time, Lionel uploads photos to communicate feelings like rootlessness in Canada. Figure 7.5 shows Lionel on his own in Toronto.

Given that Lionel has moved to different parts of the world from Jordan to Oman back to Jordan and then to Toronto, Canada, he has had to shift the tone and nature of his Facebook accounts as he moves from one context to the next. For instance, when he lived in Jordan, he shared everything with his friends and family, however, when he moved to Oman there was more censorship and his everyday Facebook practices and compositional practices shifted.

FACEBOOK AND THE CULTURAL SELF

Inflected into all of the interviews was a strong sense of the relationship between culture and identity. Williams (2008) argues that the merging of media technologies and popular culture practices create new ways of performing identity and describes Facebook pages as a collage of meaning, in which identities are presented through 'the composition of fragmented, associative collages of popular culture texts'(2008: 37). He also found that Facebook users were aware that the identities they were creating were provisional and were open to multiple interpretations, which could result in a misreading of their identities by their audience.

Bouvier's (2012) study of Facebook users in Wales also found dominant ideologies playing a role in self-presentation in her study of regimes of identity. Using social actor analysis, she defines regimes of identity as national identity (expressing allegiance to a nation state), lifestyle/consumerist identity, or belonging to an ethnic or cultural classification. Bouvier suggests that the forces of globalisation, deterritorialisation and consumer society offer compelling forms of identity that appear to serve the interests of institutions such as the nation state and global corporations. Her research also finds the majority of participants align themselves with the relational category, in terms of what they do, think, and consume: in other words, the lifestyle/consumerist identity. Bouvier says that while new forms of media have the potential to foster new kinds of identity patterns, to be a space for disseminating and engaging in new discourses and global interactions, her research on Facebook shows individuals engaging in superficial discussions centering on lifestyle and consumption and narrow communities of interest, presenting identities that are shaped by the dominant hegemonic forces in society.

In our research, one of the strongest examples of cultural and spiritual self within our case studies is Sam. During Julianne's interview he spoke about converting to Christianity from Buddhism and how Facebook became his vehicle to showcase his conversion. Sam's actual name is a Burmese Buddhist name that he received at birth, and the first and only place where he marked his conversion and symbolically shared his Christian name is on Facebook. As he says, 'I love the Facebook name because when the people see my Facebook name they can see my religion, I am Christian'. Sam talked about materialising two fundamental parts of himself on his Facebook accounts—religion and music. He is religious first and a musician second. Of the four case studies, Sam feels the most at home in Canada. His cultural self is comfortably diasporic and polyphonic—Sam was motivated to share his two strong influences by uploading songs about his religion and about his culture on Facebook.

ENGLISH LEARNERS AND MATERIALISING ONLINE IDENTITIES

Whilst most of the literature on identity construction and Facebook has focused on mainstream youth, there is a growing interest in how English language learners (ELLs) negotiate identity and interact with social media. According to Sockett and Toffoli (2012), English learners engage in significant informal English language learning outside of school through their online activities. Their participants' activities included social networking with English speakers on Facebook, Internet research for areas of interest, reading news sites, listening to music and accessing lyrics and downloading videos (movies and TV shows) with English subtitles. The authors see ELLs' emerging identities as active *users* of language and social agents engaged in complex personal learning environments. Black's (2009) exploration of ELLs' activities on fan fiction websites also reveals complex literacy and technology practices in collaborative online spaces. Researchers have noted that, in spite of language and cultural barriers, online communities afford ELLs the opportunity to adopt multiple roles, including peer, mentor, learner, collaborator, technology expert, webmaster, author, reader, reviewer and consultant. Black (2009) regards ELL engagement with literacy and technology as a way for diverse students to develop identities as 'powerful learners, language users, and as active producers of their own social, cultural and ideological materials' (Black, 2009: 696).

Across our case studies there were obvious language motifs. Melissa was the only case study participant who had one Facebook account as opposed to having one for her 'home' identity and one for her Canadian identity. As a result, she talked about moving between linguistic systems on her one account. This is where a phenomenological lens helps across interviews, but particularly with Melissa, when she talked about missing Vietnam and writing about how homesick and sad she was when she arrived in Canada and during the ensuing months in the program and how she used her dominant language, Vietnamese, to describe these feelings. She claims, 'when I post some emotion on Facebook, I can share with my friends, and they comment back for me. They give me support'. During our interview, Melissa described a felt connection between her own feelings and her home language. She always uses Vietnamese on Facebook; however, she is increasingly using English when she corresponds on her wall space with a Canadian friend or classmate whom she has met in Canada. There is a generational piece to language switching on Melissa's Facebook. Melissa moves in and out of Vietnamese and English on Facebook but exclusively speaks Vietnamese with her parents and family on Facebook.

Considering identity play in the research points to ways in which individuals take felt sensibilities and materialise them in texts. Acknowledging and elucidating this kind of creativity offers pedagogic spaces where teachers can draw on communicational repertoires that are frequently left silent. Sam, Narmin, Lionel, and Melissa struggle with their English language—building on their tacit understandings about media ecologies is one way to connect linguistic systems and their understandings of them. However, if these four adults follow the typical pedagogical path of ELL college programs, they will learn how to speak, write and read printed texts relatively competently but they will not stretch the existing, sophisticated skills and ideas that they carry with them.

EDITORS' COMMENTARY

As many of the previous chapters have explored, meaning-making is a situated practice embedded in specific places and relational contexts and can be seen as a kind of social action. But, as Scollon and Scollon (2004) suggest, meaning-making practices also draw on wider discourses, which are then instantiated in everyday experiences along with individual histories, ideas and attitudes and indeed the whole spectrum of situational influences. Whilst earlier chapters in this book explore how global forces are reworked in local contexts (e.g., Lemphane & Prinsloo; Davies), this chapter highlights how individuals negotiate their own translocal identities.

In Rowsell and Burgess's case studies, the wider discourses of nationality, ethnicity and religion pattern the particularities of these young people's lives and the ways in which they communicate and interact with others on Facebook. Although all of them are newcomers to Canada, they face different challenges and mobilise their linguistic resources in diverse ways in relation to their audiences, both in the countries they have left as well as their current context—often using several languages and different Facebook accounts. There is a sense in which they inhabit different versions of what Wellman (2002) referred to as 'glocalised' communities.

Social media provide a context for exploring the challenges of learning how to live and learning how to be literate in the context of linguistic diversity; studying young people's meaning making draws our attention to the role of multimodal and hybrid practices in the changing economy of communication. The importance of the negotiation and renegotiation of identity through sociocultural practices in conditions of superdiversity (Blommaert & Rampton, 2011) is highlighted here. These hybrid and multimodal practices underline the changing purposes of literacies across different contexts—a pattern that is repeated in different language groups as local and transnational literacy practices interweave to create rich and complex contexts for language development. Recognition of this complexity demands an approach that acknowledges how cultures and identities play out in both formal and informal learning contexts. Like Li's study of Vietnamese students in the US, which illustrates how identity development is an ongoing process of negotiation defined by everyday experiences in which cultural affiliation, gender norms and parental expectations all play a key role (Li, 2013), Rowsell and Burgess emphasise the creative ways in which this work is done and how activity in social media opens new pedagogic spaces for language learning.

These themes suggest that literacy is both a deeply personal and an undeniably social achievement. Individuals draw on a wide range of linguistic and semiotic resources in communicating with those who are close and distant in geographical terms, and this often connects to deeply felt identifications with collectivities such as nationality, religious and ethnic heritage. There can be no template as each individual is positioned by, and constructs meanings from different influences from family, peer group and popular culture. Literacy education may then, be at its most effective when it is in sympathy with this fundamental work of communicating oneself to others, providing the tools for production, negotiation and reflection on the very act of 'writing oneself into being'.

As previous commentaries have explored, pedagogy and practice must be grounded in an acceptance of individuals' social, cultural and linguistic resources. This chapter highlights the need to build on these resources in ways that are sensitive to students' fluid and multiple performances of identity. An acknowledgement of the digital tools that children and young people use is important here, and the ways in which these are deployed to establish and sustain multiple connections. In these settings, active participation in new literacy practices could become an explicit instructional goal, with at least some element of the student experience being digitally mediated. This perspective involves thinking about how digital practices can themselves be utilised in the process of developing language and literacy. The potential of using Web 2.0 tools as writing spaces for developing and publishing student content and to promote student collaboration and interaction is a key element of this (see Davies & Merchant, 2009).

Whilst Rowsell and Burgess's chapter illustrates the rich potential of digital tools to meaning-making, it is important to see such activity in relation to embodied interactions with the devices that mediate these tools and texts. In the next chapter we return to focus on the materiality of literacy encounters. Merchant's observations of children using story apps involves accounting for the physical and material aspects of iPads, as well as the movements, gestures and interactions that typify their use in context. Reframing traditional notions of story sharing, iPads materialise different sorts of literacy practices that Merchant signals as new sets of competencies that are as yet not fully understood.

8 Young Children and Interactive Story-Apps[1]

Guy Merchant

INTRODUCTION

In many sectors of society and in many parts of the world, early childhood is now infused with digital technology. A wide range of pacifiers and activity centres designed for young babies have digital components, and so do baby walkers, early games and children's first toys. Products for the very young, such as those produced by the highly successful specialist company V-Tech, characterise this new shift in edutainment. Digitally reproduced nursery rhymes, counting games and alphabet songs have become commonplace in the lives of many infants and toddlers (Burnett &Merchant, 2012). And these toys themselves are certainly not passive objects—not only are they carefully scripted but they are often programmed to 'wake up' after a period of inactivity, to begin an audiovisual action sequence prompted by gentle touch, movement or accidental collision. A proper analysis of these objects would need to account for both their active and interactive properties, as there are no grounds to doubt that their materiality is entangled with children's playful explorations as well as being ubiquitously located in the broader terrain of contemporary child-rearing practices. Along with this burgeoning of technological toys, it is now increasingly common for adults to use their own smartphones and tablet computers (such as the iPad) as an integral part of their interactions with babies and young children. Here again, apps designed for the very young can be highly interactive, prompting actions and responses from babies and toddlers. Counting games (such as *My First Numbers*[2]) and alphabet apps (such as *Endless ABC*[3]) are a highly visible part of the early-years edutainment 'curriculum'. In fact, one could say that literacies, both new and old, are writ large on the digital landscape of early childhood. And since literacies are patterned by the tools that we use to make meaning, there is much change afoot in the early years—so much so that it may well be time to rethink how we describe literacy development. Furthermore, as Wohlwend (2009) suggests, the new ways of meaning-making that young children participate in at home cannot simply be put aside as children enter the more formal institutions of early childhood education.

At the same time, there is a paucity of research on literacy and technology in the early years. Successive surveys and literature reviews have pointed to significant gaps in existing research whilst repeatedly underlining the need for more systematic and wider-scale investigations. For instance, in a review of empirical studies of technology and literacy within educational settings for young children, Burnett (2010) found only thirty-six papers published between 2003 and 2009. The review concluded that 'new ways of thinking about the relationship between literacy, technology and learning in the early years are needed' (2010: 265). Meanwhile new technologies continue to evolve and develop, and as part of this they enter into the communicational ecology of families and early-years settings. Touchscreen devices constitute part of the new wave of portable digital devices, and smartphones and iPads have become part of the shared activity of adults and children in many home settings (Kirkorian & Pempek, 2013). Despite the predictable moral panics about new technology in the lives of children and young people (see Seales & Harding, 2013, for example), many educators have been enthusiastic about their use in the more formal settings of early-childhood education. Education-focused social media and teacher conferences have, for the most part, witnessed unbridled enthusiasm for the iPad, often with little critique or awareness of the commercial interests at stake or the complexities of the literacies involved (for example: http://www.learningwithipads.co.uk/). Although the portability of these devices confers some advantages, it is often taken for granted in these accounts and, along with the idea that iPads have an 'intuitive' interface, used as a justification for their suitability for young children (O'Mara & Laidlaw, 2011). In this paper, I contribute to our growing understanding of new technologies in the literacy lives of the very young by drawing on empirical work focused on the introduction of iPads into an early-years setting. In particular I focus on how the devices are taken up in the context of adult-child interaction.

MAPPING THE TERRITORY

In their study of iPads, Rowsell et al. argue that 'mobile devices inflect local practices' (2013: 351) and suggest that sociocultural approaches to literacy studies help us to understand and theorise new technoliteracies. Drawing on Prinsloo's (2005) notion of new technologies as placed resources, they argue that divergent practices emerge within different and localised uses of the same devices. The introduction of iPads into early-years settings in a particular context is likely then to be flavoured by the local as instantiated in the routines, relationships and day-to-day operations of the institution as well as by the beliefs, understandings and experiences of both children and adults. In framing this current research, I build on this work by adopting a theoretical perspective that is based upon two propositions. The first asserts that *people and the material things they use are inextricably bound together*. In other words, looking at either in isolation provides a somewhat impoverished account. This is the point that Ihde makes when he suggests that 'Were technologies merely objects totally divorced from human praxis, they would be so much 'junk" lying about. Once taken into praxis one can speak not of technologies "in themselves", but as the active relational pair, human-technology' (Ihde, 1993: 34).

Based upon this I argue that 'the things in use', in this instance the incorporation of touchscreen devices into the early-years environment, have to be of central concern. This necessitates developing an analytical approach that includes the materiality of the iPad, its technological affordances, and how it is positioned in adult-child interaction. Extending from this, it must also be acknowledged that the relationship between iPads, adults and children does not take place in a social vacuum; it is situated in a larger context, constituted by the discourses and practices of mobile technology (Caron & Caronia, 2007). As a consequence, the second proposition is that the concept of *social practice is a helpful way of thinking about the role that technology plays in our lives.* Here I draw on the practice theory of Schatzki (2002) and Reckwitz (2002). Schatzki defines practices as 'organized nexuses of activity' that involve bodily 'doings', 'sayings' and 'relatings'. These doings, sayings and relatings take place in, and constitute, the human interactions that comprise social order (Schatzki, 2001: 56). Reckwitz, on the other hand, defines practices as 'forms of bodily activities, forms of mental activities, "things" and their use' (Reckwitz, 2002: 5). According to both sources, practices are rather like social routines, in that they are carried and transmitted by human actors; but they are also susceptible to innovation and change, and vary between locations and over time. This is important because it provides an account of the ways in which new technologies become integrated into existing social practices, in turn developing them as they are then taken up and absorbed into daily life.

In this investigation of iPad story-apps, existing social practices exert a strong contextualising influence. After all the practice of story sharing is a cornerstone of early-years practice, enshrined in policy documents, the training of early-years professionals as well as in the day-to-day schedules of most settings. Whilst current academic debate may be concerned with understanding the relative effects of the frequency of story sharing and the quality of adult-child interaction, there is broad agreement that through the sharing of books young children are able to describe pictures, label objects, explain events, ask questions and relate stories to their everyday life experience (e.g. Flood, 1977; Hammett et al., 2003; Levy, 2010). Of course, the empirical base of this work is primarily concerned with print, and although there have been some studies of e-books (e.g., de Jong & Bus, 2003), these have not involved touchscreen devices or app-based story forms. This is significant, because what Ihde (1993: 34) calls the 'active relational pair, human-technology' takes on a particular significance when the humans concerned are very young ones who are still developing their fine motor skills and the technological interface is characterised by the immediacy as well as the vagueness of the touchscreen itself.

CONSIDERING THE MATERIAL (AND THE PHYSICAL)

Materiality has become a complex and contested term in current academic circles (Kallinikos, Leonardi, & Nardi, 2012), and some of this debate has begun to spill over into literacy studies (e.g., Burnett, 2011; Gillen & Merchant, 2013). This is particularly noticeable in contexts in which 'virtual' objects have become the research focus. Partly because of the specific context of this study but also because of an interest in describing technologies as 'things in use', the material properties of the iPad are foregrounded here. The analysis that follows attempts to capture a sense of the device as a physical object, with a particular heft and a definable shape—an object that can be held in one or both hands, balanced on a lap or rested on the floor. But analysis also has to grapple with the specifics of the iPad, its various buttons, switches and essential design features, what might be called its mechanical features. And finally, there has to be some account of the particular vocabulary of gestures that work both generically on the device and specifically within individual apps (taps, swipes, drag and drop and, occasionally blowing).

In our study, we identified three types of body movements that accompanied adult-child-iPad interactions (Table 8.1). These movements take their place alongside the more familiar everyday body movements, gestures and facial expressions that are an integral part of communicative interaction (see Kendon, 2004) and are particularly significant, I would argue, in the kinds of co-constructed meaning-making that occurs in adult-child story sharing (see also Murphy, 1987). We can distinguish between (1) *stabilizing movements*— responses to the weight and shape of the iPad that are necessary in order to hold the device steady, so that users can see sufficient detail on the screen; (2) *control movements*, which are essential for basic operations, accessing apps, and navigating texts on-screen; (3) *deictic movements*, used to draw attention to the screen or to point out specific features. Although operationalising these threw up some challenges from a coding point of view, they emerged as useful ways to distinguish elements of the iPad interactions in the data.

Thinking about the material dimension and particularly the ways in which the research participants worked with the material aspects of the iPads also

Table 8.1   A Typology of Hand Movements used with the iPad

1. Stablilizing movements

Holding—*using one or both hands to support the tablet as one might hold a tray*
Holding and resting—*as above but using the knees for additional support*

2. Control movements

General tapping—*using three or four fingers in a slapping motion*
Precision tapping—*using the forefinger (like the pointing gesture) or with the hand palm downwards slightly lowering one of the first three fingers so that it activates the screen*
Swiping—*hand palm downward using one or more fingers to drag across the screen*
Thumb pressing—*using the thumb to tap, swipe or operate the home button*

3. Deictic movements

Pointing, nodding and other gestures—*directing attention to the screen or visual items framed by the screen* revealed that the physical adaptations they made were for the most part seamlessly woven into the ongoing interactions, taking their place in the wider context of communication. For instance music or voices generated by the app occurred at the same time as the fine-tuning of stabilizing movements, and took their place alongside nodding, pointing and conversational exchanges between children and adults to constitute a complex choreography of events.

RESEARCH DESIGN

The data presented here are drawn from a project guided by two overarching aims:

- to examine the interactions of young children when accessing books on ipads;
- to identify the ways in which the technology supports early literacy development.

The research team was interested to know exactly how young children respond to story- and story-related apps on the iPad, the types of interactions that they have with them and what sorts of comparisons could then be made with what we know about the use of print texts, particularly picture books, in early childhood. In addition to this, we were keen to identify the affordances of the iPad for supporting young children's early reading development, both with and without adult support.

Accordingly members of the research team worked in two early-years settings that cater for babies and toddlers. Both were located in an urban area of South Yorkshire in the north of England. Researchers conducted observations of babies and toddlers under 3 years of age as they used iPads, sometimes for the first time, to look at interactive apps both with and without adult support. These iPad encounters were video-recorded for subsequent analysis. Filming took place over three days in each setting, and two researchers were present on each occasion. This provided video footage of encounters from different points of view (where possible from behind and facing the screen). Ethical practice was ensured at all times and parental consent for the filming was agreed.

In this paper, I use extracts from the data gathered by my colleague and coresearcher Karen Daniels, focusing on two different and contrasting iPad encounters. These have been selected not because they are typical but because they highlight the ways in which the device, as a material object, enters into the ecology of adult-child interaction in the early-years setting as a 'thing in use' and becomes absorbed into routines of educational practice. By looking at the physical interactions involved, I shed some light on how the iPad's weight, portability and interface take on significance with young children and how these become part of a complex negotiation of meaning between adults and children. In developing a descriptive framework for understanding the data, I drew freely from the literature on gesture, touch and pointing (e.g., Clark, 2003; Kendon, 2004; McNeill, 2000) as well as some of the work on haptics (Minogue & Jones, 2006).

In order to look more closely at the data, I used an analytical method that highlights the significant work done by the body and hands in sharing and using iPads. This incorporates some of the features of multimodal discourse analysis such as that employed by Flewitt et al. (2009), Wohlwend (2009) and Taylor (2012). In this I use the *time code* as an anchoring device; *speech*, to include what was said by the participants as well as the voices and music generated by the app; *movement* to describe the action in terms of posture and gesture using the three kinds of movement described above; and Latour's term *actants* to describe both the actions and interactions of humans, iPads and iPad apps. I placed less emphasis on the visual content of the app because of the focus on the material and physical dimensions of interaction. Where this information seemed important to understanding the interactions, I included details of what was occurring on screen in the movement category.

INTERACTIONS WITH IPAD STORY-APPS

Apps now include a large range of commercially produced children's stories and games, from new versions of familiar texts to stories based on TV characters as well as 'books' and games specifically designed for iPads. In what follows, I present a microanalysis of two different episodes from the data, which show children and adults interacting with contrasting apps. The first involves interactions around a story-related game included as part of the *Peppa Pig's Party Time* app (P2 Games). Here we see a four-way interaction involving an experienced adult professional, two children and the *Peppa Pig's Party Time* app. The second episode is more familiar in terms of story sharing. It focuses on the telling or retelling of a chronological narrative and a rather traditional one at that: *The Three Little Pigs* (Zubadoo Media). This episode centres on the story-app, the child and the adult; thus in the terms used here, it is a three-way interaction. In this sense, then, it has much in common with the familiar practice of story sharing.

Cake-Mixing with *Peppa Pig's Party Time*

Peppa Pig is a children's television programme distributed by Channel5/Nick-Junior in the UK. First broadcast in 2004, it has rapidly extended its global reach and is now a firm favourite with under-fives in many countries. Its animated cartoon characters revolve around the everyday exploits of a pig family (5-year-old Peppa, her younger brother George, Mummy and Daddy Pig, and a small extended family). Firmly located in the traditions of anthropomorphic narrative for young children, *Peppa Pig* features pigs and other animal characters. Episodes revolve around everyday situations such as riding bikes, going to the playground and visiting relatives. In many ways the series upholds liberal middle-class values in the activities depicted, the speech patterns of the central

characters and their relationships—for instance, Daddy Pig regularly overesti-
mates his capabilities, and this is pointed out to him, whereas Mummy Pig is
quick to criticise some (but not all) implied gender inequities. *Peppa Pig* tie-ins
continue to proliferate in line with the show's popularity and global distribution; they include toys, vehicles, bathroom products, children's clothing and so
on. There are currently ten licensed *Peppa Pig* apps in Apple's App Store.

The *Peppa Pig's Party Time* app is based around organising a party to celebrate Peppa Pig's birthday. Party preparations include designing invitations,
creating party bags and baking and decorating 'yummy' cakes. In the following episode, we see Harry (22 months) and Kaitlin (18 months) engaging in
the cake-making activity with Emma, an early-childhood professional. At one
point in the sequence they are joined by Lucas (23 months), brandishing a
plastic mixing spoon. Figure 8.1 gives an impression of the physical space.
The iPad is flat on the floor throughout and all participants sit on the carpeted
floor. Kaitlin sits between Emma's legs for the duration of the episode, and
although some small postural adjustments are made by both of them, their
close physical proximity is a constant. To the right of the iPad Harry adopts a
kneeling position and moves more frequently—at one stage he is on all fours
above the iPad.

In the first sequence, which lasts for about 20 seconds, the children begin to
respond to the Peppa Pig app. Emma has started the app, and the noises it then
generates fulfil an attention-gaining function. Emma's comments support this

Figure 8.1 Adult-child interaction with *Peppa Pig's Party Time*.

Table 8.2   Initial Orientation to *Peppa Pig's Party Time*

T-code	Speech	Movement	Actants
00:00		Kaitlin taps repeatedly with right *index finger* on screen image of Peppa Pig.	App makes sound
	Boing!		
	E: That's a funny noise!		Kaitlin activates app:
00:02	Snort! Snort ! He-He-He!	Kaitlin grins with satisfaction and rocks backwards, *index finger* still extended.	Peppa's mouth moves
	K: Ha! Ha! (laughing)		
		Harry leans in with interest.	
	E: Is that a funny noise?		
		Throws her head back into Emma's lap.	Kaitlin reacts
	K: Yeah (whispers)		
	E: Yeah, press there.	Emma leans forward towards the iPad bringing Kaitlin with her; Harry extends his hand	Harry indicates interest
00:10		to touch the iPad.	
00:19		Emma extends *index finger* (other fingers slightly crooked) to demonstrate as she taps Peppa.	Emma demonstrates
	Snort! Snort !		Emma activates app:
	E: Ow! (in mock surprise)	Kaitlin strokes her *index finger*; Harry looks intently at the screen	app makes sound
			Harry repeatedly activates app:
	Snort! Snort ! Snort! Snort !	Harry, with *index finger* outstretched repeatedly taps the screen, moving	app makes sound
	Snort! Snort ! Snort! Snort !	from Peppa to Mummy Pig and then across all the characters; then looks up at Emma for approval.	

initial orientation and both children make some tentative control moves. Kaitlin is the first to attempt this (Table 8.2).

The children engage in relatively little verbal interaction here, and the sequence is characterised by the ways in which Emma and the app work in tandem to focus attention. Reactions from the children indicate their interest as they lean forward and hold the screen in their gaze; this is underlined by their willingness to interact with the touchscreen interface, aware, one assumes, that this is likely to change what is seen or heard. They are more predisposed to make things happen and to enact successful control movements than to engage in dialogue. Emma supports all this verbally with 'Yeah, press there', and she also demonstrates where and how to tap on the screen. The accuracy of the tap can be quite crucial here, and young children have a variable success rate.

This sequence is followed by the selection of a particular game. The transcript in Table 8.3 picks up at the point at which cake making has been chosen; Emma is showing how ingredients are to be selected and then added to the virtual mixing bowl. What is immediately noticeable here is that interaction is governed by the visual display on the screen. In this sequence, the app responds to actions at the interface by showing butter and sugar being added when a tap is accurately made. Adding in the eggs (which happens after this sequence) is the only action that includes a sound—the cracking noise of the shells. As a result of this Emma demonstrates and guides children's attention mainly by pointing. The children make a number of attempts to tap, and some meet with success.

Lucas's one contribution adds a fascinating dimension to the interaction. He is clearly already aware of the *Party Time* app and the cake-making game and interrupts the activity by tapping a real plastic mixing spoon on to the screen image, as if to act out a connection with the real world of spoons and stirring actions. Unfortunately the effect that this has is to distract both Harry and Kaitlin. Harry looks away, and Kaitlin begins to play with her shoe. Later, when Emma refocuses the children's attention on the game, they try out the simulated mixing that the app provides. This involves placing a finger on the screen image of a spoon and maintaining contact with the screen whilst moving the finger backwards and forwards—in other words, it is a linear movement on the horizontal plane of the touchscreen. Both Harry and Kaitlin are successful in this symbolic enactment of mixing.

This whole episode contains relatively little dialogue and focuses mainly on the control movements required to play the cake-making game. The adult role is noteworthy here—Emma works to focus the children using the sort of attention-gaining strategies observed in book sharing (Deloache & DeMendoza, 1987). She does this through verbal explanation, pointing and demonstration. Whilst doing this, she also allows for plenty of exploration and gives feedback to the children on their control movements. The game itself connects with children's enthusiasm for the *Peppa Pig* stories, draws on their everyday experience of cooking routines and allows them to refine the technical skills needed to work on the iPad.

Table 8.3 Mixing Cake in *Peppa Pig's Party Time*

T-code	Speech	Movement	Actants
00:43	E: You have to touch the things here. E: Touch the egg and the butter.	Emma points with index finger (*deictic movement*). Harry touches an icon and slides his *index finger* along the screen in a *swipe gesture*.	Emma focuses attention.
	E: Kaitlin do it, look put the butter in.	Lucas leans in. Emma uses *index finger* to point at the butter icon (*deictic movement*).	Emma guides
00:51		Kaitlin taps (unsuccessfully) with *index finger*.	Kaitlin and Harry interact with the app.
	E: Well done!	Kaitlin repeat taps the butter.	
		Harry moves forward over the screen so he is on all fours staring down at the mixing bowl on the screen.	
	E: And the sugar, touch the sugar. E: Put the sugar in.	Lucas enters the frame he is holding a plastic mixing spoon in his hand and gently rests it against the screen.	Lucas intervenes, changing the dynamic.
	H: yeah! E: Are you touching it?	Harry looks up at Emma/ the camera.	
01:05		Lucas crawls back to his original position, still *clutching the plastic spoon*.	Activity pauses.
		Harry sits back on his haunches, Kaitlin starts to play with her shoe.	

Story-Sharing with *The Three Little Pigs*

Pigs also feature in the second sequence, but on this occasion it is *The Three Little Pigs*—a traditional tale of three anthropomorphic pigs who build their houses of different materials and are pursued by a hungry Big Bad Wolf. Written versions of this story date back to the 1880s, but it is likely that it has a much longer history in oral storytelling. Some of the phrases that characterise the narrative and the morals that can be drawn from it are deeply embedded in Western culture. Global circulation of the story was no doubt accelerated by Disney's 1933 remake, *Silly Symphony*, which was followed by a variety of related versions in different media and different languages. The story itself is probably one of the best-known traditional tales in the UK. Because of its provenance, the three little pig characters are not specifically branded or licensed, although in common with *Peppa Pig* they are depicted in toys, clothing and other items produced for young children. The three little pigs also feature as characters within the four *Shrek* films, as indeed they do in other children's stories, such as the Ahlberg's iconic picture book *Each Peach Plum*. In this way the story characters of *The Three Little Pigs* and *Peppa Pig* are similarly positioned in children's culture in that they are both popular and familiar, widely depicted and part of a global mediascape (Appadurai, 1996).

In the first extract (Table 8.4) we encounter an adult professional, Ruth, sitting on the floor with Max (23 months). The iPad app *The Three Little Pigs* is playing in 'Read it to me' mode; therefore no page turning or other control movements are necessary. The app commentary simply reads the story whilst the animations run on autopilot. This then constitutes a three-way process in which the app takes the lead, with Ruth acting sometimes in support and at other times as audience. Max is an active participant, responding to the narrative verbally, gesturally and with occasional taps on the screen of the iPad. His contributions continue through the episode: his short, and relevant utterances, 'No!' and 'Wolf off!' are typical and are regularly accompanied by gestures such as nodding, pointing and finger wagging. On a subsequent rendering of 'chinny chin chin', Max raises his index finger to his chin, and when the wolf attempts to blow the house down, Max purses his lips in an exaggerated imitation of blowing. His gestures are in this way intimately connected to his participation, comprehension and enjoyment of the narrative.

In many ways these interactions seem to rehearse the familiar practices of story sharing, but the medium is, of course different. The challenges of holding a book and turning its pages are removed, but they are replaced by new challenges. The iPad is a material object that Max is keen to hold! In the beginning of the sequence it is on his outstretched

Table 8.4　The Three Little Pigs *and the Language of Gesture*

T-code	Speech	Movement	Actants
00:00	'Great, I can come in!' R: No cried the pig, no! R: ooh!* M: nah.	Max and Ruth are sitting next to one another on the floor. Max has the iPad on his outstretched legs. He raises both arms, and then grips the iPad in both hands.	App-story commentary. Ruth and Max join in.
	'Little pig let me come in!'	Ruth reaches quickly across to tap and turn off the 'connection' warning.	*iPad generates warning.
	M: No! M: Wolf Off! 'No!' cried the pig. 'Not by the hair on my chinny chin chin'	Max raises his *index finger* in a pointing gesture (*deictic movement*). Max rapidly moves his whole arm across the screen in emphasis, and repeats the gesture.	App initiates Max's response.
00:16	R: ..on my chinny chin chin (overlapping) M: see (? inaudible) 'Little pig little pig'	Max holds up his right hand, index finger still raised and nods his head in synch with the commentary.	
00:31	R: Try not to keep touching it Max, do you want me to hold it, lovey?* 'Little pig little pig'	Max returns to the two-handed iPad holding position. The 'connection' warning appears again. Max makes an unsuccessful attempt to tap it off. Ruth intervenes, gently restraining his hand, holding it around the wrist and takes the iPad balancing it on the flat of her left hand. Max moves as if to hold it again and then stops.	*iPad generates warning. App initiates responses from Max and then Ruth.
		Max holds his right hand *index finger* in a pointing gesture (*deictic movement*) which tracks the movement of the wolf across the screen. He then shakes this finger to emphasise the 'no' (admonishing gesture). Max returns his left hand to grasp the iPad—it's perilously close to the Home button	

legs, and he grips it with both hands. Later, we see that Ruth takes control, balancing it on the flat of her hand. This is to overcome two technical issues. Firstly, there is the 'connection lost' warning message that keeps on flashing up on the page—Ruth needs to tap this quickly to turn it off, so that the momentum of the narrative is preserved. Secondly, she is concerned that Max might inadvertently press the Home button, which would terminate the app. There are no direct parallels in sharing print books.

This reading of *The Three Little Pigs* continues in similar vein until the wolf is finally captured by the last pig after a botched attempt to gain access through the chimney. The second sequence shows what happens when the story concludes (Table 8.5). At this point the iPad is resting on Ruth's left knee, and as the camera pans across we notice that she has a second iPad balanced on her right knee. However, this does not detract from the interactional sequence, and Max's attention remains with *The Three Little Pigs*. At the end of the story-app the book's virtual cover is displayed, and what ensues is a good example of what under other circumstances might be referred to a book talk (Senechal et al., 1995), with plenty of labelling of objects and some conversation about the visual elements.

Ruth underscores the story's ending with her 'Goodbye, big bad wolf', but it is Max who draws her attention to the detail on the cover by pointing and saying 'That'. She quickly follows his lead, building on Max's interest. In what follows there is plenty of pointing (and although fingers often touch the screen, they remain as deictic gestures), and it accompanies Ruth's questioning and Max's labelling talk as they jointly construct meaning. This is not without some familiar complications. It is not entirely clear what Max is referring to when he says 'Rattle'—he appears to be pointing at some geese, but what is he trying to say? And in a similar exchange, when Ruth points at and labels the tortoise, Max responds with 'Crab'. Ruth's response —'Good trying, Max. It's a tortoise. He's got a shell on his back like a crab'—quickly affirms what he has said and makes a surprisingly astute (and presumably accurate) connection.

In this whole sequence relatively low technical demands are placed on the participants and there are far fewer control movements than in *Peppa Pig's Party Time*. Nevertheless there are still some issues related to the materiality of the iPad. The repeated intrusion of the 'connection lost' error message may be unwelcome but it is never disruptive. The story-app seems to support fairly intimate and sustained adult-child storytelling in which the adult finds a comfortable role and the child actively participates too. Many of the attention-gaining strategies observed in book sharing (Deloache & DeMendoza, 1987) are performed by the app, but these are sensitively supported by Ruth. The final work with the visual

Table 8.5   Talking about the Images in *The Three Little Pigs*

T-code	Speech	Movement	Actants
			App story concludes.
02:30	and that was the end of the wolf and the three little pigs . . .		
	R: Goodbye, big bad wolf!		Ruth leads with concluding remarks.
	M: Go.		Max draws attention to the App's 'book cover'
	R: . . . lived happily ever after.		
	M: Yes.	Max points at an image of the three little pigs (*deictic movement*, and then taps the screen (*control movement*).	
	R: Ooh!		
	M: That.		
	R: The pigs there . . . what else can you see?		Ruth builds on Max's interest in the images.
	M: R . . . rattle. (inaudible)		
	R: Can you see the hedge-hog?	Ruth uses her right index finger to point to the hedgehog, tapping the screen (*deictic movement*).	
	R: . . . . and the		Max responds to Ruth.
	M: rattle rattle	Max has his right index finger raised—as if in readiness.	
	R: Tortoise.	Ruth moves the finger onto a picture of a tortoise.	
	M: Crab!		
	R: Crab, where's crab?	Max uses his right index finger to indicate what he thinks is a crab (*deictic movement*).	
	M: There.		
	R: Good trying, Max. It's a tortoise. He's got a shell on his back like a crab.		Ruth tunes in to Max's error and with positive feed-back re-models it.
	R: Can you see the balloons—one, two . . .	Ruth waves her right index finger above the group of bal-loons (*deictic movement*). She then steadies this to more direct pointing to accompany the counting.	Ruth initiates bal-loon counting.
	M: three, three.		Max responds.
	R: Good. Let's have a look.	Ruth presses the Home button with the thumb of her left hand (*control movement*).	Ruth concludes the session.

elements of the app's 'book cover' shows how images on the iPad might promote book talk or simply become part of pointing and labelling inter-actions in early-years settings.

DISCUSSION

In watching the video data, one is immediately struck by the way in which multiple actions and interactions are woven together in a com-plex choreography of events. Turn taking is hard to identify, as voices and music generated by the apps overlap with the fine-tuning of sta-bilizing movements, conversational exchanges between children and adults and the related gesturing, pointing and tapping. But if there is one thing that stands out, it is the way in which hands, and particu-larly index fingers, play a key role. Figure 8.1 is a typical illustration of this. Here Emma uses her index finger as an attention-guiding strategy to point to the cake tin on screen, whilst Harry rests his right index finger on his left hand. Even Kaitlin appears to have an index finger at the ready! This is highly salient throughout the data—the young chil-dren, in particular, often pause with ane index finger resting on a knee or frozen in midair, either mimicking the adult or in preparation for their turn. On some occasions, when it seems that touchscreen control eludes them, they will drag the adult's index finger onto the screen to tap on their behalf. The pointing gesture is used by both adults and children in different ways, as both a deictic and a control movement. On regular occasions the boundary between pointing and tapping becomes very vague and what seems to start off as pointing ends up as a touchscreen tap.

Pointing takes its place alongside other gestures as well. For exam-ple, in the *Three Little Pigs* extract, Harry's communicative turns often take on a gestural form. He nods his head, waves his finger in admoni-tion, and raises his arms in exasperation. But he, like the children in the cake-mixing episode, also uses a variety of different control move-ments. Tapping is nearly always done with the index finger, but it is quite clear that the hand position can vary. This is evident in both adults and children. In these data the pointing gesture (Figure 8.2: frame 2) is most commonly used for control; but the outstretched hand with index finger slightly lowered is used, too (Figure 8.2: frames 1 and 3). Swiping nearly always involves the pointing gesture, and so does the drag-and-drop function; this is perhaps because these actions need more precisely weighted contact with the screen. Sometimes children engage in swiping movements by using all fingers simultaneously (Figure 8.2: frame 4).

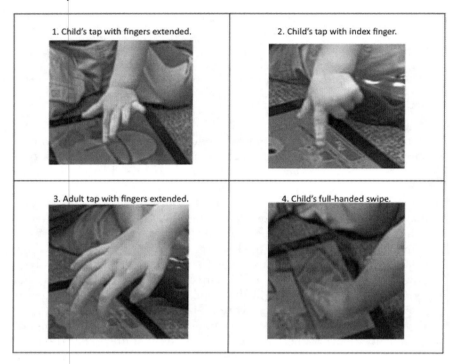

Figure 8.2   Some commonly used control movements.

This fine-grained analysis highlights how a complex gestural vocabulary is woven into the broader communicational ecology of adult-child iPad interactions. These gestures are accompanied by particular bodily movements, physical adjustments and stabilizing movements, which are needed in order to accommodate the device in the immediate setting. In this way the focus on technologies as 'things in use' (Ihde, 1993) brings the material and physical dimensions of interaction to the fore.

Parallels could be drawn between cake mixing in *Peppa Pig's Party Time* and traditional board games; between *The Three Little Pigs* story-app and book-sharing, and each instance would produce different gestures, different control movements and different physical adjustments to the material and technological affordances of the medium. These parallels are of interest because they begin to suggest how touchscreens may integrate into existing social practices or transform them. Schatzki's (2001) notion of practices as 'organized nexuses of activity', that involve bodily 'doings', 'sayings' and 'relatings' is useful here, because it shows how routines that are familiar to early-years practitioners and commonplace in early-years settings can adapt. Both board games and story sharing constitute well-established nexuses of activity. Although I have shown how these alter with the introduction of iPads, they do not appear to be as potentially disruptive as earlier technologies, such as desktop computers.

iPad apps may also map on to social practices in more subtle ways. In the introduction I pointed to the increased presence of technological toys in the early years, which occurs alongside parental uses of tablets and smartphones. If these technologies are an integral part of young children's lives, it seems inevitable that they will eventually find a place in more early-years settings. Both of the apps referred to in this paper are located, in their distinct ways, in global media narratives. In this sense they contribute to the everyday experience and popular culture of toddlers and young children just as much as the activities of cake mixing, the actions of blowing and the naming of animals, becoming part of the translocal assemblage. Although print literacies still have an important role to play, the new literacies of digital technology are now making significant inroads into early childhood, and it seems that portable touchscreens, such as the iPad, have a place in educational provision at home and in early-years settings. Some practices—such as book-sharing and game-playing—familiar in some cultural contexts, can now just as easily involve an iPad as they can a print book or a board and counters.

EDITORS' COMMENTARY

In describing new reading practices associated with iPads in an early-years setting in England, Merchant notes a similar ludic element to that described by Beavis in relation to Harry Potter. Children can read about Peppa Pig but also play in Peppa's world by planning a party and decorating cakes. The tapping, typing and swiping that children performed as they worked through apps and stories in Merchant's study signal new ways of 'reading' and thinking through texts. Physically moving and interacting with digital texts challenges models of reading that have been associated with parent-child book sharing. Merchant's chapter shows how little we understand about the intricacies of iPad reading. This chapter draws attention to the multidirectional and haptic nature of reading praxis and reading paths, demonstrating the need for multiple levels and types of analyses to capture the processes at work when children use iPads. His work highlights the need to keep revisiting our understandings of literacy processes as new opportunities for meaning-making are enabled by new technologies.

Of course the materiality of the devices or objects that mediate texts are always significant to meaning-making and the kinds of social relationships that surround and are mediated through literacies are important too. In earlier chapters, for example, we saw how two girls in Minecraft Club (Chapter 3) created a private space by using their laptop screen, and how the hairdressers (Chapter 4) were able to carry their friendships with them as they took their mobile phones to the bank and the bar. Kucircova et al.'s study of a mother-child interaction around a story-sharing app focuses on the affective dimension of the placing and holding of the iPad, drawing parallels with the intimate relationships associated with book sharing (Kucircova et al, 2013). This 'intersubjective and intercorporeal sense of embodiment' (Blackman 2012: 12) highlights how interactions between bodies and things can be deeply connected to the affective dimension of literacies. Research into use of tablet computers foregrounds the significance of 'things in use', but these relationships are always in play in meaning-making. Digital devices—and the texts they mediate—gain their significance partly through how they are taken up as objects.

Again we need to be wary of arriving at universalities. As Law (2004) argues, objects mean different things are they are put together in different assemblages in different local circumstances. However, arrangements of bodies and embodied relations with the stuff that mediates texts have and always will be significant. As Verbeek explains,

> When things are used, people take up a relation to the world that these things, thanks to their 'handiness' coshape. In this coshaping, not only does the human interaction with products have a sensory character, so does the human-world relation that is mediated by the products. Human experience and existence can only acquire a specific shape on the basis of sensory perception and sensory dealings with the world. (Verbeek, 2005:211)

The sensory—even visceral—dimension of literacies is one that deserves further investigation.

In the next chapter, Bronwyn Williams retains a focus on the significance of digital devices to new literacies. Whilst Merchant explored the handling of the device, Williams considers the significance of mobility (of device and text) and mutability to our thinking about meaning-making. Drawing on interviews with young people in the US and UK, he describes their textual practices as 'mobile, remixed, independent, collaborative, and developed through peer-based learning'. Whilst warning against assumptions about universality of experience, he contrasts the confidence with which the young people he interviewed engaged in digital practices with the anxiety they experienced in relation to schooled literacy and suggests that schools need to understand, value and extend the understandings about texts their students generate through such practices.

NOTES

1. I am indebted to my coresearchers Julia Bishop, Karen Daniels, Jackie Marsh, Jools Page and Dylan Yamada-Rice for this work, which was funded by Sheffield Hallam University and the University of Sheffield under the Collaboration Sheffield initiative.
2. *My First Numbers* is a counting app produced by GrasshopperApps.
3. *Endless Alphabet* is a letter-play app produced by Callaway Digital Arts.

9 Mobility, Authorship, and Students' (Im)material Engagement with Digital Media and Popular Culture

Bronwyn T. Williams

INTRODUCTION

Stand outside of many schools or universities and you'll witness a common sight once classes finish. As students walk through the doors, they pull out their phones and the literacy practices begin. They check social media, follow links to web pages, use downloaded applications, play games, plug into their music and send messages. Their actions are fast, mobile, social and deeply involved with texts that range across and combine print, video, sound and image. Young people find these literacy practices meaningful and engaging; their activities serve their interests and are under their control.

It's not news that, for many young people, phones function as the mediating technologies for many literacy practices. Students communicate with friends and negotiate relationships through texting, posts on social media, taking and sharing photos and video and sometimes even email. As they negotiate relationships students also perform their identities in networks and texts, shaping and reshaping these identities as audience, time and contexts shift. At the same time, their phones have become the technologies through which they encounter new texts, often from popular culture, from games to movies to music. Their encounters with popular culture involve reading and interpretation; but now, in a time of participatory popular culture, there is also the opportunity for commenting and sharing. All these activities happen on the phones they carry in their hands. In fact, calling these devices 'phones' rather than 'mobile computers' hinders our understanding of the literacy practices they enable and mediate. (In this chapter, in an attempt to rethink this labeling, I refer to them as 'mobiles' or 'mobile devices'.) For some students, mobiles are the dominant computers in their lives. Eric, a college student in England, was typical of many when he showed how he used his mobile for everything from taking photos to using the Web to watching videos. He said, 'I use this to do everything I want to do on this. Except when I have to write a paper for school, I just use my phone'. Briana a university student in the US, regarded her mobile in a similar way, 'I can do basically anything with my phone that I can do on the computer, but it's just a handheld phone. So I can't live without my cell phone, I don't know too many people who can that are my age who can live without the cell phone, you have to have it'. What's more, young people often learn how to do new things with their mobiles from each other rather than from adults. If you ask young people to show you what they can do with their mobiles, they respond with enthusiasm and confidence.

The motivation and agency students display when they discuss their mobiles often contrast with how the same students discuss literacy practices in school. Their comments about reading and writing in the classroom often revolve around concerns, even anxieties, about assessment and testing. What's more, many students perceive literacy practices in school as controlled by teachers and working toward the teachers' agendas. Instead of enthusiasm and confidence, they relate narratives of anxiety and tentativeness (and often point out that using mobiles is banned in many schools and classrooms). According to Kevin, 'Reading for school is more nerve-wracking and less interesting because you've got to get the way you read it right to satisfy the teacher. Otherwise, your grade is down the tubes'. In a similar way, Peter said that writing for school was not enjoyable, 'I'm pretty picky so I try to do a good job, but that doesn't mean I enjoy writing. I don't enjoy it much because it's still too much work and there is still the grade hanging over it'. Of course many teachers work tirelessly to create environments that will engage students' imaginations and interests. Yet even in those classrooms, teachers are working within the limitations of regimes of testing and standardisation that can overwhelm their best efforts and make students perceive the focus of school as one of judgment and inflexibility.

The writing and reading taking place as young people walk down the street with their mobiles reminds us that, if we are to teach them effectively, we need to consider the entire range of literacy practices young people engage in. Such considerations also touch on how participatory popular culture pervades and shapes reading and writing from genre awareness to perceptions of audience. It's not a matter of 'bringing' digital media or popular culture into the classroom, they are already there in students' experiences when they walk in the door. Just as important is the need to pay attention to how material technologies, such as the widespread use of mobiles, shape how students interpret and compose texts in multiple modes.

In this chapter I explore the ways in which students' daily literacy practices with mobile digital media, particularly with participatory popular culture, influence their conceptions of reading and writing. Although there has been a growing discussion about how digital media move and merge between online and material lives, less has been made of the effect of movement, both virtual and embodied, in students' engagement with texts. Once they leave school, students engage with digital texts that are mobile and mutable. Instead of acting as single authors of stable texts, they are more often collaborators of changing, impermanent texts. In addition, they encounter these texts through mobiles in which physical movement and location—the materiality of literacy—further blurs the lines between the online and the embodied. Drawing from interviews and observations with secondary and postsecondary students in both the UK and the US over the past several years, I examine how they use collaboration, commentary, and remix as strategies in everyday literacy practices. Such strategies have implications for how these students negotiate the fluid nature of authorship and text online and how this shapes perceptions and practices or reading and writing. In addition I suggest how these student practices can inform effective literacy pedagogies.

THE (IM)MATERIALITY OF LITERACY AND DIGITAL MEDIA

Recent scholarship (Burnett, et al., 2014; Pahl & Rowsell, 2010) has high-lighted the complex relationship between literacy as something that is simul-taneously material and immaterial. On the one hand, literacy is understood to be a set of internal practices—reading, writing, interpreting, composing, analyzing, reflecting—that are immaterial. Sometimes these practices are observable to others, sometimes not. Certainly the understanding that a person is able to read and write and the perception and confidence of being able to do so cannot be seen or measured by itself. Similarly, cultural norms and definitions of literacy are not, by themselves, material. At the same time, the evidence of literacy practices is material and abundant. Literacy functions through the encoding and decoding of symbols, and that encoding and decoding has to happen through material artifacts. We can't write without something to write on or read without something to read with. The material manifestations of literacy are ubiquitous, from books on shelves to billboards and signs on buildings. The material and immaterial aspects of literacy, then, are inextricable and sometimes even simultaneous. For example, to consider authorship and text is to imagine simultaneously the material and immaterial—the person composing the material artifact and the immaterial representation of self through words and images.

The advent of digital media has not changed the reality of literacy as something that is material and immaterial, but it has introduced new complexities to our considerations. The very nature of digital media, that information is encoded in 1's and 0's, means that it can be compressed, transported, transmitted and altered with ease and speed. The same abil-ity to alter digital data, to change the medium and text depending on the software you have on your computer, allows for the material nature of any text to be more flexible, more malleable (Manovich, 2001). The text can change in appearance or be altered with relative ease. As many others have noted, such technologies allow work to be created and read that combines modes of image, print, video and sound. What does not change, however, is the need for the materiality of the computer through which the text is mediated. Technologies, such as mobiles and desktop computers, have adopted and developed their own set of cultural traditions and meanings in the same way that books, over the years, developed conventions in terms of size, cover design, storage on shelves and so on (Manguel, 1996). As Miller (2010: 31) points out, the material objects in our lives are shaped by our behaviors and values, which in turn are shaped and reinforced by the objects. In the same way that the clothing common in a culture makes a person someone 'who interacts with others and with the self through this constantly shifting material', the other objects in our lives both aid us in accomplishing some of the tasks in our lives and limit our ability to do others. In terms of digital hardware, some elements, such as the centrality of a screen and the need to be able to type in words, have remained relatively consistent even as devices have changed. Yet in other ways the development of a mobile device allows for a very different set of interactions with the text, from the size of what can be read to what connections can be made to other texts and how interactions with the text can take place. What's more, the ability to use mobiles in any range of places results in accessories that allow the devices to function (protective cases, nonglare screens, headphones) as well as to act as material displays of identity, such as decorative cases. Using mobile devices today is a distinctly different experience than sitting at a putty-colored desktop computer twenty years ago.

Understanding how the design of digital media shapes literacy practices is only partially a matter of hardware, however. The conventions of software—the images of icons, the conventions of web-page design, and so on—reflect traditions of power and ideology of the dominant culture (Hayles, 1999; Selfe & Selfe, 1994; Williams, 2003). So the use of icons and terms such as *files* that reflect the cultural artifacts of corporate offices, for example, rather than some other metaphor—such as baskets or barrels—shape conceptions of uses of digital media. Also, in some ways the material text has become more of a representation, more unreal, even as the technological hardware remains tactile and visible. The illusion of transparency provided by the screen that represents images of material texts can seem to make the necessity of the material technology less evident—until we drop the mobile and it breaks (Burnett et al., 2014). What's more, digital media, through software interfaces and even coding, create a further layer of representation for texts. The visual representation of a document on word processing software is made to look like ink on paper, but it is only a representation of such an artifact.

In different, but related, ways the popular culture that is such a central focus of student literacy practices can also be understood as working through the intersection of material artifacts and immaterial practices and perceptions. The materiality of popular culture is what we usually think of when we use the term, from holding a book to sitting in a movie theatre to putting on headphones. Yet the practices of engaging with or using popular culture are, like literacy practices, ephemeral and immaterial. A film, a videogame, a recording only represent the physical objects they have recorded. And when we grow to understand a genre of movies or music or computer games, for example, our knowledge of those genre conventions and the intertextual connections we make to create our expectations for what will be included in such a text, are internal and not material. Similarly, digital media now allow people to use popular culture content as an immaterial semiotic and rhetorical resource for the expression of ideas and the performance of identity. For example, for many students, interpreting, sampling and reusing popular culture content is a regular part of their performance of self, from pasting movie clips to a Facebook page or using a song clip as a cell-phone ringtone (Merchant, 2010; Weber & Mitchell, 2008; Williams, 2009). At the same time, whether through the creation of an avatar in a videogame or the construction of a profile page on a social media site, these online, seemingly immaterial performances are deeply entwined with the embodied lives of the people sitting at the computer or holding the mobile device. Though there is still discussion of people's 'online' or 'offline' lives, increasingly it is difficult to draw clear distinctions between the two statuses. Offline factors such as personal experiences, language histories or geographical locations shape online practices, which, in turn, affect embodied, physical responses and interpretations of the surrounding world.

Examining the ways in which students negotiate the material and immaterial demands of their daily literacy practices, including their work with participatory popular culture, can help us understand more fully the experiences that shape how they approach—and perceive—reading and writing in our classrooms. We must, of course, be cautious about the assumptions we make about what students are doing outside of school. The digital media students have access to and the facility with which they use it can vary widely. It's unproductive to assume that all students are 'digital natives', in the way Prensky (2001) has notably labeled them, or are engaged in the same set of practices. Young people, like all of us, adapt media to local needs and purposes, if the local contexts allow for it (De Block & Buckingham, 2007). That said, if we take the time to talk with students and listen carefully to what they tell us about their daily literacy activities, we can create connections that make them more effective readers and writers in their daily lives. As two examples of the ways in which these literacy practices work in students' lives I focus now on perceptions and practices of texts and authorship.

TEXTS AS ALWAYS CHANGING, NEVER FINISHED

The development of digital media and mobile technologies has made the idea and reality of a text mobile and fluid in ways that challenge earlier conceptions. The more traditional conception of a text was something that, once produced, was relatively stable. Whether as print on paper or images on film, a text might be reproduced for mass distribution, but the reproductions were simply copies of the original. The mass popular culture that developed in the late 19th century with the advent of electronic reproductions of image and sound required large amounts of economic capital to produce movies or musical recordings, with the result that mass popular culture became organised along industrial modes of production and distribution. Most individuals, then, could not make their own films or television programs, but they could read and interpret the identical copies that were distributed. If I made reference to *Middlemarch*, others who have read the book assume I am discussing the same text with the same words in the same order. As Manovich (2001) points out, however, the digitising of information makes it possible to break down, remake, store and transmit texts in ever-changing and never-ending versions. A number of scholars have addressed the malleable, impermanent nature of text in the digital age, focusing primarily on the technology that allows the text to be changed. Less is made, however, of the effect of movement, both virtual and embodied, in the evolution of the changeable, mutable text.

A digital text is malleable because it can be changed with software but also because it moves and its pieces move so easily. Digital media are marked by the movement of texts, often online but also by their use in explicitly intertextual ways. The expectation among many people now is that they will be able to encounter connected texts across multiple media and multiple genres. Participatory popular culture offers many of our students daily experiences of this kind (Jenkins, 2006). For example, rather than simply watch a movie on its own, they may just as likely read and contribute fan responses to the movie, play games based on the movie, look at other news about the movie that is linked to a website, and so on. Literacy practices on digital devices involve cross-cutting through mode and medium and genre, moving from one text to the next on the screen.

Students expect that texts which they access digitally are changeable and impermanent, and that is often part of the attraction. One aspect of such change involves changes over time. Catherine, a student in the US, said that part of what she liked about checking her Twitter account was that 'things are always new. It's new things so quickly that there is always going to be something interesting. Or something interesting soon'. Other students echoed this idea about the appeal of the constant updating of social media sites such as Twitter and Facebook. 'There's a lot of stuff that I see on Facebook that I could click on', Eric said. 'I don't always, but I do sometimes and I find fun stuff I wouldn't expect . . . If I don't check back on it I'd miss that'. Other students mentioned that they also liked how news feeds they followed, on Google or BBC or Yahoo, for example, were continually updated. Linda, a UK student, said, about her newsfeed on Google, 'if it catches my eye, like if it pops up on there, I'll be like "Ooh, I need to read about that". And like as far as all the silly stuff, all the celebrities and stuff, I never read that, I think that's silly'. The constant changes make such websites fundamentally different from the pages of a print newspaper, for example, a medium that, a century ago, was criticised as the epitome of a transitory text.

Even when the changes are not as rapid as a Twitter or news feed, students talked of their awareness of how digital texts were open to change. Mike, a US student, described his practice of 'wikiwandering', where he would start reading one page on Wikipedia, moving from one entry to the next when he came upon an intriguing link. He said that even when he might be reading about similar subjects, 'the way I read things is never going to be the same. Sometimes I end on a page where I've been before, but it might have changed if people have changed what's there. And, if it hasn't been changed by people, I still got to it differently, and that's not boring'.

The comfort with changing texts is not limited to websites. Students also mentioned that they were not surprised when other texts that were not originally created digitally, such as movies or music, ended up altered and reposted online. Popular culture is regarded as available content for appropriation and remix by young people both because it makes familiar intertextual connections but also because the appropriation of it is regarded as a culturally low-stakes activity (Williams, 2009). Elena, a student from Brazil at university in the US, said that, when she wanted to create a remixed video to go with a popular song, using both the song and images were obvious choices. 'I knew what I was going to do. Taking some images of people in the world, people together, different cultures . . . and using people from movies, good examples that would fit the song. And I was just putting them with the song. It came kind of naturally'. And Mike, again, talked about how much he not only enjoyed remixed, parody videos of films posted on sites such as YouTube, but that he expected there to be such texts posted. 'As soon as a big movie comes out, I'm just waiting for the YouTube videos that will come so I can see what people do with it. I can even like the movie, I liked *The Dark Knight Rises*, and I want to see the (remixed) videos'.

Although students expected to find or create remixed content, some also said that the origins—and destinations—of remixes were not always something they considered. Adam, in the UK, was interested in photography, and much of the photo editing work he did was on his own images. Yet he also followed memes—the popular culture genre where images are altered or given amusing captions and then circulated so that others can enjoy them, change them, and send the new version along. Well-known memes range from captions added to funny images of cats to political satire to pop culture images such as *Doctor Who*. Memes have become a widespread genre online (Knobel & Lankshear, 2007; Lewis, 2012) and are often circulated through social media such as Facebook and Twitter. Adam enjoyed popular culture-based memes, sometimes downloading and remixing them with his own message. When asked if he knew where the memes originated or where his remixes would end up, he said, 'I don't think I usually know. They don't start with me. I don't start those kinds of things. I just add my bit and send it on'. These comments from students point out that not only is sampling and remixing a part of meaning making in their literacy practices but that the meaning making is networked and continual. Although there are undoubtedly digital sites that students would be less inclined to see change—and, like others, they sometimes complain about changes to the format of pages such as Facebook—they have learned to expect that digital texts may never be finished.

Students were often as likely to regard themselves as nodes in an ongoing movement of digital text rather than its originators or receivers. Part of the fun and meaning students find in digital texts is their movement. Catherine said the point of Twitter was not just reading what other people had done but in retweeting as well as adding and responding to the posts of other people.

> When I'm reading my feed I'm always looking for the things I can retweet, or rewrite, though I don't favorite much. Sometimes the things I retweet are things are things my friends will like, or that I think represent something I believe or that I'm interested in. . . . Oh, yeah, I hope they retweet those too, and I think I'm getting better at figuring out which they'll retweet. It keeps going. I mean, why would someone be on Twitter and not retweet?

Composing with a consideration to how a text might be moved along and remixed online, what Ridolfo and DeVoss (2009) call 'rhetorical velocity,' is an awareness a number of students displayed in their comments. The point of composing and posting is not simply to create an original work others might read again and again as copies of the original version but is just as often to provide material that engages the network and gets remade before being passed along.

Digital texts are not only in motion through software, however. The material devices used to access and transport the texts are in physical motion as well, from laptops to tablets to memory sticks to mobiles. The physical movement of the device may be ephemeral, but it can have an impact on what happens with the text. We may think of digital texts primarily as shared online, but people with mobiles often hold them up to friends to share a text, just as might be done with a printed book or magazine. What's more, an action such as typing a message on a mobile device while walking may influence the length, tone and language of the text. Lee, for example, said that physical location is something that is another factor in her uses of her mobile.

> I mean I'd rather text message somebody rather than call them. I mean I probably have a text message right now more than likely. I don't know, it's just easy and like if you're in the middle of class and you just remember something that you really have to tell somebody then it's a lot quieter than calling them. But because I'm in class, it means I have to be short.

The interplay among the material devices, social contexts, physical locations and rhetorical knowledge when students use mobile devices 'are all dynamically interrelated; the meanings, uses, functions, flow and interconnections in young people's daily lives located in particular settings are also situated within young people's wider media ecologies' (Horst, Herr-Stephenson, & Robinson, 2007: 31). The person sitting on a bus and using a mobile phone is putting the text in physical motion as well as moving it through the virtual world. Adam said, 'When I'm on the bus or tram I've got my phone out, texting, maybe looking up things. I'm not doing serious work on the bus because there's too much else going on, even when I'm listening to music, but I'm always doing something.' On the bus Adam continues to be a node in the online network, where he may travel virtually far beyond his city. Others students talked about the way their online devices connected them with people in other locations in ways that were more significant for them than what might be happening directly around them. Caroline, in the US, for example, is a fan of opera, an interest not shared by many of her face-to-face friends. 'Sometimes I'm listening to my music, and I'll text friends I know from Facebook about what opera I'm listening to and what I think about it, rather than talk to my friends with me, because they won't care'. Yet Adam and Caroline, and the texts they are accessing or composing, are also nodes in the public transport network of the city (Nordquist, 2012). Their physical movement influences everything from their online access, to the size of the files they can engage with, to their responses to the actions of others around them on the bus or the sidewalk.

THE COMMUNITY AS AUTHOR

If the text is malleable and in motion, so then is the concept of authorship. Although, when asked to define an 'author', students invariably responded with a definition right out of 19th-century Romanticism of a singular genius producing stand-alone, immutable texts, in practice, students were as likely to treat digital authorship as simply a starting point for a process of textual creation that is additive and communal. The author of a work in the online context provides a text and a template, but others can take those texts and, in changing or reposting, become authors as well. Adam, in discussing memes, said he didn't know where they began, which means that he did not know who started them either. But he also said that, when he remixed and posted his own version, that he did not expect any kind of authorial credit for the work. 'My friends probably know it's mine, maybe they know. That's not the point . . . When I look at Tumblr, I don't care who put stuff there, that's not what I'm thinking about at all'. Instead, he said, taking part in the phenomenon of a particular meme was the more important motivation. The importance of taking part, of making a mark on a text and being involved in the process and practice of creation, has been noted by others as a driving force in many participatory popular culture activities (Knobel & Lankshear, 2007; Lewis, 2012). Authorship has, in many online settings, become a daily practice of call and response, of posting and comment, in which the distinction between audience and author has become blurred.

Students do point, however, to some conceptions of singular authorship that continue to have social power. For example, many students said they would not copy a Facebook status or Twitter post from a friend word for word and pass it off as their own. Instead, they followed the conventions established on social media of giving credit when retweeting or sharing posts. Yet students' authorial identity in such collaborative spaces is not singular. While a student may develop and curate a particular identity in a particular community such as Facebook (Davies, this volume), it is also the case that the same person may perform a different aspect of identity in another online community. Even in collaborative spaces, the authorial presence may not be singular but performed to fit the conventions and culture of that site. As with embodied performances of identity, online identities respond to the cultural context and may be readjusted and responded to on the fly.

Collaborative authorship online also engages in what Jenkins (2006), drawing on Pierre Levy, labels as 'collective intelligence'. With collective intelligence, virtual communities can 'leverage the combined expertise of their members. What we cannot know or do on our own, we may now be able to do collectively' (Jenkins, 2006: 27). Students draw on this communal sense of meaning-making, where people pool knowledge to solve problems—for everything from help with homework to popular culture choices. In doing so, some students talk of their preference for the opinions of their peers over published sources of recommendations such as newspapers or magazines. Caroline said that the songs she saw that people were listening to on the Facebook pages were better recommendations for her than reading professional critics. 'I don't really listen to what the critics say because I don't trust them. And, you know, critics are usually experts in that field, but just because an expert likes it doesn't mean that it's a good piece of music. It might be technically good, but it might not be aesthetically pleasing'. At the same time, however, students are not uncritical consumers of the recommendations of their peers. Briana said that the social media sites she accessed on her mobile also served as sites for discussion and disagreement. 'People have blogs or post on Facebook and, basically, they bring up a topic and they invite people to be in on that topic, I've been invited to a lot of those type of debates: "Who's the best rapper?" "Who's the best group?" or stuff like that.' Both Briana and Caroline said they valued the opportunity to hear from many people about ideas and recommendations, including the disagreements, rather than just one person's opinion. They pointed out that the additive and communal nature of writing online often made them more likely to trust such opinions than those of a single author unless the single author was a close friend. Mike also pointed to the collaborative nature of sites such as Wikipedia as influencing how he interpreted the material he read there. He understood that any given entry could be changed but that if the changes were 'wrong or just weird', the community of writers would likely change them back. Mike's comments reflect the sense that Wikipedia, though a site where content is regarded as community property, is also one in which the community has agreed to a set of principles in which work that is verifiable will be rewarded and other material will face checks from the community (Bruns, 2008). Students' conceptions of collective intelligence are also influenced by the fact that much of their learning about using their mobile devices comes from peers. New applications are shared among friends; people turn to their peers to get help to solve problems or learn how to use new software. Again, it is not uncommon to see two students with mobiles side by side, loading an application and figuring out how it works. Obviously collective intelligence is an approach to understanding texts and ideas that has some limitations, such as the reality that communally agreed upon ideas may be wrong and innovation might be excluded. Still, approaching texts as collaborative and developing from collective intelligence has implications for how some students interpret the texts that emerge from collaborative spaces.

CLASSROOM IMPLICATIONS

When we consider those students leaving a school building and pulling out their mobiles, we should think about them engaging in literacy practices that are mobile, remixed, impermanent, collaborative and developed through peer-based learning. These daily practices, and the perceptions of concepts such as text and authorship, help shape how students engage in reading and writing in every moment of their lives. In learning about and engaging in these practices students demonstrate high levels of motivation, agency, and self-sponsored learning. Students not only know what they are doing when they are using these devices to engage with their friends and with participatory popular culture but also have a clear idea *why* they are doing it. At the same time, they often describe school assignments and assessments as having little connection to their lives and leaving them with little sense of agency. And, for too many teachers, there is little awareness of what is really taking place when students are reading and writing on their mobile devices. The stereotype is that, because these practices involve digital media and popular culture, they are mindless and antithetical to what should be taking place in the classroom. Yet as the comments from students above indicate, students engage with and reflect on these practices in ways that can be thoughtful and nuanced.

There are several pedagogical implications for recognising that students' online literacy activities enter our classrooms. First, these practices are a reminder that, in order to teach effectively, we must begin by finding out what students know. If we do not dismiss what they are doing with their mobiles but instead ask them to describe not only what they do but also how and why they do it, we will learn a great deal about specific practices as well as perceptions of concepts such as authorship, text and audience. Given that antecedent genre knowledge and other reading and writing experiences have been demonstrated to shape responses to new reading and writing situations, it is essential we have a more detailed, complex understanding of those experiences. What's more, just as we should not fear addressing immaterial out-of-school literacy practices in the classroom, we should not fear having the material technology in our classes. So many schools and classrooms ban the use of mobile phones because they think first of their function as *phones*, which will distract students from classroom work. If we instead consider what is possible when each student has a handheld computer, we can open up new possibilities for adapting these technologies to the classroom. Of course we do have to think carefully about how we want students to use the technologies they have in their hands. Like any technology, it is only as good as the ideas for using it, but I think we have more to gain than to lose by imagining what might be possible.

To draw effectively on students' antecedent knowledge requires thinking carefully about where such knowledge connects to the goals of the classroom. We shouldn't assume that students will easily connect in-school and out-of-school knowledge without help. If we talk with students about how they use mobile technologies, we can see that certain qualities appeal to them, such as speed, collaboration, mobility and response. When we have work in class that touches on such qualities, we can make important connections to their out-of-class experiences. For example, Twitter feeds offer useful resources for quick and fluid collaborative responses, ideal for brainstorming activities or group work in its invention stages. Blogs are slower but still good for informal writing that offers response to works in progress or to sequential work. Wikis provide excellent platforms for collaborative projects that draw on collective intelligence to solve problems. In addition, there are more and more mobile applications available every day that connect directly to reading and writing. In these and other uses, the key is first to think about how these devices are used well and what literacy practices students are adept at before trying to make our connections into the classroom.

When thinking about what is possible with out-of-school material and immaterial literacy practices, however, it is equally important to understand and discuss the limitations of such devices and practices. Every technology has strengths and limitations. There are certainly limitations with mobile devices and participatory popular culture, but they are not necessarily the obvious complaints that they are easy and shallow (Crook, 2012; de Block & Buckingham, 2007). If, for example, we think about the strengths of such practices as those of speed and collaboration, then a weakness is that such practices do not teach students how to slow down, how to work alone through a complex idea. There is certainly value in learning how to read and write a single-authored, extended print work that deals with concepts in nuance and detail. We cannot, however, just assume that the value is obvious without articulating to students what can be gained in such work. We can work with students to explore how they will gain from engaging in a wide range of practices in a wide range of media, from the fast and collaborative to the slow and singular (Miller, 2011). Then we must be more explicit in teaching how the genre conventions of something like a print article or story work and how to decode and see the moves that writers make and how to make those moves themselves.

Finally, it is important that we understand that knowledge can and should move both ways, in and out of the classroom. It is certainly valuable to draw on students' out-of-school experiences into the classroom. Yet understanding out-of-school literacy practices should be more than a one-way bridge of using those practices to further the ends of the classroom. We should also be thinking about how we help students become more effective in their daily literacy practices. By this, I do not just mean increasing their effectiveness at reading and writing that is similar to their work in school but also how what we do in the classroom can develop their skills as writers and readers on their mobile devices. What can we teach them that will make them more critical readers of Wikipedia, more creative on their Twitter feeds, more thoughtful about the selves they construct on Facebook pages? Even as new media and devices are developed, certain rhetorical concepts such as audience, authorship, genre and style will continue to be important for students to understand and apply in an ever-changing range of contexts. If we have ongoing conversations with students about what they do when they leave school, we can help make these connections and make them more effective at communicating and thinking creatively and critically across their lives.

EDITORS' COMMENTARY

In exploring the 'effects of movement' on the process of meaning-making, Williams considers both the physical movement of devices and movements of texts across media. He describes how material and immaterial dimensions intersect in an ebb and flow of the physical, the imagined, the textual, the social, the onscreen and offscreen. This, he suggests, troubles notions of 'location', as digital networks of friends, family and acquaintances are always present and may be more salient to users than the people they are physically with. At the same time, physical location and embodied reaction are important dimensions of meaning-making; as devices move, they can therefore enable new juxtapositions of text and place.

Williams highlights how, because of mobility, digital texts are 'never finished' but always open to reimagining and reworking. One way of understanding literacy is to see it in terms of creating texts that stabilise ideas, thoughts, feelings, understandings and perspectives for others (or maybe ourselves); texts become markers in time that represent or mediate certain ways of being. Notions of mobility and provisionality destabilise this. The young people Williams describes loved to anticipate how others might change a text, and when faced with a text, they played with what they might do with it; it was the movement—or expectation of movement—not the stasis that was significant. Their excitement was as much about what a text might become as about what it already was, and they were interested in how the text changed as multiple authors played it into new forms. Williams's descriptions of textual creation as 'additive and communal' and meaning-making as 'networked and continual' prompt us to see this provisionality in terms of the ongoing movement of texts.

The provisionality of digital texts is forefronted in many chapters in this book—for example, in how children improvise as they make animations (Chapter 3) or play in *MinecraftEdu* (Chapter 4). The process of creation—with all its significance for social relationships—is as important as the texts produced. We see an example of mobility in Davies's piece, as the young women she describes maintain and engage in friendships as they go about their day, dialoguing with and performing to those around them, whereas Rowsell and Burgess provide examples of ways in which networks mediated by social networking sites cross national boundaries. The mobility of texts and devices means that texts are not fixed or individually owned/authored but provisional and communal, 'changeable and impermanent'. Literacies cross sites and domains and mediate connections between them. This mutual embeddedness of text, site, artifact and identity seems to make it impossible to bound location.

The mobility of texts and devices offers much to pedagogy. Greater use of mobile devices would enable us to de-site learning from classrooms and promote engagement with varied and even imaginary landscapes, as exemplified by various case studies using mobile devices (e.g., DEFT, 2012; Facer, 2004). And of course the Internet potentially enables learners to access and engage with wide-ranging communities and environments. Coordinating, navigating and negotiating such liaisons would seem to be an important focus for education. The lived experience of mobility described by Williams, however, suggests more radical implications. Williams's emphasis on provisionality and continual remixing highlights possibilities for students to engage in powerful collaborations that move beyond the individual production of the fixed and often individual outcomes we so often associate with schooled literacy. Importantly, such work needs to acknowledge and build upon the diverse practices generated in response to these possibilities.

10 New Meaning-Making Practices
A Charter for Literacy Education

INTRODUCTION

In Chapter 1 we explored two key areas of contemporary debate with which this volume engages: firstly, the complex nature of relationships between the local and global, and secondly, what counts as 'new' in the study of literacies. Through the chapters and editorial commentaries, these themes have been explored in greater depth, drawing on varied theoretical perspectives and detailed analyses of everyday literacies in different contexts to illuminate how individuals and groups—at different ages within and outside formal education—are making meanings in the changing communicative context. In these chapters we have 'looked down' (Kwa, 2002) into the detail to understand how different flows—technological, economic, cultural and aesthetic—play in and through practice. Here, we 'look up' again to consider the implications of such work for how we think about literacies and how we might best prepare children and young people for the future.

The title of this chapter hints at closure and a definitive set of proposals for educators and policymakers. However, we emphasised from the outset that this was not what we were attempting to achieve. Indeed it is this urge to define and fix that we suggest has been problematic for literacy education in recent years. In many ways it is a refusal to arrive at answers or neatly bounded frameworks that is at the heart of our argument. To suggest that literacy can be fixed or bounded implies that it is something universal, something that can be counted and targeted, used to draw comparisons and to hold individuals, communities and institutions to account. Such measures define or reinforce certain ideas about literacy and literacy teaching in educational settings, and this 'fixing' of literacy is upheld by the texts and products used in its implementation, such as tomes of classic works, textbooks, workbooks, interactive whiteboard programmes, standardised tests and so on. Research plays a part too. In analysing the establishment of scientific 'truths', Kuhn explored how underpinning assumptions are rendered invisible as methodologies become institutionalised leading 'to an immense restriction of the scientists' vision' (1970: 64). As Law (2004) argues, the research infrastructure sets limits on what it is possible to know, and so research framed by reductionist models of literacy can only tell us about literacy as framed in those terms; the 'truths' it generates work to uphold an adherence to the model. In England we see this as funding streams favour studies that assess impact through measurable outcomes. The evidence generated is all too easily used to steer policy. This retrenchment means that certain ways of understanding literacy stick, gain credence and inform an 'overcoded' literacy curriculum (Masny & Cole, 2012) that is unable to respond to changing contexts.

In this volume, we have presented studies that draw from qualitative methods, often ethnographic in texture, describing literacies that are hard to gauge in terms of fixed measurable outcomes: literacies that are mobile, fluid, multimodal and meshed with other social practices. We focus on the everyday, the transgressive and the playful. As Williams suggests in this volume, we can no longer easily know where one text ends and another begins or even who wrote what; texts are constantly reworked and remixed, writing shades into design, and reading is not only dialogic (Ivey & Johnstone, 2013) but often has a ludic dimension. Below we reflect on what such studies bring to our understanding of literacies, with a particular focus on the theme of (im)materiality—a theme that has emerged in many of the chapters. Next we consider why it is important to take stock of our conceptualisation of literacy and what this might mean for curricula. Finally, we identify a series of foundational principles, some already well discussed and some new, which we argue should inform curriculum and pedagogy in the future. These we present as a Charter for Literacy Education.

MULTIPLE CONTEXTS FOR LITERACY: THE (IM)MATERIALITY OF LITERACY

The significance of context to a social model of literacy, and the focus on literacy events as 'observable instantiations of practice', was underlined in our opening comments. As the chapters in this volume illustrate, however, it can be difficult to isolate the boundaries of specific events, and contexts too are more often than not multiple and ambiguous. Digital technologies in these examples show us how complex the notion of the 'observable event' is; the boundaries and spaces of meaning-making become hard to define. Taking this further, we might then begin to question the porosity of context and the fuzziness of boundaries that previously seemed clear. Thus when a child is reading to her teacher, for example, the understandings she has may reach back into other contexts, joining on to different experiences and contexts to establish meanings (see Merchant, this volume).

Defining and describing the contextual spaces that the children playing *MinecraftEdu* inhabit (Burnett & Bailey, this volume) is problematic. Are they in the classroom or in a virtual world? If they inhabit a space designed at home and enter this space from the classroom, what is the context then? When the young people Davies describes in Chapter 5 are in a bar, are they also in another space with friends online? If their friends contribute text messages to a conversation that is happening in a bar, how do we describe that context? These are not insignificant questions. The blurring of boundaries between public and private and the resulting ambiguities of context raise complex issues, as we see in media stories about miscommunications and libellous or racist tweets (BBC, 2013; Urquhart, 2013).

A number of authors in this volume attempt to conceptualise provisionality and contingency in terms of the reflexive relationships between the material and immaterial dimensions of practices—a reflexivity encapsulated in the idea of (im)materiality (Burnett, 2014; Burnett et al., 2014). This includes an interest in what happens at the interface between on- and offscreen but also all the other relations, materially present and absent, that are brought into play whenever we make meaning. Different chapters foreground different (im)material relationships. Some (Burnett & Bailey; Davies) share an interest in how material and embodied dimensions of literacy practices are significant in the hybrid on/offscreen spaces that are generated as individual preferences, orientations, experiences, feelings and intentions coalesce through improvisation with digital tools.

Similarly, Williams considers the relationships between immaterial practices and the material manifestations of literacy (texts, equipment, bodies, gestures), while for Lemphane and Prinsloo, (im)material relations foreground political and economic dimensions as well as the sociocultural: we see how children's immaterial imaginings are shaped by their access to material resources. For Rowsell and Burgess, individuals' ability to negotiate the movement between immaterial and material and back again is important; for them, supporting the process of materialising the immaterial is a key part of literacy learning. A focus on (im)material relations also brings into sharper focus the diverse global flows that pattern literacy practices as threads of practices that have originated elsewhere play into and through literacy practices. So we see how *IMVU*, *Peppa Pig* and *Minecraft-Edu* are constituted in particular ways and how individuals and groups write themselves into being in transnational sites like Facebook.

A focus on (im)materiality, then, highlights relationships between embodiment, materiality and affect. The objects that mediate texts are important to how we make meanings, as are the ways our bodies interact with those objects and the feelings that shape or are shaped by those interactions. It highlights, as Burnett and Bailey illustrate, how composition and production are not just driven by the kinds of linear intentions associated with preplanned design but also how improvisations in different modes create new possibilities as material and immaterial spark each other in different ways and generate new 'lines of flight' (Deleuze & Guattari, 1987). Taking together the different (im)material relations described above, we can see how multiple relationships interweave as we make meaning. Local and situated literacy events, which we might perhaps more usefully see as 'happenings' or 'encounters', are rhizomatically linked to what *is* happening 'here' and *has* happened elsewhere. Any encounter with texts then sits momentarily at the nexus of a range of diverse ideas, experiences, discourses and flows, any of which may be called into play or shape the kinds of meanings made and taken in the here and now (Burnett, forthcoming). In her chapter, Davies describes relationships between the material and immaterial as 'kaleido-scopic,' which helps us to see how the local and global, the now, then and next, the discursive and the felt are imbricated with one another.

Of course the tools we use to convey meaning have always shaped the kinds of meanings made (Haas, 1996), and meanings have always been inflected by economics, society, culture, embodiment, affect and so on. (Im)material relations are not new. The affordances of digital media and digital devices—perhaps highlighted through research methodologies that capture interactions between bodies and things—bring (im)material relations into sharper focus. These relations, however, are always there and always, we suggest, need to be taken into account in discussions about the breadth, scope and quality of literacy in educational institutions. This, we suggest, is particularly pressing in the current policy context as explored below.

REFRAMING LITERACY IN POLICY AND PRACTICE

In Chapter 1 we outlined how national and regional responses to the changing 'translocal' environment tend to be framed within broad state-ments of pedagogical or curricular intent, linked, for example, to confi-dence, agency, ethics, community, participation, critical thinking, inquiry and problem solving. These are aspirational principles that have been espoused by literacy researchers and educationalists for many years (e.g., Comber, 2005; Janks, 2009; Larson & Marsh, 2005). The problem arises when policy statements around 'literacy' are not clearly articulated with policies around new technologies or, worse, seem to contradict these prin-ciples. In England, for example, this manifests in the contrast between the discourses of transformation associated with '21st-century literacies' and those of accountability and alphabetic competences pervading policy state-ments around 'literacy'. These contradictions are problematic. If literacy is conflated with broad pedagogical moves or, worse, extracted from debates about innovative or 'transformative' education, we miss learning from the *specific* contribution of literacies research and making *specific* recommen-dations for formulating literacy education in the contemporary context and in years to come.

In other cases we do see digital media integrated within curriculum frameworks. The Common Core State Standards in the US (National Gov-ernors Association, 2012) integrate references to digital media and tech-nology into standards for English and Language Arts (with an emphasis on critical appraisal, information gathering and presentation) but, at the time of writing, the common assessment systems have yet to be developed. The Australian Curriculum's English (ACARA, 2013) goes further. It specifies a cross curricula 'capability' informed by a social view of language, providing a framework that supports critical and creative engagement with a range of media. Specifically it requires schools to address multimodal textual design using a range of software and body language; gestures and other modes are explicitly addressed (see Exley & Mills, 2012, for discussion of theoretical underpinnings). However, the standardised National Assessment Program (NAPLAN) in Australia, which is tagged to school accountability, focuses on much narrower definitions of print literacy (Lu & Cross, 2012; Mills, 2008), and this tends to distort the emphasis of teachers' and schools' literacy provision (Comber, 2012). It is beyond the scope of this chapter to explore the continuities and contrasts between curricula and assessment frameworks across the world, but we do feel that such comparisons are useful. Assessment frameworks and associated accountability systems have significant implications for how curricula are interpreted. As we argue below, revisions do not just require the insertion of the digital into the curriculum but call for a more expansive reworking of literacy curriculum, pedagogy and assessment regimes to better recognise the scope and complexity of meaning-making. For us, it is not just new texts that we need to integrate but new understandings about literacy more generally.

Teasing out where literacy as a curriculum area, or at least a curriculum concern, sits with these aspirations for the future is complex. Debates about what constitutes literacy—and what should be included in a literacy curriculum—have ebbed and flowed. Multimodality and digital media have been dominant themes in the last decade, themes developed through the chapters in this volume. However, despite broad consensus within the New Literacies community that the curriculum should address these areas there is less agreement on what the particular contribution of 'literacy' should be, if indeed the term *literacy* is still useful in framing policy, curriculum and pedagogy. Researchers in the field of New Literacies have argued in the past for retaining the word *literacy* for the written word, whether in print or digital form (Marsh, 2003; Merchant, 2007)—for what Kress (1997) called 'lettered representation'. Over recent years, however, literacies research has drifted ever further away from this. Sheridan and Rowsell in their book *Design Literacies* (2010) argue for engagement with a wide range of modes and media, whilst others have developed models and ideas that decentre the text (Burnett & Merchant, 2014; Leander & Boldt, 2013; Norris & Jones, 2005). In moves designed to highlight affective, material and embodied dimensions of meaning-making, such work has explored the role of feelings, objects and bodies in interactions around and through texts, and we see examples of this in the exploration of (im)materialities in this volume. We could argue that, in much contemporary work in the field, printed and screen-based texts are not simply *decentred* from literacies research but *erased*, or that literacy is defined so broadly that it seems to incorporate any product, event or medium.

We have much sympathy with this work, as is illustrated in the chapters selected for this volume, and are committed to the idea of literacies as living, being, making and meshed with other social practices. However this perspective is problematic, particularly for education. It begs the question, 'Where does literacy begin and end?' On the one hand we have literacy policies that reduce literacy to a decontextualised set of skills, and on the other we have literacy researchers whose interest seems to be moving ever further away from written texts. How then does and should new literacies research speak to literacy policy? And what is the mandate, if there is one, for literacy as a separate concern in the curriculum?

As a basis for our Charter for Literacy Education, we identify a number of dimensions of literacy described in the chapters in this volume. These are presented in the first column of Table 10.1 and contrasted in the second column with qualities we might associate with school literacy as sanctioned and recognised by print-focused accountability regimes.

Whilst assessment regimes and accountability structures often ignore the characteristics listed in the first column, it is important to note that we are not suggesting that these characteristics do not *apply* to literacy as experienced in educational settings. Research exploring how children and young people negotiate school literacies highlights that these things are very much part of how children make meanings in classrooms (Burnett, 2013; Maybin, 2006; Nespor,1997), and curricula and pedagogies need to take them into account.

A CHARTER FOR LITERACY EDUCATION

In recent years, there have been a number of influential proposals from educators and researchers working in the field of New Literacies for structuring learning about meaning-making that recognise new communicative practices (e.g. Cope & Kalantzis, 1999; Jenkins et al, 2006; Lankshear & Knobel, 2010), and work on in this book builds on this. Here we add to these proposals by foregrounding recent research-based notions of *literacy* that are important to consider in the ongoing national and transnational debates about curriculum and pedagogy. These are conceived of as a set of principles that could usefully inform policy and curriculum development and reform. We present these as a Charter for Literacy Education (see Table 10.2)—foundational principles that can be interpreted differently to suit different local circumstances and which are flexible enough to respond to changing communicative practices and possibilities in the future. In doing so, we restate calls made previously by influential literacy

Table 10.1   Literacy in Life and School

Literacy in Experience and Action	Literacy in Print-Based School Contexts
Literacies as multiple Literacies are used and learned in everyday social settings. Individuals and groups use meaning making resources in purposeful activity. Differences between communities reflect variances in access and norms of use.	**Literacy as singular** Literacy is a set of specific skills and understandings that are taught. Intervention may be needed to 'compensate' for differences in prior experience. Success is defined in terms of individual developmental progress.
Multiple modes and media Communicative practices draw on a variety of modes. They require orchestration of print and digital media and are loosely bounded as meaning-making draws on extratextuality and intertextuality.	**Paper-based texts** Verbal written texts are prioritised. These are often decontextualised to emphasise the structural features of print literacy. Accuracy and correctness are given priority over meaning.
Provisionality Texts are ephemeral and provisional and often rewritten or remixed over time. These processes do not take place in bounded time periods.	**Fixity** Finished or 'polished' texts are produced within set time-space periods in specific lessons. There is limited revision and texts are developed in a linear fashion.
Multiple authorship Collaborative and individual contributions are valued and easily facilitated. Contributions can be made within shared time-space sites or across boundaries.	**Individual authorship** Individual contributions are highly valued enabling individuated assessment. Collaboration and unclear authorship may be penalised.
Objects, bodies and affect Literacy has a material and embodied dimension that is significant to the subjective experience of literacy.	**Cognitive skills and understandings** Literacy is a set of objective skills that are learned cognitively, determined by notions of correctness or appropriacy.
Social Literacy has a social function and is experienced within relationships with others. Meaning-making practices are participatory.	**Individual** Literacy is about the individual construction of meaning. It is an individual achievement with fixed meanings and single authorship.
Socially situated Meaning-making practices are significant to the diverse ways we position ourselves and others and are positioned by others in the present, past and future.	**Future-orientated** Literacy learning is necessary for later economic success and civic participation. Literacy learning is preparation, something that will be used 'later'.
Unruly Literacy is about experimentation and innovation.	**Ordered** Literacy is about adhering to a set of established rules.
Changing New meaning-making practices will continually emerge in response to technological, economic, social and cultural shifts.	**Fixed** Literacy involves a set of defined and durable competencies.

educators and researchers but also foreground considerations that emerge from reading across the studies presented in this collection.

Whilst the provenance for this charter is our review of New Literacies, these recommendations do not relate solely to the digital. Recommendations are mapped against the dimensions of literacy summarised in Table 10.1. They are intended to support what we describe as an 'empowering' literacy education.

Table 10.2 A Charter for Literacy Education

Dimensions of literacy in experience and action	Qualities of Empowering Literacy Education
Literacies as multiple	1. Empowering literacy education involves a recognition of the linguistic, social and cultural resources learners bring to the classroom, whilst encouraging them to diversify the range of communicative practices in which they participate.
Multiple modes and media	2. Empowering literacy education involves understanding how socially recognisable meanings are produced through the orchestration of semiotic resources.
Provisionality	3. Empowering literacy education involves a range of activity that includes improvisation and experimentation as well as the production of polished texts.
Multiple authorship	4. Empowering literacy education values collaboration in text-making and is emancipatory in the way is facilitates access to others' texts and ideas.
Objects, bodies and affect	5. Empowering literacy education involves a recognition of the affective, embodied and material dimensions of meaning-making.
Social	6. Empowering literacy education involves engaging with others in a variety of different ways.
Socially situated	7. Empowering literacy education involves exploring how you position yourself and how you are positioned by others through texts.
Unruly	8. Empowering literacy education occurs within safe, supportive spaces that promote experimentation.
Changing	9. Empowering literacy education involves developing an understanding of the changing nature of meaning making.

1. **An empowering literacy education involves a recognition of the linguistic, social and cultural resources learners bring to the classroom whilst encouraging them to diversify the range of communicative practices in which they participate.**

If literacies are multiple (New London Group, 1996), then educational institutions need to adopt a 'strength orientation' (see Chapter 3) or 'asset model' (e.g. . see Mackey, 2002). which recognises the social, cultural and communicative resources that children and young people bring with them to classrooms. For the most part, the children and young people described in these chapters operate with confidence and skill, in using mobiles, computer games, video cameras and story apps and moving rapidly between different registers, languages, media and so on. At the same time, as the chapters explore, children and young people approach these practices in different ways, and as Lemphane and Prinsloo's chapter highlights, their uses may reproduce inequalities rather than eradicating them. We must avoid assuming children and young people have an innate ability to use new technologies or make meanings associated with social, cultural or economic capital. We need to identify the barriers—economic, physical, social, cultural and institutional—to using different forms of meaning-making and challenge these at all levels: within policy, amongst educators and directly with learners.

2. **An empowering literacy education involves understanding how socially recognisable meanings are produced through the orchestration of semiotic resources.**

The chapters in this volume contribute to an understanding of literacy as the orchestration of different resources for meaning-making. Children and young people need to be equipped to select, critique and use different modes and media and use them creatively, persuasively and for different purposes. Building on previous arguments for multimodality and multiple literacies, however, we also need to enable children and young people to traverse and combine media. A literacy curriculum must: provide opportunities for children and young people to draw from a range of resources—digital and other; help students to articulate transmedia connections; foster understandings of how texts draw on the affordances of different modes; and provide a metalanguage that is helpful in the appreciation of how texts work.

3. **An empowering literacy education involves a range of activity that includes improvisation and experimentation as well as the production of polished texts.**

In this volume, the authors show how creativity is generated through the improvisational quality of the practices described. Children and young people are not engaged in neatly planned tasks, but schemes unfold as they play or improvise. We need to create environments and provide resources that allow children to set their own agendas and are flexible enough to accommodate possibilities that emerge through children's engagement with meaningful projects.

4. Empowering literacy education values collaboration in text making and is emancipatory in the way it facilitates access to others' texts and ideas.

Institutions need to find ways of valuing collaborative work and to resist the dogma of individualised assessment policies. Whilst assessment is important, the collaborative work that we see as unproblematic in many other contexts outside education needs to be valued in school contexts. The benefits of learning from others, of working on texts together, of embedding links and sources from multiple sites are all skills that the young are likely to need in their future lives if not in school.

5. An empowering literacy education involves a recognition of the affective, embodied and material dimensions of meaning-making.

The chapters in this volume highlight the significance of embodiment, materiality and affect which, we would suggest, have been underplayed in official accounts of literacy. This emphasises that meaning-making is inflected by what we feel, what has just happened and who we are with, as well as how we are positioned by those people and things around us. Rather than aiming for a dispassionate objective literacy curriculum, we need to allow for students to explore what texts mean to them and share emotional, personal and situated responses. We also need to be alert to how architecture, resources and relationships are significant to meanings made and support students in negotiating and reviewing these. As Lewis (2013) explores in her work on 'emotions as mediated action', such work can lead to the kind of critical engagement explored below.

6. An empowering literacy education involves engaging with others in a variety of different ways.

The chapters in this book echo influential studies that have highlighted the collaborative and participatory dimension of engagement with new technologies (Jenkins et al., 2006; Lankshear & Knobel, 2010). At the same time they have explored how on/offline communities dissolve and hybridise, suggesting that the structured approaches to collaboration often encountered in schools may not adequately address the needs of work across the hybrid contexts described above. We would echo those, therefore, who have argued for looser models of collaboration: examples include Gee's take on 'affinity spaces' (Gee, 2004), whereby individuals collaborate around areas of shared interest and then disperse again, and Engestrom's (2009) notion of 'wildfire activities', through which people come together in apparently ad hoc ways from time to time to share, critique, resource and act.

7. An empowering literacy education involves exploring how you position yourself and how you are positioned by others through texts.

Literacy education has to be about more than facilitating economic growth and competitiveness, as important as these may be. It needs to support our present and future participation in a range of communities and activities. This means being aware of a range of meaning-making opportunities and being confident in their use, reviewing how we position ourselves and how we are positioned by others as we do so. This includes a critical engagement with digital environments. The research presented in this book (e.g., Davies; Lemphane & Prinsloo; Rowsell & Burgess) highlights the need for education to support critical engagement to help children and young people understand how texts and related materials position readers, players and consumers. Given that so much of life is played out online, this critical dimension needs to go beyond the text analysis often associated with critical literacy to include a focus on how individuals can and want to be presented online, the kinds of communities they participate in and how these relate to 'broader social and broader textual networks' (Burnett & Merchant, 2011: 50). We endorse Greenhow and Robelia's call for educators to 'help students enact legal, ethical, responsible, safe and advantageous online community practices' (Greenhow & Robelia, 2009: 136).

8. An empowering literacy education occurs within safe, supportive spaces that promote experimentation.

An argument for an expansive, student-led exploratory curriculum could lead us to question whether schools are the best places to support the literacy education of children and young people. For us, schools do have an important role to play, not least *because* they bring together individuals who would not normally come together to engage in a range of practices they may not normally encounter. Educational settings, at their best, offer safe environments and resources where children and young people can experiment or 'tinker' (DiGiacomo, Gutierrez & Schwartz, 2013), supported and challenged by their peers and adults: 'being together' can provide opportunities to resource, critique, evaluate, review, try out, think and create.

9. An empowering literacy education involves developing an understanding of the changing nature of meaning-making.

We need to recognise that the affordances and demands of texts are likely to remain in flux, and this has implications for the any literacy curriculum. The chapters in this book suggest a range of competencies and sensitivities that should be supported: rhetoric and design (Rowsell & Burgess; Williams), the negotiation of new digital objects (Merchant) and aesthetic and critical perspectives (Beavis). As new technologies and new practices become commonplace, we need to continually review the kinds of learning that are needed and prioritised.

CONCLUSION

Like previous writing on new literacies, much of the work in this volume highlights the need to redefine and re-frame literacy. It challenges established ideas relating, for example, to literature (Beavis), authorship (Williams), collaboration (Burnett & Bailey), emergent literacy practices (Merchant) and literacy in the early years (Wohlwend & Buchholz). Such reframings, however, can only ever be temporary. Rather than trying to arrive at a new curriculum orthodoxy—a new fixity—we need to continually weigh the curriculum in terms of everyday life, and this has radical implications for the systems through which educational institutions are held to account.

Judgments about the efficacy of literacy education must work to *open up possibilities* rather than close them down. Systems of accountability need to be built on understandings of literacy that are relevant to individuals' active, critical, creative, safe and economically secure participation in civic and social lives. This means recognising the work that teachers and schools do to support the relational and affective dimensions of learning. It needs to be recognised that these things are not easily measured, and we need to be prepared to follow the lead of those countries who have ditched simplistic indicators of attainment for purposes of accountability in favour of informed, considered debate about education. Debates around the future of literacy in education need to be inclusive and ongoing if we are to recognise and take advantage of the 'lines of flight' generated through experimentation by teachers and the children and young people with whom they work. Wohlwend and Buchholz's 'strength orientation' is just as important in looking at the work of teachers and schools as in looking at the work of their students. This means being alert to and learning from new literacy practices in everyday life.

The chapters in this volume describe an array of practices in selected sites and are not intended as a representative sample of literacies across the globe. There are many dimensions of literacy and lives as experienced and in action that are not considered here, and many policy contexts remain undescribed. These chapters do, however, illustrate why it is so important to develop curricula and pedagogies that see meaning-making as a convergence of the rhetorical and aesthetic, the embodied, material and affective, as well as the social, cultural and economic. Our Charter for Literacy Education has at its heart a respect for the creativity and resourcefulness of individuals and groups—a creativity and resourcefulness that is often missing from official accounts of literacy education. It suggests that decisions about resources, curriculum and assessment frameworks need to be underpinned by an ethic of care and social justice that sees literacy as a deeply human activity inseparable from relationships, ideologies and the politics of power.

Bibliography

Aarseth, E. (2001). Computer games studies, year one. *Game studies*, vol. 1, no. 1. Retrieved from: http://www.gamestudies.org/0101/editorial.html

Aberton, H. (2012). Material enactments of identities and learning in everyday community practices: Implications for pedagogy. *Pedagogy, Culture & Society*, vol. 20, no.1, pp. 113–136.

Abrams, F. (2012). US idea of cultural literacy and key facts a child should know arrives in UK. *Guardian Newspaper*, 15 October, 2012. Retrieved from: http://www.theguardian.com/education/2012/oct/15/hirsch-core-knowledge-curriculum-review

ACTS (2013). *The assessment and teaching of 21st century skills*. Retrieved from: http://atc21s.org/

Alper, M. (2013). Developmentally appropriate new media literacies: Supporting cultural competencies and social skills in early childhood education. *Journal of Early Childhood Literacy*, vol. 3, no.2, pp. 175–196.

Anderson, B. (1983). Imagined Communities: Reflections on the Origins and Spread of Nationalism. London: Verso.

Appadurai, A. (1996). *Modernity at large: Cultural dimensions of globalization*. Minneapolis: Minnesota University Press.

Apperley, T., & Beavis, C. (2013). A model for critical games literacy. *E-learning and Digital Media*, vol.10, no.1, pp. 1–10.

Auld, G., Snyder, I., & Henderson, M. (2012). Using mobile phones as placed resources for literacy learning in a remote indigenous community in Australia. *Language and Education*, vol. 26, no. 4, pp. 279–296.

Australian Curriculum and Reporting Authority (ACARA). (2013). *The Australian curriculum*. Retrieved from: http://www.australiancurriculum.edu.au/

Bakhtin, M. M. (1981). *The dialogic imagination: Four essays*. M. Holquist, Ed., C. Emerson & M. Holquist, Trans. Austin: University of Texas Press.

Bakhtin, M. M. (1986). *Speech genres and other late essays*. C. Emerson & M. Holquist, Eds., V. W. McGee, Trans. Austin: University of Texas Press.

Bakhtin, M. (1999). *Problems of Dostoevsky's poetics*. C. Emerson, Trans. Minnesota: University of Minnesota Press.

Barton, D., & Hamilton, M. (1998). *Local literacies: Reading and writing in one community*. London: Routledge.

Barton, D. 2007. *Literacy: An introduction to the ecology of written language*. (2nd ed.). Oxford and Cambridge, MA: Blackwell.

Barton, D., Ivanic, R., Appleby, Y., Hodge, R., & Tusting, K. (2007). *Literacy, lives and learning*. London: Routledge.

Bazalgette, C. (2010). *Teaching media in primary schools*. London: Sage.

BBC News England, updated online 9 April 16:57. Retrieved from: http://www.bbc.co.uk/news/uk-england-22083032

Beavis, C. (2013). Multiliteracies in the wild: Learning from computer games. In G. Merchant, J. Gillen, J. Marsh, & J. Davies (Eds.), *Virtual literacies: Interactive spaces for children and young people*. New York and London: Routledge.

Beavis, C., & Charles, C. (2007). Would the real girl gamer please stand up? Gender, LAN cafes and the reformulation of the girl gamer. *Gender and Education*, vol. 19, no. 6, pp. 691–705.

Beavis, C., OMara, J., &. McNeice, L. (Eds.). (2012). *Digital games: Literacy in action*. Adelaide: Wakefield Press.

Berger, R., & McDougall J. (2013). Reading videogames as (authorless) literature. *Literacy*, vol. 47, no. 3, pp.142–149.

Black, R. (2009). English-language learners, fan communities, and 21st century skills. *Journal of Adolescent & Adult Literacy*, vol. 52, no. 8, pp. 688–697.

Black, R., & Reich, S. (2013). A sociocultural approach to exploring virtual worlds. In G. Merchant, J. Gillen, J. Marsh, & J. Davies (Eds.), *Virtual literacies: Interactive spaces for children and young people*. New York and London: Routledge.

Blackman, L. (2012). *Immaterial bodies: Affect, embodiment mediation*. London: Sage.

Bloch, G. (2009). *The toxic mix: Whats wrong with South Africas schools and how to fix it*. Cape Town: Tafelberg.

Blommaert, J. (2005). Situating language rights: English and Swahili in Tanzania revisited. *Journal of Sociolinguistics*, vol. 9, no. 3, pp.390–417.

Blommaert, J., & Rampton, B. (2011). Language and superdiversity. *Diversities*, vol. 13, no. 2, pp. 1–21.

Bolter, J., & Grusin, R. (2000), *Remediation: Understanding new media*. Cambridge, MA: MIT Press.

boyd, d. (2006). Friends, friendsters, and top 8: Writing community into being on social network sites. *First Monday*, vol.11, no.12, pp.1–13. Retrieved from: http://firstmonday.org/htbin/cgiwrap/bin/ojs/index.php/fm/article/view/1418/1336

Bourdieu, P. (1990). *The logic of practice*, R.Nice, Trans. Cambridge, UK: Polity Press.

Bouvier, G. (2012). How Facebook users select identity categories for self presentation. *Journal of Multicultural Discourses*, vol. 7, no. 1, pp.37–57.

Bradford, C. (2010). Looking for my corpse: Video games and player positioning. *Australian Journal of Language and Literacy*, vol. 33, no. 1, pp. 54–64.

Brandt, D., & Clinton, K. (2002). Limits of the local: Expanding perspectives on literacy as a social practice. *Journal of Literacy Research*, vol. 34, no. 3, pp. 337–356.

Bruns, A. (2008). *Blogs, Wikipedia, second life, and beyond*. London: Peter Lang.

Burgess, A. (2010). The use of space-time to construct identity and context. Ethnography and Education, vol. 5, no. 1, pp. 117–131.

Burn, A., & Parker, D. (2003). *Analysing media texts*. London: Continuum.

Burnett, C. (2010). Technology and literacy in early childhood educational settings: A review of research. *Journal of Early Childhood Literacy*, vol. 10, no. 3, pp. 247–270.

Burnett, C. (2011). The (im)materiality of educational space: Interactions between material, connected and textual dimensions of networked technology use in schools. *E-Learning and Digital Media*, vol. 8, no. 3, pp. 214–227.

Burnett, C. (2014). Investigating pupils' interactions around digital texts: a spatial perspective on the 'classroom-ness' of digital literacy practices in schools. *Educational Review*, vol. 66, no. 2, pp. 192–209.

Burnett, C. (forthcoming). *(Im)materialising literacies*. In K. Pahl & J. Rowsell (Eds.), The Routledge handbook of literacy studies. London: Routledge.

Burnett, C., & Merchant, G. (2011). Is there a space for critical literacy in the context of social media? *English Teaching, Practice and Critique*, vol. 10, no. 1, pp. 41–57.

Burnett, C., & Merchant, G. (2012). Learning, literacies and new technologies: the current context and future possibilities. In J. Larson, & J. Marsh (Eds.), *The handbook of early literacy*. London: Sage.

·Burnett, C. & Merchant, G. (2014). Points of View: reconceptualising literacies through an exploration of adult and child interactions in a virtual world. *Journal of Research in Reading*, vol. 37, no. 1, pp. 36–50.

Burnett, C., Merchant, G., Pahl, K., & Rowsell, J. (2014). The (im)materiality of literacy: The significance of subjectivity to new literacies research. *Discourse: Studies in the Cultural Politics of Education*, vol. 35, no. 1, pp. 90–103.

Caron, A. H., & Caronia, L. (2007). *Moving cultures: Mobile communication in everyday life*. Montreal: McGill-Queens University Press.

Carr, D., Buckingham, D., Burn, A., & Schott, G. (2006). *Computer games: Text, narrative and play*. Cambridge, UK: Cambridge University Press.

Carrington, V. (2005). The uncanny: Digital texts and literacy. *Language and Education*, vol. 19, no. 6, pp .467–482.

Clark, H. (2003). Pointing and placing. In Kitta, S. (Ed.), *Pointing: Where language, culture, and cognition meet*. Hillsdale NJ: Erlbaum.

Cohen, M., Hadley, M., & Frank, M. (2010). *Young children, apps & iPad*. New York: Michael Cohen Group. Retrieved from: http://mcgrc.com/publications/publications/

Collier, S. (2006). Global assemblages. *Theory, Culture & Society*, vol. 23, no. 2–3, pp. 379–381.

Comber, B. (2012). Mandated literacy assessment and the reorganisation of teachers work: federal policy, local effects. *Critical Studies in Education*, vol. 53, no. 2, pp. 119–136.

Comber B., & Kamler, B. (2005). *Turn-around pedagogies: Literacy interventions for at-risk students*. New Town, New South Wales: Primary English Teaching Association.

Cope, B., & Kalantzis, M. (Eds.). (1999). *Multiliteracies: Literacy learning and the design of social futures*. London: Macmillan.

Crook, C. (2012). The digital native in context: Tensions associated with importing Web 2.0 practices into the school setting. *Oxford Review of Education*, vol. 38, no. 1, pp.63–80.

Danath, J., & boyd, d. (2004). Public displays of connection. *BT Technology Journal*, vol. 22, no. 4, pp. 71–82.

Davies, J. (2004). Negotiating femininities on-line. *Gender and Education*, vol. 16, no. 1, pp. 35–50.

Davies, J. (2005). Nomads and tribes: On line meaning-making and the development of new literacies. In Marsh, J., & Millard, E. (Eds.), *Popular literacies, childhood and schooling*. London: Routledge/Falmer.

Davies, J. (2007). Display, identity and the everyday: Self-presentation through online image sharing. *Discourse: Studies in the Cultural Politics of Education*, vol. 28, no .4, pp.549–564.

Davies, J. (2013). Trainee hairdressers uses of Facebook as a community of gendered literacy practice. *Pedagogy, Culture and Society*, vol. 21, no. 1, pp. 147–169.

Davies, J., & Merchant, G. (2009). *Web 2.0 for schools: Learning and social participation*. New York: Peter Lang.

Davies, J., & Merchant, G. (2013). Digital literacy and teacher education. In P. Benson & A. Chik (Eds.), *Popular culture, pedagogy and teacher education: International perspectives*. London: Routledge.

DEFT. (2012). *Using hand-held devices to develop digital literacy.* Retrieved from: http://www.digitalfutures.org/section/4–1-case-studies-in-school-settings/ ?table_of_content_post_id=87

De Block, L., & Buckingham, D. (2007). *Global children, global media: Migration, media, and childhood.* New York: Palgrave Macmillan.

De Jong, M. T., & Bus, A. G. (2003). How well suited are electronic books to supporting literacy? *Journal of Early Childhood Literacy,* vol. 3, no. 2, pp.147–164.

Deleuze, G., & Guattari, F. (1987). *A thousand plateaus: Capitalism and schizophrenia.* London: Continuum.

Deloitte (2012). *Sub-Saharan Africa Mobile Observatory 2012: Report to Groupe Speciale Mobile Association (GSMA).* London: GMSA. Retrieved from: http://www.gsma.com/publicpolicy/wp-content/uploads/2013/01/gsma_ssamo_full_web_11_12–1.pdf

Department of Children, Schools and Families (DCSF). (2009). *Your child, your schools, our future: Building a 21st century schools system.* Norwich, UK: The Stationery Office.

Deleuze, G., & Guattari, F. (1987). *A thousand plateaus: Capitalism and schizophrenia,* B. Massumi, Trans. Minneapolis: University of Minnesota Press.

DeLoache, J., & DeMendoza, O. (1987). Joint picturebook interactions of mothers and 1- year-old children. *British Journal of Developmental Psychology,* vol. 5, no. 2, pp. 111–123.

DiGiacomo, D., Gutierrez, K., & Schwartz, L. (2013). Relationships and tinkering: The generative power of the relationship as a tool for expansive literacies and learning. Literacy Research Association Conference, Dallas, Texas, 3–6 December 2013.

Dick, L. (2012). Riffing on the Pied Piper: Combining research and creativity. In A. Webb (Ed.), *Teaching literature in virtual worlds: Immersive learning in English studies.* New York: Routledge.

Dickens, C. (1859). *A tale of two cities.* London: Chapman and Hall.

Digital Media Awareness. (2010). *Digital literacy in Canada: From inclusion to transformation.* Digital Economy Strategy Consultation. Retrieved from: http://mediasmarts.ca/sites/default/files/pdfs/publication-report/full/digitalliteracypaper.pdf

Donehower, K., Hogg, C., & Schell, E. E. (2012). *Reclaiming the rural: Essays on literacy rhetoric, and pedagogy.* Carbondale, IL: Southern Illinois Press.

Durrant, C., & Green, B. (2000). Literacy and the new technologies in school education: Meeting the l(*IT*)eracy challenge? *Australian Journal of Language and Literacy,* vol. 23, no. 2, pp. 89–108.

Dyson, A. H. (1993). *Social worlds of children learning to write in an urban primary school.* New York: Teachers College Press.

Dyson, A. H. (2003). *The brothers and sisters learn to write: Popular literacies in childhood and school cultures.* New York: Teachers College Press.

Dyson, A. H. (2008). Staying in the (curricular) lines: Practice constraints and possibilities in childhood writing. *Written Communication,* vol. 25, no. 1, pp. 119–159.

Eggins, S., & Slade, D. (1997). *Analysing casual conversation.* London: Cassell.

Ellis, V., with Fox, C., & Street B. (2007). Why English? Rethinking the school subject. In V. Ellis, C. Fox, & B. Street (Eds.), *Rethinking English in schools.* London: Continuum.

Engestrom, Y. (2009). Wildfire activities: New patterns of mobility and learning. *Journal of Mobile and Blended Learning,* vol. 1, no. 2, pp. 1–2.

Exley, B., & Mills, K. (2012). Parsing the Australian English curriculum: Grammar, multimodality and cross-cultural texts. *Australian Journal of Language and Literacy,* vol. 35, no. 1, pp. 192–205.

Facebook Newsroom. (2013). Retrieved from: http://newsroom.fb.com/News

Facer, K. (2004). Savannah: A Futurelab prototype research report. Retrieved from: http://www2.futurelab.org.uk/resources/documents/project_reports/Savannah_research_report.pdf

Featherstone, M. (2006). Genealogies of the global. *Theory, Culture & Society*, vol. 23, no. 2–3, pp .367–399.

Fields, A. A., & Kafai, Y. B. (2010). Knowing and throwing mudballs, hearts, pies, and flowers: A connective ethnography of gaming practices. *Games and Culture*, vol. 5, no. 1, pp. 88–115.

Fleisch, B. (2008). *Primary education in crisis: Why South African schoolchildren underachieve in reading and mathematics.* Cape Town: Juta.

Flewitt, R., Nind, M., & Payler, J. (2009). "'If she's left with books she'll just eat them'": Considering inclusive multimodal practices. *Journal of Early Childhood Literacy*, vol. 9, no. 2, pp. 211–233.

Flood, J. (1977). Parental styles in reading episodes with young children. *The Reading Teacher*, Vol. 30, May, pp. 864–867.

Foucault, M. (1982). The subject and power. In H. Dreyfus & P. Rabinov (Eds.), *Beyond Structuralism and Hermeneutics.* Brighton, UK: Harvester.

Foucault, M. (1988). *Technologies of self.* Boston: The University of Massachusetts Press.

Freebody, P., Barton, G., & Chan, E. (2014). Literacy education. In C. Leung & B. V. Street (Eds.), *Handbook of English Language Studies.* London: Routledge.

Freebody, P., & Freiberg, J. (2008). Globalised literacy education: Intercultural trade in textual and cultural practice. In M. Prinsloo & M. Baynham (Eds.), *Literacies, global and local.* Amsterdam and Philadelphia: John Benjamins.

Fuchs, C. (2007). *Internet & society: Social theory in the information age.* London: Routledge.

Gallas, K. (1994). *The languages of learning: How children talk, write, dance, draw, and sing their understanding of the world.* New York: Teachers College Press.

Galloway, A. (2006). *Gaming: Essays in algorithmic culture.* Minneapolis: University of Minnesota Press.

Ge, X., Ruan, J., & Lu, X. (2012). Integrating information and communication technologies in literacy education in China. In C. Leung & J. Ruan (Eds.), *Historical, philosophical, & sociocultural perspectives on literacy teaching & learning in China.* New York: Springer.

Gee, J. P. (1991). *Sociolinguistics: Ideology in discourses.* London: Falmer Press.

Gee, J. P. (2003). *What videogames have to teach us about learning and literacy.* New York: Palgrave Macmillan.

Gee, J. P. (2004). *Situated language and learning: A critique of traditional schooling.* London: Routledge.

Gee, J. P. (2007). *What video games have to teach us about learning and literacy* (2nd ed.). New York: Palgrave MacMillan.

Gillen, J., & Merchant, G. (2013). From virtual histories to virtual literacies. In G. Merchant, J. Gillen, J. Marsh, J. & Davies (Eds.), *Virtual literacies: Interactive spaces for children and young people.* New York and London: Routledge.

Golding, W. (1954). *Lord of the flies.* London: Faber.

González, N., Moll, L. C., & Amanti, C. (Eds.). (2005). *Funds of knowledge: Theorizing practices in households, communities, and classrooms.* Mahwah, NJ: Erlbaum.

Green, B. (1999). The new literacy challenge? *Literacy Learning: Secondary Thoughts*, vol. 7, no. 1, pp. 36–46.

Green, B., & Beavis, C. (Eds.). (2012). *Literacy in 3D: An integrated perspective in theory and practice.* Melbourne: ACER Press.

Greenhow, C., & Robelia, B. (2009). Informal learning and identity formation in online social networks. *Learning, Media and Technology*, vol. 3, no. 2, pp. 119–140.

Gregory, E., Long, S., & Volk, D. (Eds.). (2004). *Many pathways to literacy: Young children learning with siblings, grandparents, peers and communities.* New York: Routledge Falmer.

Griffin Wolff, C. (1979). The Radcliffean gothic model: A form for feminine sexuality. *Modern Language Studies*, vol. 9, no. 3, pp. 98–114.

Gura, P., & Bruce, T. (1992). *Exploring learning: Young children and blockplay.* London: Paul Chapman.

Gutierrez, K. (2008). Developing a sociocritical literacy in the third space. *Reading Research Quarterly*, vol. 43, no. 2, pp.148–164.

Gutiérrez, K. D., & Rogoff, B. (2003). Cultural ways of learning: Individual traits or repertoires of practice. *Educational Researcher*, vol. 32, no. 5, pp. 19–25.

Haas, C. (1996). *Writing technology: Studies on the materiality of literacy.* Abingdon, UK: Routledge.

Hammersley, M., & Traianou, A. (2012). *Ethics and educational research. British Educational Research Association on-line resource.* Retrieved from: http://www.bera.ac.uk/category/keywords/ethics

Hammett, L., Van Kleeck, A., & Huberty, C. (2003). Patterns of parents extratextual interactions during book sharing with preschool children: A cluster analysis study. *Reading Research Quarterly*, vol. 38, no. 4, pp. 442–468.

Hannaford, J. (2012). Imaginative interaction with Internet games. *Literacy*, vol. 46, no. 1, pp. 25–32.

Harris, R. (1995). *Signs of writing*, London: Routledge.

Hayles, N. K. (1999). *How we became posthuman: Virtual bodies in cybernetics, literature, and informatics.* Chicago: University of Chicago Press.

Hayles, N. K. (2005). *My mother was a computer: Digital subjects and literary texts.* Chicago: University of Chicago Press.

Heath, S. B. (1983). *Ways with words.* Cambridge, UK: Cambridge University Press.

Heath, S. B., & Street, B. V. (2008). *Ethnography: Approaches to language and literacy research.* London: Routledge.

Held, D., McGrew, A., Goldblatt, D., & Perraton, J. (1999). *Global transformations: Politics, economics and culture.* Stanford CA: Stanford University Press.

Hind, D. (2010). *The return of the public.* London: Verso.

Hine, C. (2000). *Virtual ethnography.* London: Sage.

Hodge, R., & Tripp, D. (1986). *Social semiotics.* Cambridge, UK: Polity.

Horst, H., Herr-Stephenson, B., & Robinson, L. (2010). Media ecologies. In Ito, M., Baumer, S., Bittanti, M. , boyd, d., cody, D., Herr-Stephenson, B., Horst, H. A., Lange, P. G., Mehendran, D., Martinez, K. Z., Pascoe, C., Perkoe, D., Robinson, L., Sims, C. & Tripp, L., et al. (Eds.). *Hanging out, messing around, and geeking out: Kids living and learning with new media.* Cambridge, MA: MIT Press.

Hyland, K. (2002). Genre, language, context and literacy. *Annual Review of Applied Linguistics*, vol. 2, pp. 113–135.

Hymes, D. (1996). *Ethnography, linguistics, narrative inequality: Toward an understanding of voice.* London: Taylor and Francis.

Husserl, E. (1913). *Ideas: General introduction to pure phenomenology.* W. R. Boyce Gibson, Trans. London and New York: Collier, Macmillan.

Ihde, D. (1990). *Technology and the Lifeworld: From garden to earth.* Bloomington and Indianapolis: Indiana State University Press.

Ihde, D. (1993). *Postphenomenology: Essays in the postmodern context.* Evanston, IL: Northwestern University Press.

IMVU. (2014). Retrieved from: IMVU.com

Interactive Games and Entertainment Association (iGEA). (2012). *Digital Australia (DA12)*. Retrieved from: http://www.igea.net/category/research-2/igea-research-reports/

Ito, M. (2011). Machinima in a fanvid ecology. *Journal of Visual Culture*, vol. 10, no .1 pp. 51–54.

Jagex Games Studio (2001). *Runescape*. Retrieved from: http://www.runescape.com/

Jenkins, H., Clinton, K., Purushotma, R., Robinson, A. J., & Weigel, M. (2006). *Confronting the challenges of participatory culture: Media education for the 21st century*. Chicago: MacArthur Foundation.

Jenkins, H. (2006). *Convergence culture: Where old and new media collide*. New York: New York University Press.

Jewitt, C. (2008). *Technology, literacy, learning: A multimodality approach*. London: Routledge.

Johnstone, K. (1981). *Impro: Improvisation and the theatre*. London: Methuen.

Kallinikos, J., Leonardi, P., & Nardi, B. (2012). The challenge of materiality: Origins, scope, and prospects. In P. Leonardi, B. Nardi, & J. Kallinikos (Eds.), *Materiality and organizing: Social interaction in a technological world*. Oxford, UK: Oxford University Press.

Kamler, B. (1997). Text as body: Body as text. *Discourse: Studies in Cultural Politics of Education*, vol. 18, no. 3, pp. 369–387.

Kell, C. (2011). Inequalities and crossings: Literacy and the spaces in-between. *International Journal of Educational Development*, vol. 31, no. 6, pp. 606–613.

Kendon, A. (2004). *Gesture: Visible action as utterance*. Cambridge, UK: Cambridge University Press.

Kirkorian, H., & Pempek, T. (2013). Toddlers and touch screens; Potential for early learning? *Zero to Three*, vol. 33, no. 4, pp. 32–35.

Kleifgen, J. (2005). ISO 9002 as literacy practice: Coping with quality-control documents in a hi-tech company. *Reading Research Quarterly*, vol. 40, no. 4, pp. 450–468.

Knobel, M., & Lankshear, C. (2007). Online memes, affinities, and cultural production. In M. Knobel & C. Lankshear (Eds.), *A new literacies sampler*. London: Peter Lang.

Knobel, M. & Lankshear, C. (Eds.). (2010). *DIY media: Creating, sharing and learning with new technologies*. New York: Peter Lang.

Kress, G. (1997). *Before writing: Rethinking the paths to literacy*. London: Routledge.

Kress, G. (2002). English for an era of instability: Aesthetics, ethics, creativity and design. *English in Australia*, vol. 134, no. 3, pp. 15–24.

Kress, G. (2003). *Literacy in the new media age*. London: Routledge.

Kress, G. (2010). *Multimodality: A social approach to contemporary communication*. London and New York: Routledge.

Kress, G., Jewitt, C., Ogborn, J., & Tsatsarelis (2001). *Multimodal teaching and learning: The rhetorics of the science classroom*. London: Continuum.

Kress, G., & Street, B. (2006). Multi-modality and literacy practices: A foreword. In K. Pahl & J. Rowsell (Eds), *Travel notes from the new literacy studies: Instances of practice*. Clevedon, UK: Multilingual Matters.

Kuhn, T. (1970). *The Structure of Scientific Revolutions* (2nd ed.). Chicago: University of Chicago Press.

Kucircova, N., Messer, D., Sheehy, K., & Flewitt, R. (2013). Sharing personalised stories on iPads: A close look at one parent-child interaction. *Literacy*, vol. 47, no. 3, pp.115–122.

Kwa, C. (2002). Romantic and baroque conceptions of complex wholes in the sciences. In J. Law & A. Mol (Eds.), *Complexities: Social studies of knowledge practices*. Durham, NC: Duke University Press.

Ivey, G., & Johnstone, P. (2013). Engagement with young adult literature: Outcomes and processes. *Reading Research Quarterly*, vol. 48, no. 3, pp. 255–275.

Janks, H. (2009). *Literacy and Power*. New York: Routledge/Taylor and Francis.

Lankshear, C. & Knobel, M. (2010). *New literacies: Everyday practices and social learning* (3rd ed.). Maidenhead, UK: Open University Press.

Larson, J., & Marsh, J. (Eds.). (2005). *Making literacy real: Theories and practices for learning and teaching*. London: Sage.

Larson, J., & Marsh, J. (Eds.). (2013). *The Sage handbook of early childhood literacy* (2nd ed.). London: Sage.

Lave, J., & Wenger, E. (1991). *Situated learning: Legitimate peripheral participation*. Cambridge, UK: Cambridge University Press.

Law, J. (2004). *After method: Mess in social science research*. London: Routledge.

Law, J. (2004). And if the global were small and non-coherent? Method, complexity and the Baroque, *Environment and planning D. Society and Space*, vol. 22, no. 1, pp. 13–26.

Leander, K., & Boldt, G. (2013). Rereading "A pedagogy of multiliteracies": Bodies, texts, and emergence. *Journal of Literacy Research*, vol. 45, no. 1, pp. 22–46.

Leander, K. M. & McKim, K. K. (2003). Tracing the everyday "sitings" of adolescents on the Internet: A strategic adaptation of ethnography across online and offline spaces. *Education, Communication and Information*, vol. 3, no. 2, pp. 211–240.

Leander & Sheehy (2004). *Spatializing literacy research and practice*. New York: Peter Lang.

Learning with iPads (2013). Retrieved from: http://www.learningwithipads.co.uk

Lefebvre, H. (1991). *The production of space*, Nicholson-Smith, D., Trans. Oxford, UK: Blackwell.

Lemphane, P. (2012). A contrastive ethnographic study of children's digital literacy practices in two homes in Cape Town. Master's minor dissertation, School of Education, University of Cape Town.

Levinson, M. P. (2007). Literacy in English Gypsy communities: Cultural capital manifested as negative. *American Educational Research Journal*, 44, 5–39.

Leung, C., & Ruan, J. (2012). *Perspectives on learning Chinese language and literacy in China*. New York: Springer.

Levy, R. (2010). *Young children reading at home and at school*. London: Sage

Lewis, C., & Tierney, J. (2013). Mobilizing emotion in an urban classroom: Producing identities and transforming signs in a race-related discussion. *Linguistics in Education*, vol. 24, no. 3, pp. 289–304.

Lewis, L. (2012). The participatory meme chronotope: Fixity of space/rapture of time. In B. Williams & A. Zenger (Eds.), *New media literacies and participatory popular culture across borders*. London: Routledge.

Li, G. (2013). Understanding English language learners literacy from a cultural lens: An Asian perspective. In K. Hall, T. Cremin, B. Comber, & L. Moll (Eds.), *International handbook of research on childrens literacy, learning and culture*. Oxford, UK: Wiley-Blackwell.

Littau, K. (2006). *Theories of reading: Books, bodies and bibliomania*. Cambridge, UK: Polity Press.

Livingstone, I., & Hope, A. (2011). *Next gen. transforming the UK into the world's leading talent hub for the video games and visual effects industries*. London: NESTA (National Endowment for Science, Technology and the Arts).

Llloyd, P. (2008). *Mamma mia*. Universal.

Lu, W., & Cross, R. (2012). Literacy and the Australian curriculum: Mixed messages, but ones that are hard to shake. Joint Australian Association for Research in Education and Asia-Pacific Educational Research Association Conference

(AARE-APERA). World Education Research Association (WERA). Focal Meeting, Sydney, New South Wales, 2–6 December 2012.

Luhrmann, B. (1996). *Romeo + Juliet* motion picture.Twentieth Century Fox. Produced by Baz Luhrmann and Gabriella Martinelli.

Mackey, M. (2002). An asset model of new literacies: A conceptual and strategic approach to change. In R. Hammett & B. Burrell (eds), *Digital expressions: Digital media and English language arts*. Calgary, AL: Detselik.

Mackey, M. (2011). The embedded and embodied literacies of a young reader. *Children's literature in education*, vol. 42, no. 4, pp. 289–307.

Madonna (1984). *Material world*. Warner Brothers: Sire Records.

Manguel, A. (1997). *A history of reading*, New York: Penguin.

Manovich, L. (2001). *The language of new media*. Cambridge, MA: MIT Press.

Marsh, J. (2003). Contemporary models of communicative practice: Shaky foundations in the foundation stage? *English in Education*, vol. 37, no. 1, pp. 38–46.

Marsh, J. (2004). The techno-literacy practices of young children. *Journal of Early Childhood Research*, vol. 2, no. 1, pp. 55–66.

Marsh, J. (2010a). *Childhood, culture and creativity: A literature review*. Sheffield, UK: Creativity, Culture and Education.

Marsh, J. (2010b). Young childrens play in online virtual worlds. *Journal of Early Childhood Research*, vol. 8, no. 23, pp. 23–39.

Marsh, J. (2011). Young children's literacy practices in a virtual world: Establishing an online interaction order. *Reading Research Quarterly*, vol. 46, no. 2, pp. 101–118.

Marsh, J., & Richards, C. (2013). Play, media and children's playground cultures. In R. Willett, C. Richards, J. Marsh, A. Burn, & J. Bishop (Eds.), *Children, media and playground cultures: Ethnographic studies of school playtimes*. Basingstoke, UK: Palgrave.

Marsh, J., Brooks, G., Hughes J., Ritchie, L,. & Roberts S. (2005). *Digital beginnings: Young children's use of popular culture, media and new technologies*. Sheffield, UK: University of Sheffield. Retrieved from: http://www.digitalbeginnings.shef.ac.uk/final-report.htm

Martin C., Williams., C., Ochsner A., Harris, S., King, E., Anton, G., Jonathon Elmergreen, J., & Steinkuehler, C. (2012). Playing together separately: Mapping out literacy and social synchronicity. In G. Merchant, J. Gillen, J. Marsh, & J. Davies (Eds.), *Virtual literacies: Interactive spaces for children and young people*. New York: Routledge.

Martin, D. (2013). Feminine adolescence as uncanny: Masculinity, haunting and self-estrangement. *Forum for Modern Language Studies*, vol. 49, no. 2, pp. 135–145.

Masny, D., & Cole, D. (2012). *Mapping multiple literacies: An introduction to Deleuzian literacy studies*. London: Continuum.

Massey, D. (2005). *For space*. London: Sage.

Mattel. (2010). *Monster high*. Retrieved from: http://www.monsterhigh.com/

Matthews, H., Limb, M., & Taylor, M. (2000). The street as third space.In S. Holloway & V. Valentine (Eds.), *Children's geographies: Playing, living, learning*. London: Routledge.

Maybin. J. (2006). *Children's voices: Talk, knowledge and identity*. Basingstoke, UK: Palgrave.

Maybin, J. (2013). What counts as reading? PIRLS, eastenders and the man on the flying trapeze. *Literacy*, vol. 47, no. 2, pp. 59–66.

McFarlane, C. (2009). Translocal assemblages: Space, power and social movements. *Geoforum*, vol. 40, no.4, pp. 561–567.

McLuhan, M. (1964). *Understanding media*. New York: Mentor.

McNeill, D. (Ed.). (2000). *Language and gesture*. Cambridge, UK: Cambridge University Press.

Medina, C. L., & Wohlwend, K. E. (2014). *Literacy, play, and globalization: Converging imaginaries in childrens critical and cultural performances*. New York: Routledge.

Merchant, G. (2006). Identity, social networks and online communication. *E-Learning*, vol. 3, no. 2, pp. 235.

Merchant, G. (2007). Writing the future in the digital age. *Literacy*, vol. 41, no. 3, pp. 118–128.

Merchant, G. (2009). Literacy in virtual worlds. *Journal of Research in Reading*, vol. 32, no. 1, pp. 38–56.

Merchant, G. (2010). View my profile(s). In D. E. Alvermann (Ed.), *Adolescents online literacies: Connecting classrooms, digital media, and popular culture*. London: Peter Lang.

Merchant, G. (2012). Mobile practices in everyday life: Popular digital literacies and schools revisited. *British Journal of Educational Technology*, vol. 43, no. 5, pp. 770–782.

Merchant, G., Gillen, J., Marsh, J., & Davies, J. (Eds). (2012). *Virtual literacies: Interactive spaces for children and young people*. London: Routledge.

Merleau-Ponty, M. (1962). Phenomenology of perception: An introduction. London: Routledge.

Mills. K. (2008). Will large-scale assessments raise literacy standards in Australian schools? *Australian Journal of Language and Literacy*, vol. 31, no. 3, pp. 211–225.

Miller, D. (2010). *Stuff*. Cambridge: Polity.

Miller, R. (2011). *Reading in slow motion, Text2Cloud*. Retrieved from: http://text2cloud.com/wp-content/uploads/2011/01/Reading_in_Slow_Motion_Final-41.pdf

MoE Finland (Ministry of Education and Culture, Finland). (2003). *Ministry of Education Strategy 2015*. Helsinki: Finland. Retrieved from: http://www.minedu.fi/export/sites/default/OPM/Julkaisut/2003/liitteet/opm_155_opm35.pdf?lang=en

MoE Finland (Ministry of Education and Culture, Finland). (2012). *Education and research 2011–2016: A development plan*. Helsinki: Department for Education and Science Policy, Finland. Retrieved from: www.minedu.fi

MoE Singapore (Ministry of Education Singapore). (2012). *Education in Singapore*. Singapore: Ministry of Education.

Minogue, J., & Jones, M. (2006). Haptics in education: Exploring an untapped sensory modality. *Review of Educational Research*, vol. 76, no. 3, pp. 317–348.

Misson, R., & Morgan, W. (2006). *Critical literacy and the aesthetic: Transforming the English classroom*. Urbana IL: National Council for the Teaching of English.

Moffatt, T., & Reinhardt, B. (1999). *Laudanum*. Ostfildern, Germany: H. Cantz.

Mol, A., & Law, J. (2002). *Complexities: An introduction*. In J. Law & A. Mol (Eds.), Complexities. Lancaster, UK: Duke Press.

Mojang. (2010). *Minecraft*. Retrieved from: https://minecraft.net/

Murphy, C. M. (1978). Pointing in the context of a shared activity. *Child Development*, 49, pp. 371–380.

National Council of Teachers of English (NCTE) (2010). The NCTE Definition of 21st Century Literacies. Retrieved from http://www.ncte.org/positions/statements/21stcentdefinition.

National Governors' Association (2012). *Common core state standards initiative: Preparing America's students for college & career*. Retrieved from: http://www.corestandards.org/ELA-Literacy

Nespor, J. (1997). *Tangled up in school: Politics, space, bodies, and signs in the educational process.* Mahwah, NJ: Erlbaum.

New London Group. (1996). A pedagogy of multiliteracies: Designing social futures. *Harvard Educational Review,* vol. 66, no. 1, pp.60–93.

Nichols, S. (2006). From boardroom to classroom: Tracing a globalised discourse on thinking through internet texts and teaching practice. In K. Pahl & R. Rowsell (Eds.), *Travel notes from the new literacy studies: Instances of practice.* Clevedon, UK: Multilingual Matters.

Nordquist, B. (2012). Economies of difference at the nexus of high school and college. Thomas R. Watson Conference on Rhetoric and Composition. Louisville, KY: University of Louisville, 19 October 2012.

Norris, S., & Jones, R. (2005). *Discourse in action: Introducing mediated discourse analysis.* Abingdon, UK: Routledge.

Oksman, V., & Rautiainen, P. (2003). "Perhaps it is a body part"; How the mobile phone became an organic part of the everyday lives of Finnish children and teenagers, in J. E. Katz (Ed.), *Machines that become us: The social context of personal communication technology.* Rutgers, NJ: Transaction.

OMara, J., & Laidlaw, L. (2011). Living in the i-world: Two literacy researchers reflect on the changing texts and literacy practices of childhood. *English Teaching Practice and Critique,* vol. 10, no. 4, pp. 149–159.

Ong, A. (2007). Neoliberalism as a mobile technology. *Transactions of the Institute of British Geographers,* vol. 2, no. 1, pp. 3–8.

Pahl, K. (2006). Birds, frogs, blue skies and sheep: An investigation into the cultural notion of affordance in children's meaning making. *English in Education,* vol. 40, no. 1, pp. 20–35.

Pahl, K., & Rowsell, J. (Eds.). (2006). *Travel notes from the new literacy studies: Instances of practice.* Clevedon, UK: Multilingual Matters.

Pahl, K., & Rowsell, J. (2010). *Artifactual literacies: Every object tells a story.* New York: Teachers College Press.

Pahl, K., & Rowsell, J. (2011). Artifactual critical literacies: A new perspective for literacy education. *Berkeley Review of Education,* vol. 2, no. 2, pp. 129–151.

Pahl, K., & Rowsell, J. (Eds.). (2012). *Early childhood literacy* (Vols. 1–4). Los Angeles: Sage.

Paley, V. G. (2004). *A child's work: The importance of fantasy play.* Chicago: University of Chicago Press.

Parry, R. (2011). Cowboy mutant golfers and dreamcatcher dogs: Making space for popular culture in animation production with children. *International Journal of Learning and Media,* vol. 3, no. 3, pp. 43–53.

Pelletier, C. (2005). The uses of literacy in studying computer games: Comparing students' oral and visual representation of games. *English Teaching: Practice and Critique,* vol. 4, no. 1, pp. 40–59.

Pelletier, C. (2007). Producing gender in digital interactions: What young people set out to achieve through computer games design. In S. Weber & S. Dixon (Eds.), *Growing up online: Young people and digital technologies.* New York: Palgrave Macmillan.

Plato. (360 BCE, trans. B. Jowett). *Dialogue with Phaedrus.* Available at: http://www.perseus.tufts.edu/hopper/text?doc=Perseus%3Atext%3A1999.01.0174%3Atext%3DPhaedrus

Potter, J. (2012). *Digital media and learner identity: The new curatorship.* New York: Palgrave Macmillan.

Premier's Technology Council. (2010). *A vision of 21st century education.* Vancouver, British Columbia: Author.

Prensky, M. (2001). Digital natives, digital immigrants. *On the Horizon*, vol. 9, no .5, pp. 1–6.

Presto Studios (2001). *Myst III exile*. Ubisoft.

Prinsloo, M. (2005). The new literacies as placed resources. i, vol. 23, no. 4, pp. 87–98.

Ravitch, D. (2010). *The death and life of the great American school system*. New York: Basic Books.

Reckwitz, A. (2002). Towards a theory of social practices: A development in culturalist theorizing. *European Journal of Social Theory*, vol. 5, no. 2, pp. 243–263.

Richards, C. (2012). Playing under surveillance: Gender performance and the conduct of the self in a primary playground. *British Journal of Sociology of Education*, vol. 33, no. 3, pp. 373–390.

Rideout, V. J., & Hammel, E. (2006). *The media family: Electronic media in the lives of infants, toddlers, preschoolers and their parents*. Menlo Park, CA: Kaiser Family Foundation.

Ridolfo, J., & DeVoss, D. N. (2009). *Composing for recomposition: Rhetorical velocity and delivery*. Kairos: A Journal of Rhetoric, Technology, and Pedagogy, vol. 13, no. 2. Retrieved from: http://kairos.technorhetoric.net/13.2/topoi/ridolfo_devoss/intro.html

Roach, J. (2010). *Dinner for schmucks*. Paramount.

Rockstar Games. (2011). *L. A. noire: The collected stories*. Glasgow: Rockstar.

Rodogno, R. (2012). Personal identity online. *Philosophy and Technology*, vol. 25, no. 3, pp. 309–328.

Rowsell, J. (2009). My life on Facebook: Assessing the art of social networking. In A. Burke & B. Hammett (Eds.), *Assessing new literacies: Perspectives from the classroom*. New York: Peter Lang.

Rowsell, J. (2013). *Working with multimodality: Rethinking literacy in a digital age*. London: Routledge.

Rowsell, J., & Pahl, K. (2007). Sedimented identities in texts: Instance of practice. *Reading Research Quarterly*, vol. 42, no. 3, pp. 388–401.

Rowsell, J., Saudelli, M., Scott, R., & Bishop, A. (2013). iPads as placed resources: Forging community in online and offline spaces. *Language Arts*, vol. 90, no. 5, pp. 351–360.

Rylands, T. (n.d.). *Myst Exile in the classroom*. Retrieved from: http://www.youtube.com/watch?v=X5xFMmK5Ujs

Saunders, T. J. (1987). Introduction to Socrates. In *Plato: Early Socratic dialogues*. London: Penguin.

Schatzki, T. R. (2001). Practice-minded orders. In T. R. Shatzki, K. K. Cetina, & E. V. Savigny (Eds.), *The practice turn in contemporary theory*. London: Routledge.

Schatzki, T. R. (2002). *The site of the social: A philosophical account of the constitution of social life and change*. University Park, PA: Pennsylvania State University Press.

Scollon, R. (2001). *Mediated discourse: The nexus of practice*. London: Routledge.

Scollon, R., & Scollon, S. W. (1981). *Narrative, literacy and face in interethnic communication*, Norwood, NJ: Ablex.

Scollon, R., & Scollon, S. W. (2004). *Nexus analysis: Discourse and the emerging Internet*. New York: Routledge.

Seales, R., & Harding, E. (2013). Four-year-old girl is Britain's youngest iPad ADDICT: Shocking rise in children hooked on using smartphones and tablets. *Mail Online*, 27 April 2013. Retrieved from: http://www.dailymail.co.uk/news/article-2312429/Four-year-old-girl-Britains-youngest-iPad-ADDICT-Shocking-rise-children-hooked-using-smartphones-tablets.html

Selfe, C., & Selfe, R. (1994). The politics of the interface: Power and its exercise in electronic contact zones. *College Composition and Communication*, vol. 45, no. 4, pp. 480–504.

Senechal, M., Cornell, E., & Broda, L. (1995). Age-related differences in the organization of parent-infant interactions during picture book reading. *Early Childhood Research Quarterly*, vol. 10, no. 3, pp. 317–337.

Sheridan, M. P., & Rowsell, J. (2010). *Design literacies: Learning and innovation in the digital age*. London: Routledge.

Snyder, I. (1998). *Page to screen: Taking literacy into the electronic era*. London: Routledge.

Sockett, G., & Toffoli, D. (2012). Beyond learner autonomy: A dynamic systems view of the informal learning of English in virtual online communities. *European Association for Computer Assisted Language Learning*, vol. 24, no. 2, pp. 138–151.

Sorrels, K. (2012). *Intercultural communication: Globalization and social justice*. London: Sage.

Steinkuehler, C. (2007). Massively multiplayer online gaming as a constellation of literacy practices. *E-Learning and Digital Media*, vol. 4, no. 3, pp. 297–318.

Steinkuehler, C. (2008). Cognition and literacy in massively multiplayer online games. In J. Coiro, M. Knobel, C. Lankshear, & D. Leu (Eds.), *Handbook of research on new literacies*. New York: Routledge.

Stipek, D. (2006). No Child Left Behind comes to preschool. *Elementary School Journal*, vol. 106, no. 5, pp. 455–465.

Stirling, E. (2009). We all communicate over Facebook: A case study of undergraduate students usage and non-usage of the Facebook group. Unpublished thesis. Sheffield, UK: The University of Sheffield.

Stirling, E. (2014). "We use Facebook chat in lectures of course!" Exploring the use of Facebook Group by first year undergraduate students for social and academic support. In M. Kent & T. Leaver (Eds.), *An education in Facebook? Higher education and the world's largest social network*. London: Routledge.

Street, B. (1985). *Literacy in theory and practice*. Cambridge, UK: Cambridge University Press.

Street, B. (1995). *Social literacies*. London: Longman.

Street, B. (Ed.). (2001). *Literacy and development: Ethnographic perspectives*. London: Routledge.

Street, B. V., & Heath, S. B. 2007. *On ethnography: Approaches to language and literacy research*. New York and London: Teachers College Press.

Sucker Punch. (2009). *inFamous*. Sony Computer Entertainment.

Sucker Punch. (2011). *inFamous 2*. Sony Computer Entertainment.

Taylor, R. (2012). Messing about with metaphor: Multimodal aspects to childrens creative meaning-making. *Literacy*, vol. 46, no. 3, pp. 156–166.

Teacher Gaming. (2013). *MinecraftEdu*. Retrieved from: http://minecraftedu.com/page/

Thomas, R. (2009). Writing, reading, public and private literacies: Functional literacy and democratic literacy in Greece. In W. A. Johnson & H. N. Parker (Eds.), *Ancient literacies: The culture of reading in Greece and Rome*. Oxford, UK: Oxford University Press.

Tusting, K. (2013). Paper 105: Literacy studies as linguistic ethnography. In *Working papers in urban language & literacies*. Retrieved from: https://www.kcl.ac.uk/innovation/groups/ldc/publications/workingpapers/the-papers/WP105-Tusting-2013-Literacy-studies-as-linguistic-ethnography.pdf

Ubisoft Montreal/Ubisoft Entertainment. (2009). *Assassin's creed II*. Retrieved from: http://assassinscreed.ubi.com/en-au/games/assassins-creed-2/index.aspx

180 Bibliography

Urquhart, C. (2013). Police question Paris Brown over Twitter comments. *The Guardian* online, 20 April 2013, Retrieved from: http://www.theguardian.com/uk/2013/apr/20/police-paris-brown-twitter

Vass, E. (2007). Exploring processes of collaborative creativity: The role of emotions in children's joint creative writing. *Thinking Skills and Creativity*, vol. 2, no. 2, pp. 107–117.

Verbeek, P. (2005). *What things do: Philosophical reflections on technology, agency, and design.* Philadelphia: Pennsylvania University Press.

Vertovec, S. (2007). Super-diversity and its implications. *Ethnic and Racial Studies*, vol. 30, no. 6, pp. 1024–1054.

Volition Inc. (2006). *Saints row.* Retrieved from: http://www.saintsrow.com/uk

Vosloo, S. (2012). *The future of education in Africa is mobile.* Durbanville: Shuttleworh Foundation. Retrieved from: http://www.shuttleworthfoundation.org/the-future-of-education-in-africa-is-mobile-bbc-article-uk-version/

Vygotsky, L. S. (1978). *Mind in society: The development of higher psychological processes*, M. Cole Trans. Cambridge, MA: Harvard University Press.

Walton, M. (2009). *Mobile literacies and South African teens: Leisure reading, writing, and MXit chatting for teens in Langa and Guguletu.* Cape Town: University of Cape Town, Centre for Film and Media Studies.

Watson, M., & Hay, C. (2003). The discourse of globalisation and the logic of no alternative: Rendering the contingent necessary in the political economy of new labour. *Policy and Politics*, vol. 30, no. 4, pp. 289–305.

Webb, A. (Ed.). (2012). *Teaching literature in virtual worlds: Immersive learning in English studies.* New York: Routledge.

Weber, S., & Dixon, S. (2007). Reviewing young people's engagement with technology. In S. Weber & S. Dixon (Eds.), *Growing up online: Young people and digital technologies.* New York: Palgrave Macmillan.

Weber, S., & Mitchell, C. (2008). Imaging, keyboarding, and posting identities: Young people and new media technologies. In D. Buckingham (Ed.). *Youth, identity, and digital media.* Cambridge, MA: MIT Press.

Wellman, B. (2002). Little boxes, glocalization, and networked individualism. In M. Tanabe, P. Besselaar, & T. Ishida (Eds.), *Digital cities II: Computational and sociological approaches.* Berlin: Springer.

Wilderness Society (2013). Retrieved 8 February 2014 from http://www.wilderness.org.au/articles/victory-australia's-nature-wa-supreme-court-rules-james-price-point-approval-'illegal'

Willett, R. (2008). Consumption, production and online identities: Amateur spoofs on YouTube. In R. Willett, M. Robinson, & J. Marsh (Eds.), *Play, creativity and digital cultures.* London and New York: Routledge.

Willett R., Robinson, M., & Marsh, J. (Eds.). (2009). *Play, creativity and digital cultures.* London and New York: Routledge.

Willett R., Richards C, Marsh J, Burn, A., & Bishop, J. (2013). *Children, media and playground cultures: Ethnographic studies of school playtimes.* Basingstoke: Palgrave.

Williams, B. T. (2003). Where should we want to go today? Some cultural implications of computers and composition. In J. Walker. & O. Ovieod (Eds.), *TnT: Texts and technology.* Cresskill, NJ: Hampton Press.

Williams, B. T. (2008). Tomorrow will not be like today: Literacy and identity in a world of multiliteracies. *Journal of Adolescent & Adult Literacy*, vol. 51, no. 8, pp. 682–686.

Williams, B. T. (2009). *Shimmering literacies: Popular culture and reading and writing online.* London: Peter Lang.

Williams, R. (1958/1983). *Culture and society, 1780–1950.* New York: Columbia University Press.

Willis, P. (1990). *Common Culture*. Milton Keynes, UK: Open University Press.

Wohlwend, K. E. (2009a). Damsels in discourse: Girls consuming and producing gendered identity texts through Disney Princess play. *Reading Research Quarterly*, vol. 44, no. 1, pp. 57–83.

Wohlwend, K. E. (2009b). Early adopters: Playing new literacies and pretending new technologies in print-centric classrooms. *Journal of Early Childhood Literacy*, vol. 9, no. 2, pp. 119–143.

Wohlwend, K. E. (2011). *Playing their way into literacies: Reading, writing, and belonging in the early childhood classroom*. New York: Teachers College Press.

Wohlwend, K. E., Buchholz, B. A., Wessel-Powell, C., Coggin, L. S., & Husbye, N. E. (2013). *Literacy playshop: Playing with new literacies and popular media in the early childhood classroom*. New York: Teachers College Press.

Wohlwend, K., Zanden, S., Husbye, N., & Kuby, C. (2011). Navigating discourses in place in the world of Webkindz. *Journal of Early Childhood Literacy*, vol. 11, no. 2, pp. 141–163.

Zhao, S., Grasmuck, S. & Martin, J. (2008). Identity construction on facebook: Digital empowerment in anchored relationships. *Computers in Human Behavior*, vol. 24, no. 5, pp. 1816–1836.

Contributors

Chris Bailey is a doctoral student at Sheffield Hallam University, with a recent background in teaching across the primary and early-years age ranges. His current research explores the role of technology in formal and informal learning contexts, with a particular focus on the use of virtual social environments as places where children make meaning and develop their identities. He is also interested in how childrens lived experiences of digital culture inflect their participation in schooled literacy.

Catherine Beavis is Professor of Education at Griffith University, Australia. She teaches and researches in the area of English Curriculum, Literature and Literacy Education and about young people and digital culture, with a particular focus on video or computer games, the changing nature of text and the nature and implications of young people's engagement with video games for English and literacy education. Her work explores contemporary constructions of English, texts and literacy; the role of game play in young people's lives, games as spaces within which young people play and connections between game play, identity and community.

Beth A. Buchholz is a doctoral student at Indiana University in the Literacy, Culture, and Language Education department. She is a teacher, writer, designer, artist and researcher. She explores the social and ideological identity work of children composing multimodal texts within and beyond school. Her research works to disrupt notions of autonomous authorship and fixed meaning that undergird much of the writing instruction occurring in classrooms by examining how children collectively compose multimodal texts in ways that complicate artificial separations between global/local, home/school and physical/digital.

Julianne Burgess currently teaches English as an Additional Language at Mohawk College in Hamilton, Ontario, where she has been a part-time faculty member since 2008. She is completing her Master of Education at Brock University, focusing her studies in the area of new literacies, multiliteracies and multimodal practices in the English language classroom.

Cathy Burnett is Reader in the Department of Teacher Education at Sheffield Hallam University in the United Kingdom, where she leads the Language and Literacy Research Group. She has published widely in the field of literacy in education and coedits *Literacy,* the United Kingdom Literacy Association journal. Her research interests are concerned with relationships between literacies within and beyond educational contexts and with meaning-making in hybrid on/offline spaces.

Julia Davies is a Senior Lecturer in The School of Education at The University of Sheffield where she codirects The Centre for the Study of Literacies. She researches vernacular digital text-making, particularly exploring how social media impact upon literacy and the ways in which we see ourselves in the world. She has also explored educational uses of new technologies and looked at the continuities and discontinuities between formal educational uses and the less formal learning that happens outside of schooled institutions. She coedits *Literacy,* the United Kingdom Literacy Association journal.

Peter Freebody is an Honorary Professorial Fellow in the School of Education at the University of Wollongong, Australia, and a Fellow of the Academy of the Social Sciences in Australia. Recent appointments have been at the University of Sydney, the University of Queensland, and the National Institute of Education, Singapore. He has contributed publications in the areas of literacy education, educational disadvantage, classroom interaction, and research methodology. He has served on Australian state and national advisory groups in the areas of literacy policy, English curriculum, and technology-enhanced teaching, and he is a member of the International Reading Association's Literacy Research Panel.

Polo Lemphane is a researcher and language educator. She received her master's degree from the University of Cape Town in 2012. Her master's research contrasted childrens digital literacy practices across divergent socioeconomic settings. She is a former English language and English literature educator at both secondary and high school levels in Lesotho.

Guy Merchant is Professor of Literacy in Education at Sheffield Hallam University, where he specialises in research into digital literacy in formal and informal educational settings. Guy has published widely in international journals and is a founding editor of the *Journal of Early Childhood Literacy.* With Julia Davies he coauthored the influential book *Web 2.0 for Schools: Learning and Social Participation* (2009) and is lead editor of *Virtual Literacies: Interactive Spaces for Children and Young People* (2013).

Mastin Prinsloo is an Associate Professor in the School of Education at the University of Cape Town, working in language and literacy studies in education. His coedited books include *The Social Uses of Literacy* (1996), with Mignonne Breier; *Literacies, Local and Global* (2008), *The Future of Literacy Studies* (2009), a reference collection, *Literacy Studies* (2103). with Mike Baynham; and the forthcoming books *Language, Literacy and Diversity: Moving Words* (Routledge) and *Educating for Language and Literacy Diversity* (Taylor and Francis), both coedited with Christopher Stroud.

Jennifer Rowsell is Professor and Canada Research Chair in Multiliteracies at Brock University in Canada. Her research interests include children's digital and immersive worlds, adopting and applying multimodal epistemologies with young people and ecological work in communities examining everyday literacy practices. Her most recent book is *Working with Multimodality: Learning in a Digital Age* (Routledge).

Bronwyn T. Williams is a Professor of English and director of the University Writing Center at the University of Louisville in the US. He writes and teaches on issues of literacy, identity, pedagogy, digital media, and popular culture. His books include *New Media Literacies and Participatory Popular Culture Across Borders* (with Amy Zenger) (2012), *Shimmering Literacies: Popular Culture and Reading and Writing Online* (2009), *Popular Culture and Representations of Literacy* (with Amy Zenger) (2007), *Identity Papers: Literacy and Power in Higher Education* (2006), and *Tuned In: Television and the Teaching of Writing* (2002).

Karen E. Wohlwend is an Associate Professor of Literacy, Culture and Language Education at Indiana University, Bloomington. She is the author of *Playing Their Way into Literacies: Reading, Writing, and Belonging in the Early Childhood Classroom* (2011); *Literacy Playshop: New Literacies, Popular Media, and Play in the Early Childhood Classroom* (2013), with Beth Buchholz and colleagues; and *Literacy, Play, and Globalization: Converging Imaginaries in Childrens Critical and Cultural Performances* (2014), with Carmen Medina. Wohlwend's articles have appeared in *Reading Research Quarterly*, *Gender and Education*, *Journal of Early Childhood Literacy*, *Language Arts* and *Contemporary Issues in Early Childhood*, among others.

Index